DATE DUE			

FENIMORE COOPER

Adventure most unto itself
The Soul condemned to be—
Attended by a single Hound
Its own identity.

Emily Dickinson

Fenimore Cooper

A STUDY OF HIS LIFE AND

IMAGINATION

BY STEPHEN RAILTON

PRINCETON UNIVERSITY PRESS

Copyright © 1978 by Princeton University Press

Published by Princeton University Press, Princeton, New Jersey
In the United Kingdom: Princeton University Press,
Guildford, Surrey

Library of Congress Cataloging in Publication Data will
be found on the last printed page of this book

Publication of this book has been aided by the
Paul Mellon Fund of Princeton University Press

This book has been composed in Linotype Baskerville

Printed in the United States of America by
Princeton University Press, Princeton, New Jersey

CONTENTS

PREFACE

My emphasis in this study is on the relationship between James Fenimore Cooper's emotional life and his literary career, between the works of his imagination and the needs of his psyche. I am most interested in the way Cooper's novels responded to the complicated and conflicting demands of his unconscious. Obviously, we are interested in Cooper at all because he was an author, and it would be a mistake to forget that his novels were written for and have appealed to a reading public. They were also part of a tradition of literature, which influenced them and which they subsequently influenced. Yet the student of literature can ask various questions of the work of art: aesthetic, historical, cultural, moral, metaphysical, or psychological. These all strike me as valid, and I do not want to preclude any other approach to Cooper by posing and trying to answer my own set of questions. Actually, my questions can be stated very well, with the largest possible reference, in someone else's words: "What is Arte?" asked Thomas Wright, author of *The Passions of the Minde in General,* in 1604; "what the Idaea in the Artificers minde, by whose direction hee frameth his woorkes, what . . . the internall speech and words of the minde?" Wright's questions about "Arte" are much too big for me to pretend that I have answered them here, but it is toward an answer that I have written this book.

And while, almost 400 years later, no one has yet convincingly and definitively answered those questions, we are in a better position than Wright was to do so. The twentieth century has devoted a vast amount of energy to the study of the passions of the mind in general; in particular, the contributions of Sigmund Freud now enable us to translate "the internall speech" of the mind, and my attempt to explicate Cooper's "woorkes" begins with Freud's account of the psyche. This is an intellectual debt I acknowledge gladly, though I know that many people still resist the

Freudian account. For the most part our culture has accepted and popularized the notion of the unconscious, but critical efforts to trace the role of the unconscious in an artist's creative life remain out of favor among what probably amounts to a majority of scholars. The conventional complaint about this kind of biographical literary criticism labels it "reductive." By that is ostensibly meant the limited scope of such an approach, a limitation that forces the critic to ignore or omit many of a literary text's claims to our attention. The complaint is legitimate, but I cannot understand why psychological interpretations are so regularly singled out by it. If not reductive, every species of criticism is at least restrictive. The cultural historian adopts his particular point of view, the formalist critic his, and so on—each approach applies a text to its purposes, applies its purposes to a text, and all leave as much unsaid about the work as they can possibly say. There can be nothing wrong with that. A painter who intends to sketch a landscape must set his easel up someplace, though his choice will necessarily bring some details into the foreground, subordinate others, and overlook some entirely. Accepting the vision of a specific perspective is what makes composition possible for the artist—and what makes it possible for the critic to say anything coherent about art. My suspicion, however, is that when someone accuses psychoanalytic criticism of reducing a text, he is actually bothered by something else: by the worry that such criticism diminishes, may even demean, the character of man. Why, after all, do people refer to a psychiatrist as "the shrink"?

The basic insights of psychoanalysis can help us explain human actions and emotions—can, for example with regard to Cooper, help make sense out of many things that have perplexed his biographers and critics—but the fear that they reduce a writer's stature to the crippled figure of a neurotic is misplaced. What matter about the course of anyone's life are his achievements; explaining them does not explain them away. Rather, to me the real danger of my perspective lies in the inevitable limitations on our knowledge about ourselves. The problem does not so much involve what is lost in the translation of the internal speech of another man's mind, as what may be changed or distorted. Here is what Cooper himself, a man who felt that he had been regularly misunderstood, said about "attempts at an analysis of human motives"; the passage is from *The Crater*, a novel written late in his career:

> The man who has been much the subject of the conjectures and opinions of his fellow-creatures, in this way, must have many occasions to wonder, and some to smile, when he sees how completely those around him misjudge his wishes and impulses. Although formed of the same substance, influenced by the same selfishness, and governed by the same passions, in nothing do men oftener err than in this portion of the exercise of their intellects. The errors arise from one man's rigidly judging his fellow by himself, and that which he would do he fancies others would do also. This rule would be pretty safe, could we always penetrate into the wants and longings of others, which quite as often fail to correspond closely with our own, as do their characters, fortunes, and hopes.

I would rephrase Cooper's warning like this: if the work of an artist is to some extent an attempt to deal with his individual psychic conflicts, then equally to some extent the secondary work of a critic must reflect the needs of his psyche. I cannot very well say that Cooper's life embodies his unconscious "wishes and impulses" without also saying that my interpretation of that life embodies mine. It is clear to me that I was attracted to Cooper in the first place because trying to understand him helped me to understand myself.

My interest in psychoanalytic theory is founded in part on a similar motive, and I believe that probably the most valuable result of examining literature in its light is what such a study can teach us, not simply about a particular work or a particular author, but also about ourselves. What "the shrink"—despite the epithet—actually seeks to accomplish is to expand the patient's knowledge of himself. How different is this purpose from that of the creative writer, who asks his reader to concern himself with the conflicts and desires of an imagined set of characters first, I suppose, merely for their sake, but finally for the reader's own? Whenever we examine our literary preferences, we realize that we prize most highly those writers who seem best to articulate our own emotional or intellectual aspirations or preoccupations. A biographical study similarly attempts to claim the reader's interest and sympathy for its subject, but to talk solely of sympathy overlooks the reason behind our interest in someone else's life. To describe the relationship between the biographical subject on the one hand and the biographer or the reader on the other, it might be better to speak of empathy. I know that in my own case, I have tried in this study of Cooper to provoke an intelligent, informed empathy for his attempt to come to terms with his life.

Of course, I am a student of literature, not a psychoanalyst. In no strict sense is my study of Cooper a Freudian interpretation of his novels. Nor is it a case history of his life. I would like to state as explicitly as possible that it is a critical and biographical study based upon the insights of psychoanalysis, not a psychoanalytic study of a literary subject. I am aware of the hazard that a book such as mine cannot easily avoid: that my reader will respond to it according to his own preconception of what "Freudian criticism" either is or is worth. I have used quotation marks because I want to suggest the error of the implication that "Freudian criticism" must necessarily mean one kind of criticism, that taking Freud's name in a Preface necessarily commits a critic to a specific methodology. It does commit me to a definite perspective: I do consider myself an orthodox Freudian, and I believe that my conclusions about Cooper's life and art are firmly based upon and are entirely

consistent with psychoanalytic doctrine. But my interpretation of Cooper's life and works does not conform to the
pattern of more orthodox psychoanalytic studies. These
usually seem to be written for a presumed audience of professional and amateur psychoanalysts. They examine a work
of art with the precision, the rigor and the thoroughness
required of a psychiatrist examining a patient. I do not
wish to take issue with that use of psychoanalytic theory,
but I want to make it clear that that is not my intention
here. The context in which I am "treating" Cooper is not
a clinical one. I have tried to write for the audience which
I believe the literary critic should address—one that has
read more novels than case histories. I have tried to make
my interpretations useful to those readers, whatever their
opinion of the applicability of psychoanalysis to the study
of literature, who are more interested in the second discipline than in the first; I have tried to shape my interpretations into a narrative of Cooper's emotional life.

With the first of these motives in mind, I decided that
my study would be more effective if, wherever possible, I
could keep it free of technical terms. The reliance upon
a clinical vocabulary may be one of the factors which have
prevented psychoanalytic literary criticism from finding
much sympathy or understanding among many people
whom it could appeal to. Among professional psychoanalysts, the terms are a necessary convenience, but the precise
categories which they imply are perhaps too rigid, too nar-
rowly defined, to be useful in a literary or biographical
context. It is the prerogative of critical prose, unlike scien-
tific prose, to be expository rather than demonstrative;
certainly the ideas which the terms represent can be developed with the full range of words and phrases already
in the vocabularies of nonpsychoanalytic readers. It is the
ideas that matter, and I felt that I could best articulate
them by avoiding a set of terms which I would have to define, terms which might even prevent the perception of the
ideas that they were originally meant to stand for. The dan-

ger of any technical vocabulary is that too often the terms serve not to encourage thought but to supplant it.

To make a consistent as well as a concise biographical narrative out of the relationship between Cooper's emotional life and his literary career, I omitted quite a bit from this account that was interesting chiefly from a theoretical point of view. For example, I have limited my analysis to certain aspects of Cooper's personality, notably his responses to the conflicts of the Oedipal period, and left other aspects, such as the influence of the pre-Oedipal stages of his development, out of my account. I do not feel, however, that I need to apologize for my omissions. The reader who considers how much longer this could easily have been may not himself feel that I owe him any apology for the missing pages; the reader who would like to consider the aspects of Cooper's life or his various novels which I do not develop is certainly free to do so. My own justification is that throughout I have sacrificed what, in terms of both the dimensions of Cooper's emotional life and the concerns which the student of literature can share with the psychoanalyst, was less interesting, less significant, less worth taking the space to discuss. Throughout this study I have kept two responsibilities in mind. The first was to Cooper: I have tried to examine his life and work in such a way as to slight or distort none of his leading preoccupations. The second was to my reader: I have tried to use the insights of psychoanalysis in a way that will make them accessible and persuasive even to someone who is not predisposed to accept Freud's account of the psyche. It is probably superfluous to say that I believe the best way to account clearly and fully for the scope and complexity of Cooper's preoccupations is by examining them from the perspective provided by psychoanalysis.

Psychoanalysis has taught us that the most important elements in an adult's mental life are the attitudes, emotions, and impulses formed in childhood around the figures of his parents. In Freud's first book, *The Interpretation of Dreams*, the Greek legend of King Oedipus was introduced as evidence of the most important of the infant's desires—his incestuous affection for one of his parents and murderous jealousy of the other. Only later did Freud and others begin to call this emotional nexus the "Oedipus complex." The name is unfortunate, because it obscures as much as it explains. Oedipus, of course, was the man who killed his father and married his mother; as Freud pointed out, and as our culture has eventually realized, every son conceives this inchoate wish. Yet as Freud also pointed out, though the popular conception of it seldom includes this, the Oedipus complex is more complex than that: each infant son similarly perceives his mother as a rival for the father's love, similarly wants to be dominated by his father. This emotional ambivalence felt by the son toward the figure of his father is fixed in the adult's unconscious. These two conflicting desires—actively to overthrow the father's authority and passively to submit to it—continue permanently to influence the behavior of the man who was the son. Were the child's desires unambivalent, murdering his father and marrying his mother might well be the easiest path to happiness. As soon as Oedipus realized what he had done, however, he punished *himself*, and his tragic fate sufficiently illustrates the fact that such a straightforward course will not overcome the infant's Oedipal conflicts. To become an adult, to outgrow the child within himself, each son has a more difficult path to pursue.

Oedipus was also the man who solved the infamous riddle of the Sphinx—that was in fact the deed that earned him Jocasta's hand. The Greek legend is only one example of the latent connection that men always seem to have made between riddles (apparently the oldest form of humor) and repressed desires. In Shakespeare's *Pericles*, the king of Antioch poses a riddle which each suitor to his daughter must answer correctly or forfeit his life:

> I am no viper, yet I feed
> On mother's flesh which did me breed.
> I sought a husband, in which labor
> I found that kindness in a father.
> He's father, son, and husband mild;
> I mother, wife, and yet his child . . .

Pericles puzzles this out to his dismay, for the solution to the king's riddle is that Antiochus himself is sleeping with his daughter.

Other literary instances of this linking of riddles and incestuous themes could be cited—there is even one in Cooper's *Wyandotté*, which I shall discuss in Chapter VII. The answers to riddles and the secrets of the unconscious have several obvious things in common: both are hidden, although there are clues that permit their discovery; tracing the unconscious sources behind a dream, a work of art or an action is very much like puzzling out a riddle, for both processes are interpretive, both bring a disguised truth to light. In one sense, therefore, in my interpretation of Cooper's works and actions, I shall be trying to make clear the riddle of his life.

But I mention the correlation between the answer to a riddle and the truths of the unconscious for another reason. The last line of Antiochus' riddle reads, "As you will live, resolve it you." And the solution to the earliest recorded riddle, the one that Oedipus unraveled, is "man." Oedipus' horrible dilemma is every man's: he saved his life by mastering the riddle of the Sphinx, but the riddle of his own existence finally mastered him. We are all presented with a similar problem—how to deal with, respond to, satisfy, or overcome the particular set of psychic needs that arise out of the emotional conflicts of our childhood. This is not a riddle we can solve—there is no simple answer—but rather one that we can only attempt to resolve. We never fully outgrow the secretly cherished and openly repugnant desires that we felt as children. The childhood needs preserved in our unconscious continue throughout our lives to demand satisfaction and to inspire guilt. But we must dress the child in grown-up clothes: our mental health, our emotional happiness, and our psychological salvation require us to accommodate these desires with the demands of living in the community of other adults. As we will live, we must resolve them; as we resolve them, so will we live.

As a man, an individual beset with the conflicting emotions common to humanity and those particular to himself, Cooper was forced to deal with the same problem. If the riddle of his life is an abstract question in the context I have created for it, it was real enough for him. Fortunately for us, he found writing a way of encountering this question, of responding to his psychic needs, of trying to master the problem of his identity.

DEBTS

I WOULD like first to acknowledge the assistance of two institutions—the New York State Historical Association, at Cooperstown, and the University of Virginia—in the research for and the preparation of this book. Joseph V. Ridgely, one of my former teachers at Columbia, and David Levin, one of my colleagues here at Virginia, read this book in manuscript. To their patient concern and friendly advice both it and I are indebted. The two men whose published work on Cooper I most respect are Henry Nash Smith and James Grossman, and I have been fortunate enough to benefit from their knowledge and their generosity. Their suggestions about this study have helped me to improve it. To Quentin Anderson I owe the most, more than his student can acknowledge, but not more than his friend can hope to be able to repay.

I owe my wife Ilene a debt of a different kind. She listened to, read, and aided this book. She suffered Cooper's presence to interfere with our life to a degree that I had no right to expect. She consistently (for this I need the present tense) encourages, inspires, and matures me, and—but for that I need the future. . . .

FENIMORE COOPER

TEXTS AND ABBREVIATIONS

Unless otherwise specified, the texts of Cooper's novels used in this study are from the first collected edition of his fiction (*Cooper's Novels*, 32 vols.; New York: W. A. Townsend and Company, 1859-1861). This is known as the "Author's Revised Edition"; for it Cooper wrote several new prefaces and added a number of footnotes, but actually made few substantive revisions in the texts themselves. Each novel is illustrated by the impressive drawings of F.O.C. Darley.

Throughout my study, all references to Cooper's letters and journals are cited in my text. These have recently been collected and edited by James Franklin Beard (*The Letters and Journals of James Fenimore Cooper*, 6 vols.; Cambridge, Mass.: Harvard Univ. Press, 1960-1968), to whom every student of the novelist owes an immense debt. References to Beard's edition are abbreviated "*L/J*," followed by volume and page numbers. Beard uses "broken brackets" (i.e. ⟨. . .⟩) to indicate words that Cooper struck out, and square brackets (i.e. [. . .]) to supply missing words or letters, or to reconstruct damaged portions of the manuscript. Unless otherwise specified, all quotations from the letters or the journals exactly follow Beard's edition. Permission to quote from Beard's volumes was generously granted by Harvard University Press.

CHAPTER I

"THE SECRETS OF
AUTHORSHIP"

IN MANY respects Cooper was the founding father of the novel in America. Although other writers had earlier aspired to the role, he was the first popularly successful American novelist, the first in the land of opportunity to prove that fiction could afford a citizen of the republic with a career. The imaginative debt that such minor nineteenth century novelists as Simms and Stowe owed to Cooper is obvious, and in general popular fiction remained in the mold that Cooper had shaped for it until after the Civil War. Yet it is equally true to say that Cooper first established many of the themes with which the major authors of the century would deal. Before Hawthorne, he wrote historical romances, including one set in Puritan New England. Before Melville, he wrote sea-going fiction in which the ocean provides a setting at once realistic and symbolic. Before James, he wrote international novels. Before Twain, he wrote the kind of tale in which, at the end, the hero lights out for the territory. Before Howells, he wrote American *romans de société*. In these instances it would be harder to measure the precise extent of Cooper's influence, though it is certain that each of these subsequent writers had read Cooper. It is also certain that Cooper supplied them with the one thing which he himself had consciously lacked: an example, for better or worse, of what the novel in America could be. Throughout his career he was very much aware of his particular responsibilities as the first popular American novelist, and of his service as a pathfinder into the possibilities of fiction in the new world. Like the later writers of the American Renaissance, Cooper attempted to be representatively and distinctly American; he was determined, to quote what Melville said about the cisatlantic author's political obligation, "to carry republican progressiveness into Literature." At the same time, Cooper was the first novelist to acknowledge, as Hawthorne and James later did, the specific sort of difficulties faced by an American writer.

Some of these difficulties, as is well known, Cooper could not overcome. We may, however, need to be reminded that during his lifetime he not only ranked among the world's most popular novelists, but also was ranked, by such European peers as Scott and Balzac, as one of the world's greatest novelists as well. Americans, whatever their opinion of Cooper's merits, recognized his preeminence. He discovered and developed many of the nation's literary resources; in the settings and subjects of his books, he helped to introduce the young country to itself—even though it did not always like what it saw there. As part of the meeting held in New York on February 24th, 1852, to commemorate and honor the novelist's death five months earlier, Irving, Emerson, Hawthorne, Melville, and most of the republic's other leading men of letters entered their praise for Cooper's accomplishments, and especially for his contribution to the cause of an American literature, into the public record. Forty years afterward, Mark Twain wrote "Fenimore Cooper's Literary Offenses" not to praise Cooper, but to bury him. Yet merely the fact that in the 1890s Twain took the trouble to destroy Cooper's reputation in his notorious and calculating essay shows how alive Cooper's presence was even at the end of the nineteenth century, two generations after his death.

Since then, despite the attention paid him by literary and historical scholars, Cooper's stature has diminished considerably. As most students learn when they are finally asked to read a Cooper novel, he himself is much better than his reputation. That they are not asked more often to read

Cooper—not as often, at least, as they are asked to read Hawthorne or Melville, Twain or James—is somewhat surprising, considering the respect with which Americans generally treat founding fathers. The problem that critics have had in deciding Cooper's place among the authors of the previous century is a complicated phenomenon, one that can be attributed to a number of causes. The list of his novels suffers from the absence of a certified masterpiece, a single work whose merit or power is beyond dispute; certainly Hawthorne's preeminence would be less secure without *The Scarlet Letter*, Melville's without *Moby-Dick*, and Twain's without *The Adventures of Huckleberry Finn*. Even Cooper's best work has often been tainted by the suspicion that it is adolescent reading, although adolescents no longer read Cooper. But Twain has survived the fact that younger readers enjoy his books, and if Cooper never wrote a masterpiece, eight or ten of his novels are works of substantial merit and power. Except for Henry James, in fact, no other nineteenth century American wrote as many good novels as Cooper.

Yet there are additional reasons why Cooper's reputation is apparently at odds with his achievement. For the twentieth century reading public in general, his assumptions about aesthetics are too firmly fixed in the early nineteenth century. Part of the task of criticism should be to bridge such temporal distances, to put modern readers in a position to appreciate works which were written to satisfy their ancestors or according to extinct literary convictions. Until recently, however, Cooper's reputation has been poorly served by contemporary critical assumptions about literary value. His work has been blamed for or ignored because of its failure to meet the standards of formalist criticism. The aesthetic expectations of New Criticism were nurtured by the Modernists, and consequently it stressed technique over narrative, the working up of language over the working out of plot. By training its audience to read carefully and reread conscientiously, the Modernist Novel on the one hand made possible the retrieval of Melville's books from the uncomprehending nineteenth century; on the other, it threatened to consign Cooper's to the oblivion of critical disregard. To the modern taste, Cooper seems incredibly unconscious of most matters of literary craft. His nonchalant attitude toward the creative process, which I shall discuss later in this chapter, made him an unattractive figure to formalists. Their manifest denial of Cooper's claims upon the tradition of American literature, however, reveals the deficiencies of this approach to art at least as much as it reveals those of Cooper's own work.

All of these factors have contributed to the uncertainty about the rightful place of the first successful American novelist, about the value of his work and the meaning of his career. The critic who would enlist in Cooper's cause could address any one of them. But these are essentially aesthetic issues; redressing them will not finally clear up the confusion about Cooper. He has been a problematic figure almost since he began to write, and the problems have involved questions of personality and temperament as well as literary merit. The course of Cooper's career has always puzzled his critics. "In his substantial character," concludes Vernon L. Parrington, "was embodied what may well appear no more than a bundle of contradictions. . . . No other major writer, unless it be Whitman, has been so misunderstood, and no other offers a knottier problem to the student of American letters."[1] I believe that the contradictions in Cooper—whether in his character or in his career—are what have most interfered with a proper evaluation of his significance. To critics and historians he is a major but intractable figure, an author whose inconsistencies and perplexities make him exceedingly difficult to deal with for the purposes of either literary criticism or cultural history. Unable to decide what to make of the novelist, scholars have often been vexed in their desire to make conclusions about his novels.

[1] *Main Currents in American Thought*, II: *The Romantic Revolution in America* (New York: Harcourt, Brace & World, Inc., 1927), p. 214.

Parrington's cautionary observation was made in 1927, when only three book-length studies and a score of essays and articles treating Cooper were available. Since then, of course, a rapidly increasing number of scholars have interested themselves in him, have researched neglected portions of his life, have focused on specific aspects of his career, have examined different novels in his bibliography, and have published their conclusions. Cooper now is better understood. Yet the knotty problem posed by the contradictions he embodied still, as we shall see, remains unraveled. Perhaps the best way to establish the meaning and importance of Cooper's achievement would be to give his life, his career, and his work a sense of coherence. This they have so far lacked, and without it, it has been impossible truly to understand his relationship with literature or society in nineteenth century America.

Cooper's contemporaries, including the sympathetic ones, were often at a loss to comprehend his temperamental behavior. Even in his own time he had two reputations: that of the romancer who entertained his society with indulgently constructed novels of adventure, that of the critic who took his society to task in unattractive and aspersive novels of social commentary. After a certain point in Cooper's career, a reader must have picked up the newest tale wondering how he would find its author—with a smile or a scowl on the face of his prose. Too often for their liking, Americans found him in print in nonliterary contexts: on the front page of their newspaper they might have read the report of his most recent public controversy or law suit; on its editorial page, either the latest journalistic attack on Cooper's social opinions or the novelist's testy defense of them in a letter. No doubt the ordinary American gave up the attempt to come to terms with this extraordinary American author. The country's first popular novelist was also its first aggressively unpopular one; the first writer to make a career out of fiction kept threatening to retire. At some moments in his work Cooper basks in his and his countrymen's mutual esteem for each other; at others, he relieves himself of his disgust with America in line after line of invective. In his books, Cooper quarreled with his country; in life, with his neighbors and countrymen; and in reality, with himself. Old friends privately expressed dismay and uncertainty. Unfriendly critics publicly and positively reached their own conclusions: Park Benjamin, an influential newspaper editor and a victim of Cooper's penchant for libel suits, pronounced him "the craziest loon that ever was suffered to roam at large without whip and keeper."[2] To this Cooper responded with another subpoena. His numerous attempts to explain himself, however, in pamphlets, prefaces and letters, even in courtrooms, did little good.

After the novelist's death, relatives and friends insisted that his character had been badly misunderstood, and especially that the bitterness of the quarrels should be forgotten. What William Cullen Bryant, who had known him for thirty years, wanted somewhat apologetically to direct the public's attention to when he addressed the Cooper Memorial Meeting in New York were "the creations of his genius, fixed in living words, [which] survive the frail material organs by which the words were first traced."[3] Yet contradictions also survive in the various books. Ideas set forth in them directly refute each other. Antithetical judgments are made upon the very same subjects. Within particular novels, two conflicting sets of values often compete not for the reader's sympathy only, but, one feels, for the author's.

We shall examine specific conflicts later, in the context of the novels and events in which they make their presence felt. I want now to turn to what others have said about this problem, without attempting to do full justice to their anal-

[2] Quoted by John P. McWilliams, Introduction to *Fenimore Cooper: The Critical Heritage*, ed. George Dekker and McWilliams (London: Routledge & Kegan Paul, 1973), p. 22.

[3] William Cullen Bryant, "Discourse on the Life, Genius, and Writings of J. Fenimore Cooper," in *Precaution*, p. xl.

yses, but simply to outline the dimensions of Cooper's contradictory character. Some of Cooper's critics ignore his
inconsistencies. Others consider them unimportant: "essentially a man of fragments" is Yvor Winters' description of
Cooper.[4] Winters is primarily interested in the writer's
stylistic achievements, and this characterization amply serves
his purpose by permitting him to discuss those passages
that succeed as prose. Aesthetically, Cooper's greatest moments are fragmentary, but psychologically, he is of course
indivisible, and unfortunately, the attempt to come to terms
with him cannot license one to dismiss bad art.

A different kind of division is made, either explicitly
or implicitly, by the majority of commentators. To most
of them, Cooper still has two reputations, and their procedure corresponds to D. H. Lawrence's in *Studies in Classic
American Literature*, where he sorts the novelist's work into
two categories—"Fenimore Cooper's White Novels" and
"Fenimore Cooper's Leatherstocking Novels." Some critics
locate the "real" Fenimore Cooper in the first of these
classes, which contains the novels of social commentary,
and some in the second, which contains Natty Bumppo,
Chingachgook, and the pathless wilderness. Most would
agree that he could not be equally in both, since the two
groups seem written from antithetical literary perspectives
and affirm radically different ethical codes. Robert E. Spiller, a pioneer critic of the "White" novels, labels the two
groups "novels of purpose" and "romances," terms which
imply the value judgment Spiller in fact endorses. About
the romances he has little to say; his thesis is that Cooper's
remaining novels "are at once a reflection and an interpretation of the emerging American civilization about
him."[5] Spiller's purpose is primarily sociological. The

[4] Yvor Winters, "Fenimore Cooper or The Ruins of Time," in
Maule's Curse: Seven Studies in the History of American Obscurantism
(1938), rpt. in *In Defense of Reason* (Denver: Allan Swallow, 1947),
p. 198.

[5] *Fenimore Cooper: Critic of His Times* (New York: Minton, Balch,
& Company, 1931), p. viii.

"White" novels have been appropriated by a number of others with a similar interest. Parrington, for one, calls Cooper "the barometer of a gusty generation." He traces the tensions and contradictions in Cooper's thought to "an underlying conflict between the man and his age. . . . The perplexities and dogmatisms that clutter so many of his later pages . . . are a testimony to the confusions of a generation in the midst of epic changes."[6] Examined separately, however, Cooper's social novels are by no means unambiguous, and even within the ranks of their critics conflicts exist. About half have decided that despite a superficial allegiance to republican democracy, Cooper was at heart an American aristocrat; half, that his inconsistencies can best be explained by regarding him as an orthodox Jacksonian Democrat. The study of the relation between an author and his age is undeniably important. Yet such a study should always recognize that society is only one of the forces that shape an individual's mental and emotional responses. Whatever cultural ideals a writer may subscribe to or reflect have to some degree been determined by his own particular history. At least in Western society we are all members of a family before we acquire membership in a community. To ignore personal influences would distort the meaning of anyone's interaction with society. And in the case of James Fenimore Cooper, a purely socio-historical perspective is especially distorting for two reasons.

The title of Spiller's book is *Fenimore Cooper: Critic of His Times.* Its index reveals the limitations of this conception of him. Listed there are Cooper's opinions on New England, a large navy, personal liberty, England, France, and women, but not slavery, manifest destiny, the Mexican War, and the other really major social issues of the times. An opinionated man, Cooper did have things to say about all of these, but in the main his most firmly held beliefs, the ones he developed at length in his books, are too idiosyncratic to be construed into judicious social commentary.

6 Parrington, p. 215.

For example, a local New York crisis, the Anti-Rent War of the 1840s, provoked Cooper into writing a trilogy of novels of purpose; abolitionism, briefly mentioned in many of his books, he considered exclusively a southern issue; it was his opinion that if the nation ever went to war with itself, it would fight over leases, not slaves.

In addition, the emphasis on Cooper's role as a social critic distorts his own opinion of his achievements: "If anything from the pen of the writer of these romances is at all to outlive himself, it is, unquestionably, the series of 'The Leather-Stocking Tales.' "[7]

With this opinion later generations of readers have unquestionably agreed, and it is with the five Leather-Stocking Tales that the study of Cooper usually begins and ends. By this means most people remain unaware of the blatant contradictions in Cooper's thought, although inconsistencies are embodied in the Tales as well. Leslie Fiedler, who is interested in the romances, perceives the problem. To solve it, he splits the novelist in two, into the "myth-maker and the man of letters," into "a half-conscious framer of legends" and "a fully conscious moralist and polemical social critic." This second man is not very interesting: "Cooper was, whenever he wrote self-consciously, above all things a gentleman"; but the first, the creator of Natty Bumppo, possesses a "mythopoeic power which, in a handful of books, delivered him from the limitations of his class and his time."[8] Consequently, one can dismiss the "White" novels entirely, a quick operation and for many critics completely painless. "It should be evident by now," writes one,

> that any mature approach to an assessment of Cooper's essential qualities must be, primarily, neither personal nor stylistic—though, in a very real sense, it is possible to speak of Cooper's art—nor sociological—though it is

[7] "Preface to the Leather-Stocking Tales," in *The Deerslayer*, p. vi.
[8] *Love and Death in the American Novel* (1960; rev. ed. New York: Dell Publishing Co., Inc., 1966), pp. 188 and 190-91.

also clear that Cooper's insights into the mainspirngs
of society are, while limited in their scope, extraordinarily clear. No, Cooper's genius was mythopoeic rather
than comic; . . . dealing, at its rare purest, in arche-
types rather than types.[9]

But can we accept either this reduction of the Cooper canon
to "a handful of books" or this promotion of an individual
from the limitations of class and time to the atemporal,
impersonal realm of myth? We cannot without, on the one
hand, doing violence to the creative energy Cooper invested
in his other novels, or, on the other, ignoring the particular
material out of which Cooper shaped his "myth."

Two facts alone are sufficient to underscore the importance of both these claims for our attention. The first- and
last-written of the Leather-Stocking Tales, the beginning
and end of the mythic cycle, are set on the site of the first
and last years of Cooper's life. The action of *The Pioneers*
and *The Deerslayer* takes place in the vicinity of Cooperstown, and if, in the final reverberations of these stories in
the reader's mind, they attain the self-contained status of
myth, in the initial imaginative impulses of their creator's
mind, they must have been linked with the circumstances of
his biography. Rather than simply positing the unexplained
existence of some mythopoeic faculty, the critic has an
obligation to explain how one man, dealing with personal
material, writing from his own experience, can at the same
time tell a story that most readers perceive as mythic, as
archetypical. And there is yet another connection he must
take into account, for there is one more Cooper novel set
on that same territory—*Home As Found*, which was written after *The Pioneers* and before *The Deerslayer*. In none
of his books was Cooper more of a "polemical social critic"

[9] Charles A. Brady, "James Fenimore Cooper: Myth-Maker and
Christian Romancer," in *American Classics Reconsidered*, ed. Harold
C. Gardiner (New York: Charles Scribner's Sons, 1958), p. 82.

than in this one; in none does he seem more constricted by "the limitations of his class and his time." Both these fictive worlds—the mythopoeic and the moral—share not only the same setting, but the same source as well. However attractive the five Leather-Stocking Tales might be in themselves, they must somehow be reconciled with the other twenty-seven, and all thirty-two must somehow be understood in terms of the one imagination that conceived them.

Those novels sit uneasily on the same shelf. Several critics have attempted to interpret the inconsistencies in both Cooper's writing and his life. Here again, even the interpretations are in direct conflict. Henry Walcott Boynton, one of Cooper's biographers, cites "a love of his own place, the soil from which he sprang, the hills and prairies and forests of his land . . . a jealous passion for the *patria*" as the emotion which "binds together and makes intelligible all those otherwise contradictory and baffling elements in his nature and conduct."[10] According to Cooper himself, patriotism was a significant motif of, and a persuasive motive behind, his work; on May 21st, 1831, he wrote to an acquaintance:

> You have appreciated my motives, in regard to my own country, and it has given me great satisfaction. Her mental independence is my object, and if I can go down to the grave with the reflection that I have done a little towards it, I shall have the consolation of knowing that I have not been useless in my generation. (*L/J*, II, 84)

Exactly the opposite cause for "that profound psychic split with which Cooper was doomed to struggle through much of his creative career" is offered by Robert H. Zoellner. He diagnoses Cooper's complaint as "a profound emotional disattachment," a "gradually developing alienation from

10 *James Fenimore Cooper* (New York: The Century Co., 1931), p. 391.

13

his American roots."[11] A very good case can be made—and Zoellner makes one—for this alienation; he quotes from Cooper's letter to another acquaintance on March 16th, 1832: "One fact is beyond dispute—I am not with my own country—the void between us is immense—" (*L/J*, II, 237).

Still, Boynton's Cooper is at bottom the successful writer of romances, Zoellner's the embittered critic of society. Marius Bewley suggests a way to reconcile the two:

> In his political and agrarian novels [Cooper] enlarged the scope of the novel itself by introducing ideas in a functional and structural way. These ideas became the very substance of the novels. Important as this was technically in the development of fictional form, the novels remain very incomplete successes because Cooper's personal feelings and imagination never seem wholly involved. In the Leather-stocking tales the reverse is true. The ideas are not present as such, although they may make their presence felt indirectly. Instead, the imagination takes over. Natty Bumppo is not a "character" . . . but a symbol thrown up from the depths of Cooper's own response to America, a response that involved both love and revulsion.[12]

As examples of books in which "Cooper's personal feelings and imagination never seem wholly involved," Bewley refers to "the Effingham novels," *Homeward Bound* and *Home As Found*. The mere presence of the word "home" in both titles, however, should indicate that, whatever they may amount to as works of art, the Effingham Novels do reflect Cooper's personal feelings. In fact, his contemporaries read them as autobiography. Around them swirled the greatest controversy in the novelist's career; they and their critical reception were at the center of his lengthy

[11] Robert H. Zoellner, "Fenimore Cooper: Alienated American," *American Quarterly* 13 (1961), 57.

[12] *The Eccentric Design: Form in the Classic American Novel* (New York: Columbia Univ. Press, 1963), p. 111.

libel suits against the press. The Effingham Novels represent a complex problem to which I shall return, but one
thing is immediately clear—they do not represent a failure
on Cooper's part to involve himself personally with his
writing. Bewley's solution to the problem posed by Cooper's
disparate novels is inadequate because he confuses the
reader's response to those novels with the author's intention
in writing them. Cooper's political novels do not stimu-
late our imagination, our feelings, to the degree that the
Leather-Stocking Tales do. But the attempt to understand
Cooper's works, while it must also accept and try to explain the appeal of his most successful books, nonetheless
must define its limits by the scope of his own—not our—
interests and preoccupations.

Henry Nash Smith and Richard Chase are two critics
who meet Cooper on his own ground, recognizing that artistic success or failure will not serve as a gauge of the novelist's involvement, that Cooper's ground includes the landed
estate as well as the virgin forest. Natty Bumppo, a man of
the forest, in fact a virgin himself, is unlettered, is tortur-
ously inaccurate in his grammar and pronunciation, is content to wipe off the drop on the end of his nose with his
hand. Ned Effingham owns a large estate, dotes on his
daughter, prides himself on his education, speaks not only
correctly but with studied carefulness of tone and diction,
and doubtless carries a spotless silk handkerchief. Yet Natty
and Ned both occupy a place in Cooper's psyche, though
they may stand at opposite poles. According to Smith, "the
antithesis [is] between nature and civilization, between freedom and law"—

> Cooper was able to speak for his people on this theme
> because the forces at work within him closely repro-
> duced the patterns of thought and feeling that pre-
> vailed in the society at large. But he felt the problem
> more deeply than his contemporaries: he was at once
> more strongly devoted to the principle of social order

and more vividly responsive to the ideas of nature and freedom in the Western forest than they were.[13]

Chase's interpretation of the conflicting forces at work within Cooper is similar:

> In short, Cooper found it necessary in America to be both a conservative and an anarchist. The vitality of his romances, the very form in which he sees things, the actions that he is able to make vivid—these stem from the political contradiction at the center of his thought . . . the contradiction between the values of a traditional society and those of the lone individual in the marginal hinterland.[14]

These very perceptive analyses provide a breakdown of most of the important elements in Cooper's thought. The terms of the polarity that they employ—nature and civilization, freedom and law, anarchy and conservatism, the individual and society—are essential to any serious effort to apprehend either the meaning of his novels or the course of his life. As we study those novels and that life, other antitheses will occur to us, for if this hasty review of Cooper criticism has uncovered the broad outlines of the "bundle of contradictions" represented by his character and embodied in his writing, it has necessarily left the details unmentioned.

Yet nothing that has been said so far satisfactorily accounts for the contents of that bundle, or explains what held it together. Most of Cooper's critics cite his relationship with his country as the source of his creative writing and his conflicting opinions. For Spiller, Parrington, and a number of others,[15] the historical and social events and shifts of perspective in the Age of Jackson provide the in-

[13] *Virgin Land: The American West as Symbol and Myth* (1950; rpt. Cambridge, Mass.: Harvard Univ. Press, 1970), pp. 60-61.

[14] *The American Novel and Its Traditions* (Garden City, N.Y.: Doubleday Anchor Books, 1957), p. 52.

[15] Cf. Dorothy Waples, John Ross, Arthur M. Schlesinger, Jr.

tellectual basis for an understanding of Cooper. But even
Smith, who believes that Cooper's imaginative preoccupations "closely reproduced the patterns of thought and feeling that prevailed in the society at large," makes one necessary qualification: "he felt the problem more deeply than
his contemporaries." Almost by definition, an author's vision is uniquely his; that he seeks to express it imaginatively is simply another way of saying that he feels a certain
set of problems more deeply than his contemporaries, who
feel no such need. So deep were Cooper's feelings that they
seem unfathomable: one critic concludes that at the bottom of his response to America was a jealous love; another,
a profound emotional detachment; and another, both love
and revulsion. To this confusion must be added Thomas
R. Lounsbury's description of the last decade of Cooper's
life:

> He had now lived for so long a time a life remote from
> the real clash of conflicting views that he had finally
> reached that satisfied state of opinion which thinks the
> little circle in which it moves is the proper orbit for the
> revolution of thought of the whole race. As he advanced
> in years he narrowed instead of broadening.[16]

As a matter of fact, at almost no point during his career
did Cooper fully participate in or represent "the real clash"
of the conflicting views of his generation; "Cooper's America," in the words of the historian Marvin Meyers, is not
"a transcript of reality."[17]

Not merely the contradictory and idiosyncratic character
of his response to events in the real world, but its intensity,
amounting nearly to hysteria at times, nearly always out of
proportion to its ostensible causes, suggests that there is a
missing factor in the equation between Fenimore Cooper

[16] *James Fenimore Cooper* (Boston: Houghton, Mifflin and Company, 1882), p. 256.
[17] *The Jacksonian Persuasion: Politics and Belief* (Stanford: Stanford Univ. Press, 1957), p. 97.

and contemporary America. As James Grossman tactfully concludes at the end of his excellent study of Cooper, the source of the novelist's quarrel with his countrymen was originally located within Cooper himself—he "may in fact have created the conspiracy against himself which he discovered and which soon by his efforts took on an objective reality."[18] It was primarily the inexplicable force of his feelings that cost Cooper his popularity. His various quarrels, his irascibility, his iterated complaints and contentions —these unlikable traits came to stand for the man himself. In the minds of his contemporaries, the image of the popular novelist was replaced by that of the belligerent and seemingly implacable faultfinder. If Cooper's actions provoked a few people to decide that he had gone mad, they puzzled many others enough to keep them from reading his later novels. For in the second half of his career, Cooper's need to respond to the forceful emotions which he clearly felt but did not himself understand often overwhelmed his obligations as a novelist: the proprieties of the story, the just expectations of the reader are violated by an author with other and more pressing things on his mind. This need was equally present, equally significant, in the earlier novels, though there it could usually be accommodated within the framework of the tale. Erupting through the story's surface over and over again, it irrevocably ruined most of the final ones. That the same unconscious energy was also responsible for his "mythopoeic power"—the spring of his successful writing cited by one class of critics—is another contradiction that confronts the student of Cooper.

To explain Cooper's complex attitude toward America, to account for his achievements as a myth-maker, to reconcile the antitheses that inform his writing, it is necessary to look at more than the history of his period and the texts of his books. The child and man who was James Cooper (the name he received from his parents) and J. Fenimore

[18] *James Fenimore Cooper* (Stanford: Stanford Univ. Press, 1949), p. 264.

18

Cooper (the name he legally adopted), the particular circumstances of his life, must have an equal claim to our attention. I believe that that life will provide the evidence to
resolve the contradictions we have noted. There are difficulties in this approach to Cooper's art. There is the fact that
he never wrote a full autobiography. There is his insistence
at the end of his life that no authorized biography be written, which led to the loss and destruction of many personal
documents. There is the scarcity of reliable information
about much of his early life. There is even Cooper's own
assertion that he never "endeavored to delineate myself in
any character of any book I ever wrote" (L/J, III, 351).

Actually, this last assertion, made in the heat of one of
Cooper's public controversies, has never convinced any of
his readers. In my fifth chapter I shall examine the palpable
relationship between the novelist and Ned Effingham, the
most explicitly autobiographical of his characters. Several
other of his books, as his critics have long realized, are
based very closely on personal experience. But the study
of a creative artist need not rely solely on personal documents or autobiographical material. The twentieth century conclusions of psychoanalysis about the creative process
have confirmed what many writers themselves always knew:
that acts of the imagination are revelatory. In the Preface to
The Snow-Image, for example, Nathaniel Hawthorne admits that a writer cannot help but disclose his own character, though the reader who notices only the author's
prefatory account of himself will be misled. To become acquainted with the man, he writes, "You must make quite
another kind of inquest, and look through the whole range
of his fictitious characters, good and evil, in order to detect
any of his essential traits." Hawthorne would doubtless
agree with what Thoreau says in *Walden*: that although
"in most books, the *I*, or first person, is omitted . . . it is, after
all, always the first person speaking." Thoreau goes on to
say that, for his part, he would require of every author "a
simple and sincere account of his own life." This require-

ment is one of the reasons behind Thoreau's impatience with romantic fiction; in his eyes, novels are insincere, that is, fictitious. But as I shall try to demonstrate, the account of Cooper's emotional life supplied by the texts of his fictions, though by no means simple, is nevertheless recoverable from them. And not only is such an "inquest" of Cooper's novels a legitimate means by which to approach the novelist; understanding his novels in this way is also, I believe, essential to a full appreciation of their meaning.

An objection which is sometimes entered against the assumption I have just made is that the process of literary composition is not, like the dream or fantasy, a primary process—which is to say that if the dreamer in his bed is wholly unconscious, the artist at his desk is not. No one would deny that the imagination reaches into a portion of the mind that is inaccessible to consciousness, but critics who are skeptical of the value of biographical and literary studies based upon the interpretive methods of psychoanalysis point out that a large part of an author's work is conscious and deliberate, that, to paraphrase T. S. Eliot, a good writer knows when to trust the unrevised offerings of his imagination, when to overrule them, and how to reshape them according to the imperatives of his art. Aesthetic needs do not enter into the mind of the dreamer, which is concerned instead exclusively with psychic needs, but both kinds of necessities are involved in the production of the creative artifact, the text of the book we read. This, too, no one would wish to deny. Since in the chapters that follow I shall use the texts of Cooper's books as the basis for an analysis of the particular emotional demands which, throughout his life, he was forced to try to fulfill, I want in this first chapter to introduce the grounds on which Cooper's novels can be used as evidence in my inquiry. It would be possible to establish that theoretically, on general principles, but because we are here concerned with a particular author, it will be more relevant and, I think, more useful to limit the discussion chiefly to what we know about the way Cooper's imagination worked.

In my next chapter I shall examine Cooper's decision, made when he was thirty, to become a writer. Apparently this decision was unpremeditated. Premeditation, in fact, was never a feature of his literary career. His only training for the occupation was a wide familiarity with contemporary British fiction, which Cooper read avidly. At the time he started writing, a novel was published in several volumes (in America as two, in England as three), and among the writer's most important obligations was supplying his publisher with enough words to fill up those volumes. Like epic poems, nineteenth century novels commonly take their time; this is one reason why Cooper's modern reader tends to run out of patience before he has run out of pages, but Cooper's imagination was perfectly suited to this scale. Having chosen to try his hand at telling a story, he quickly learned that it suffered with writer's cramp only from restrictions, never from use. Reviewers of his second novel, *The Spy*, observed that the book's denouement seemed rushed and muddled. When he revised *The Spy*'s Introduction for a later edition, Cooper confessed what had happened:

> As the second volume was slowly printing, from manuscript that was barely dry when it went into the compositor's hands, the publisher intimated that the work might grow to a length that would consume the profits. To set his mind at rest, the last chapter was actually written, printed and paged, several weeks before the chapters which precede it were even thought of. This circumstance, while it cannot excuse, may serve to explain the manner in which the actors are hurried off the scene.[19]

In regard to his first book he told Andrew Thompson Goodrich, the man who printed it, that "I commenced the writing of a moral tale—finding it swell to a rather unwieldy size—I destroy'd the manuscript and chang'd it to a novel" (*L/J*, I, 42). That novel, *Precaution*, was published in

[19] *The Spy*, p. xi.

1821. In 1851 the novelist died. During those thirty years as an author, Cooper produced almost fifty books, thirty-two of which were novels, a number of pamphlets, reviews, and miscellaneous items, even a play: an impressive inventory, and one that confirms the soundness of his ultimate choice of a career. It also implies a characteristic that Cooper shared with other contemporaneous writers, the method of composition that made it possible for him to be so prolific. "No book," he wrote Goodrich about *Precaution*, "was ever written with less thought and more rapidity . . . from 14 to 28 pages of the book were written between 9 o clock in the Morning and 9 at night . . . and it is a fact that *no plot* was fix'd on until the first Vol. was half done" (*L/J*, 1, 66). Unlike the rest of his novels in many respects, *Precaution* did provide Cooper with a model in this one: what he said about its composition applies more or less to them all, with one difference—it is doubtful that he ever destroyed another manuscript.

From his letters to various publishers one can reconstruct the mechanics of Cooper's craft. These might dismay the reader who appreciates the trouble later authors like Flaubert or Joyce took with each sentence, but they were typical enough for his time. When his English publishers asked him to revise nine of his novels for new editions, Cooper requested fifty pounds per book, adding however that he would do it for five, "if you will leave me the sole judge of the execution—This is an age when good company makes an author rather shameless, and I believe it is very generally understood that the genius finishes to order" (*L/J*, 11, 64). Nor have authors always accepted Eliot's assumptions about good writing. Also in keeping with his age was Cooper's belief that inspiration, not perspiration, produced the best work—"Graham had three parts [of *Jack Tier*] stolen in manuscript, and I have been obliged to rewrite them. This has impaired their interest, for one never writes as well, on such subjects, as at the first heat" (*L/J*, v, 198-99). *Jack Tier*, one of Cooper's later novels, was the only one published serially before it was issued as a book. Like Charles Dickens, who had popularized this form of publication, Cooper was still writing the book's final chapters while the earlier ones were being read. But once Cooper had established himself as a novelist, he regularly sent manuscript to the publisher without waiting until he had finished the tale: "I should like to print as I go," he said about *The Prairie*; "It will be a great relief to me, as I detest looking over my own rascally scrawls" (*L/J*, I, 131). This practice of course meant that the writing of a book's second volume had to keep pace with the typesetters at work on the first, but Cooper rarely gave his publishers any reason to complain of delay. What he promised them in regard to *The Bravo*—"I shall work as fast as possible, and do justice to the book" (*L/J*, II, 71)—was true in almost every other case. That a book was sometimes sacrificed to expediency was an occupational hazard familiar to many professional authors of the period.

At all times substantial revisions were practically impossible in the face of this publishing procedure, a result which Cooper occasionally regretted, as in this comment to a publisher:

> I ought in justice to myself to say, that in opposition to a thousand good resolutions, the Pioneers, has been more hastily and carelessly written than any of my books—Not a line has been copied, and it has gone from my desk to the printers—I have not to this moment been able even to *read* it— (*L/J*, I, 86)

Yet despite such regrets, he retained the basic procedure throughout his career, although shortly after *The Pioneers* was finished he began to employ a secretary to make his "rascally scrawls" more legible. Another letter details how the average Cooper novel made its way to the public. Aaron Vail, American chargé d'affaires in London, had written the novelist soliciting an autograph for Princess Victoria; Cooper responded lavishly:

> I send a rough manuscript precisely as it was written, and which contains a chapter of the Bravo. The work in question was written in this manner by myself and then copied by a secretary. The copy was corrected again by myself, and then it passed into the hands of the printers. The sheets were subjected to another correction, and the result was the book. Now it is more than probable that the work will differ materially from this manuscript, but they who take the trouble to compare them will have an opportunity of getting an insight into the secrets of authorship. (*L/J*, III, 144-45)

Note that the copy and the galleys were "corrected"—not revised. And judging from other Cooper manuscripts, a comparison of Victoria's gift with the published *Bravo* would probably not in fact reveal many material differences. But if major revisions, stylistic improvements, and careful rewriting were not often among the secrets of Cooper's authorship, their absence greatly assists an effort to gain insight into another class of secrets: where the student of literature as aesthetics would apologize, one interested in how artists employ their imagination to respond to their psychic needs is encouraged to proceed.

Because for the most part Cooper's manuscripts passed through the process of publication unchanged, his fictions reflect faithfully "the first heat" of their creation. As we might have guessed, for the act of creation itself, which the ancients attributed to the visitation of a divine spirit, Cooper felt no awe. He candidly recounts a conversation with Sir Walter Scott, an author the American ranked with Shakespeare:

> Curious to know whether a writer as great and as practised as he, felt the occasional despondency which invariably attends all my own little efforts of this nature, I remarked that I found the mere composition of a tale a source of pleasure; so much so, that I always invented

twice as much as was committed to paper, in my walks, or in my bed, and, in my own judgment, much the best parts of the composition never saw the light; for, what was written was usually written at set hours, and was a good deal a matter of chance; and that going over and over the same subject in proofs, disgusted me so thoroughly with the book, that I supposed every one else would be disposed to view it with the same eyes.[20]

Cooper happily reports that Scott agreed with him about the effect of rereading his own work, but much more interesting is what Cooper reveals about the workings of his imagination. Quoting this passage, William Charvat notes one implication: "that he threw away many inspirations and inventions simply because they did not turn up at the right point in the course of composition."[21] Charvat's indictment is well-founded, and consistent with Cooper's reckless attitude toward authorship. But for my purposes emphasis should be placed not on the inspirations that were lost, but on those that indeed turned up "at the right point." The following description by Susan Fenimore Cooper, who served for many years as her father's secretary and copyist, underscores the point I wish to make:

On this occasion, as on all others when writing a book, he first adopted some general leading idea, sketched vaguely in his mind a few of the more prominent characters, and then immediately began his work in its final shape, leaving the details to suggest and develop themselves during the progress of the volume. Excepting when writing history, he is not known to have ever drawn up a written plan, and in one or two instances only were a few brief notes thrown on paper, regarding some particular chapter. In all the details he depended

20 *Gleanings in Europe* [*France*] (Philadelphia: Carey, Lea & Blanchard, 1837), II, 19.
21 William Charvat, "Cooper as Professional Author," *New York History* 52 (1954), 497-98.

in a great measure on the thought and feeling of the moment.[22]

Susan is talking specifically about *The Spy*, but throughout his career Cooper maintained the same writing habits that he acquired in 1820, when he composed *Precaution* with so much more rapidity than thought. Understanding the novels that he published in 1830 or 1840 or 1850 will mean taking into account the way in which the circumstances of his life changed between the beginning and the end of his career, but this one professional circumstance remained unchanged.

Though he called his imagination a source of pleasure, Cooper was impatient with the more formal aspects of writing. Both his own instincts and the usages of his time led him to create as spontaneously as possible. He intentionally limited the degree of conscious control—either premeditated or ex post facto—he could exert over his stories. He seldom planned his plots; he seldom revised them. Rather, as Susan tells us, he depended upon the thought and feeling of the moment to supply his material whenever he sat down, at fixed hours, to his job as professional novelist. Obviously, much of what the moment suggested was dictated by conscious, even professional, considerations. No writer was more committed than Cooper to contemporary literary conventions. He was, for example, simply unable to conceive a tale without a love story, without a comic character, without a narrow escape. Neither chance nor impulse is accountable for these details, and their presence in the majority of instances reveals more about the influence of Cooper's reading than about the facts of his life. In the nineteenth century literary conventions fulfilled the terms of an unwritten, tacit contract that a popular novelist had agreed upon with his audience: readers demanded

[22] Susan Fenimore Cooper, *Pages and Pictures, from the Writings of James Fenimore Cooper* (New York: W. A. Townsend and Company, 1861), pp. 29-30.

novelty and suspense, but they also expected to be entertained in a familiar way, and the writer was pledged to satisfy those expectations. By the end of the century this bond between author and reader had almost disappeared (with the Modernist Novel it disappeared completely, though it persists in all less serious forms of imaginative entertainment, such as paperback gothics and television serials). But this was the rule of composition that Cooper believed himself bound by. His imagination obeyed it so strictly that he would ruin a story (as several of them testify) rather than omit an essential ingredient. Yet in spite of this subservience to convention, what W. C. Brownell says about Cooper is also true: "He never thinks of the reader. He follows his own inclination completely, quite without concern for company."[23] Reading any of his novels will convince one of this. It can also be true because an author was always permitted a lot of imaginative freedom within the fixed limits of convention, freedom which Cooper, who often trespassed on his readers' rights, could use more for his own ends than for their entertainment. And while appreciating its aesthetic merits or tracing its indebtedness to convention are both valid ways to analyze Cooper's imaginative activity, the analysis most faithful to the way his imagination worked would concentrate on what its workings reveal about his spontaneous—we would say unconscious—thoughts, feelings, and inclinations.

We should say unconscious because it is no longer possible to accept Cooper's assertion that his writing "was a good deal a matter of chance." Of course even now we are better able to interpret creative processes—art, dreams, daydreams, fantasies, children's make-believe—than to account for them. No one can precisely say why an artist creates at all, but that the creator is as responsible for what he creates as the dreamer is for his dream, that much is unde-

23 W. C. Brownell, "Cooper," in *American Prose Masters* (1909; rpt. Cambridge, Mass.: Harvard Univ. Press, 1967), p. 10.

niable. Like all such imaginative activity, Cooper's writing was the product of his psyche. That he feels no conscious responsibility for a large part of it means that we must look for its undisclosed psychic sources.

Susan Cooper was at least partially correct when she said that the incidents and descriptions in her father's novels suggested and developed themselves, although a psychoanalyst's explication of the deepest springs behind the working of the imagination is more precise. In his terms, an author's hidden mental impulses—emotions and attitudes hidden even from himself—can become conscious in the act of artistic creation. These unconscious desires do not express themselves directly, but rather are disguised in accordance with the demands of the mental agency that keeps them repressed, and transformed in accordance with the requirements of the particular story in progress. Unrecognized, unacknowledged by the writer, these impulses are nonetheless recognizable in his works. Thus to Cooper, sitting at his writing desk, the offerings of his imagination could seem to come from nowhere, when in fact they were suggested by the unconscious portion of his mind. Thus for us, studying the relationship of a man to his writing, those offerings provide the clues by means of which we can reconstruct the needs of Cooper's psyche, and examine how his writing responded to those needs.

Such an analysis is what literary criticism based upon psychoanalytic theory conventionally undertakes to provide. To me, one of its chief merits is that, by insisting upon an author's emotional involvement with the products of his imagination, it firmly establishes the connection between literature and life. I do not think, however, that such an analysis should be confined within the boundaries of the relationship between Cooper's life and Cooper's writing. The traditional function of criticism has been not only to interpret the work of art, but also to articulate whatever greatness is inherent in it. The kind of critical attempt I am engaged in here should, like all good and useful criticism, be able to explain the felt aesthetic appeal of particular creative works. Since a novel, unlike a dream or a fantasy, is also in one sense a public production—written by one man to be read by others—we must also consider the way in which the imaginative response of the novelist to his personal conflicts, his inward experiences, has subsequently been appropriated by his audience. If an author is always the implicit "first person" speaking in a book, the implied "second person" present is the reader. The best way to account for what critics have called Cooper's mythopoeic power, I believe, would be to examine the unconscious sources of that power in the reader's as well as the writer's mind; my sixth chapter, which looks particularly at the figure of the Leather-stocking, will undertake such an examination.

In several places, Cooper himself appears almost to acknowledge unconscious sources for his imagination. He once wrote his publishers that he intended to defer one book he had already begun, "in order to throw off at a heat . . . 'The Headsman of Berne' an idea that has seized me with such force, that there is no resisting it" (L/J, II, 353-54). There were internal causes for this heat and force, as we shall see when we arrive at the novel in question. About the creation of another work he said that he "had a crotchet to be delivered of, and *produced it must be*, though it were stillborn" (L/J, II, 178; italics mine).

Surely one conclusion that can be drawn simply from the number of novels Cooper wrote is that the psychic forces beneath his imagination were very compelling. Once tapped, they became almost irresistible. Again and again during his life he resolved that the novel he was working on would be "the last of the series." Halfway through his career, in fact, he publicly announced his retirement. Each time he discovered that there was another that he had to be delivered of. By the time he finished *The Ways of the Hour*, he had grown cautious: "I write no more novels, so far as one can foretel[l] his own career" (L/J, VI, 157). Unhappily, he

29

was finally correct—less than two years after making this prediction he died, although apparently he had begun to contemplate a new tale.

Using his imagination pleased Cooper. On the other hand, the decision not to employ it could only have been made at great psychic cost. Sanctioned by his role as novelist, Cooper could attempt to deal with unconscious conflicts in elaborate fantasies that he would otherwise have been forced to repudiate. Unless he is an artist, an adult must suppress, or at least feel ashamed of, the rich world of make-believe in which he played as a child. Because people never outgrow the need for this make-believe, they have granted the artist a dispensation from this shame, allowing him to continue to construct imaginary worlds for his own and their pleasure. Perhaps people have always suspected artists of indulging themselves in this way. There was an old lady in Cooperstown, where Cooper spent the last seventeen years of his life, who would call to the renowned novelist whenever he walked by her house: "James, why don't you stop wasting your time writing those silly novels, and try to make something of yourself!"[24]

But imaginative creation can also have overt rewards and satisfactions, and Cooper enjoyed his share of them. He could afford to ignore the old lady. By writing those novels he had made himself world-famous and, in his good years, a lot of money. Fame and wealth might seem sufficiently explicit reasons for any man to pursue a literary career. Why is it necessary to look for hidden ones? When I discuss in more detail the thirty-year-old Cooper's decision to write a novel, I shall keep these motives in mind. But he had opinions of his own about why he wrote.

It is probably unfair to expect a man to be very convincing or even articulate about the motives behind his behavior. The ones Cooper offers are contradictory. While he

[24] Mentioned by Ralph Birdsall, *The Story of Cooperstown* (Cooperstown: The Arthur H. Christ Co., 1917), p. 245.

told Walter Scott in 1826 that he found "the mere composition of a tale" so enjoyable that he "always invented twice as much as was committed to paper," in 1830 he wrote an old friend: "I have another novel nearly printed, and still another on the carpet. I begin to think this will be the last. I have now the means of doing something else, and I have never liked the employment, except as a ready resource against poverty" (*L/J*, I, 424). Another statement of his—"A good, wholesome, profitable and continued pecuniary support, is the applause that talent most craves"[25]— also suggests that writing appealed to him primarily as a livelihood. His publishers did pay him, often handsomely, and his letters to them frankly refer to this important transaction, insisting on every dollar he thought he was worth. But when in 1838 some of his critics charged Cooper with having written certain novels "in order to raise money, by selling abuse against his country," he not only sued them for libel, but invited his American publisher, Isaac Lea, to appear in court in his behalf: "Now your testimony will be of importance to us . . . by showing generally that I have not consulted my pecuniary interests as a writer, but have sacrificed them to my opinions" (*L/J*, III, 420-21). Mr. Lea could not be present, but had he been, he would sadly have backed up Cooper's claim—sadly, because Cooper's opinions on what he should write had by then cut deeply into his own and his publishers' profits. Despite the best efforts of Lea and the others to change his mind, Cooper continued to sacrifice his "pecuniary support" at the altar of his personal convictions. About writing as a source of income we can conclude with Cooper that he "never wrote any thing with a view to higher or lower prices" (*L/J*, III, 351).

About writing for fame and popularity Cooper is again contradictory. Flushed with the best-selling success of his second novel, he declared in the original (1823) Preface to

25 *Notions of the Americans: Picked Up by a Travelling Bachelor* (Philadelphia: Carey, Lea & Carey, 1828), II, 106.

The Pioneers: "This is the third of my novels, and it depends on two very uncertain contingencies, whether it will not be the last;—the one being the public opinion, and the other mine own humour." In that Preface he also boasted that since *Precaution* had been unpopular, *The Spy* "was written to see if I could not overcome this neglect of the reading world."[26] Only ten years later, however, he confessed to an old friend, "If I were anxious for popularity I should cut my throat in despair" (*L/J*, III, 10-11). "I no longer care what the public here, thinks of me," he wrote another friend. "Fame never had many charms for me, and posthumous reputation, apart from its influence on my children, just none at all" (*L/J*, III, 233). If he had ever been preoccupied with them, by the middle of his career Cooper had been forced to abandon wealth and popularity as goals. They were abandoned not because they were unattainable: he had repeatedly demonstrated at the beginning of his career that he could write to please a large audience. They were abandoned because they were somehow undesirable: there was something other than an audience that he needed to satisfy. Numerous passages in his letters reveal how difficult it was for him to relinquish the world's applause, for of course he was anxious for popularity, and fame did have its charms. His decision to sacrifice them often must have seemed as inexplicable to Cooper as it did to his friends and well-wishers. Whether he published another novel, however, was no longer contingent upon public opinion. "Mine own humour"—that, and that alone, was what he wrote for.

What it was that Cooper most needed to satisfy can be suggested by standing the disclaimer I quoted earlier on its head. To say that he endeavored to delineate himself in every character of every book he ever wrote would be inaccurate, but I do think that each of his novels, and his literary career as a whole, quintessentially represented his imaginative effort to delineate himself: to assert or achieve

[26] Preface to *The Pioneers*, 1st ed. (New York: Charles Wiley, 1823), pp. vii-viii.

his own identity. Identity was the leading imperative to which his art responded. Defining himself meant attempting to resolve the various contradictory and demanding impulses that not only originally created but also consistently threatened his personality. These psychic conflicts had their roots in Cooper's childhood, but we should be able to discover the emotional motifs of his early years in the novels he wrote during the second half of his life. We should also be able to analyze the way his early life influenced, and can even help to explain, those novels. Perhaps most important, we should be able to put the image of Cooper back together: to understand, without distorting his achievements or ignoring his preoccupations, the full dimensions of Cooper's existence. His critics have found Cooper as difficult to delineate as he found himself, but it is possible to restore to him a coherent identity.

Assessing the evidence of Cooper's early life will at times involve conjecture, at other times involve the use of undocumentable family traditions. In both instances, we should be guided by what seems sensible. Conjectures must be consistent with the facts about Cooper's childhood that can be documented. On the other hand, family traditions, which used to be preserved and passed on with more care than we can easily conceive, almost always have some truth to them. As Hawthorne, also a member of a nineteenth century American family, says in *The House of the Seven Gables* about "chimney-corner tradition," it "often preserves traits of character with marvellous fidelity." If a particular event did not in fact occur, it nonetheless is usually consistent with the kinds of events that did, else it would not have become traditional. A henpecked husband will not descend to his posterity as a domestic tyrant. And when family tradition informs us that a man was a domestic tyrant, we can safely believe it, though not every act of tyranny with which he is charged may have been committed.

Assessing the evidence of Cooper's novels requires one to take into account his conscious obedience to literary convention and the contextual necessities of the particular story. For these reasons we should be cautious, but we need not be deterred. And whenever a text presents us with an unaccountable element or an unexplained tension, whenever, in short, something seems senseless, we shall be especially justified in seeking its meaning outside the text and within Cooper's psyche. Of course, because his habits of composition were so casual, Cooper committed more than his share of simple gaffes. The most well-known of these concerns Natty Bumppo's age in *The Prairie*—at one point he is just eighty; a few days later, eighty-six (aging at that rate he obviously must die by the end of the story). These problems are easy to explicate: another novelist would have had notes about his characters to which he could refer as he wrote; Cooper had none.

According to his daughter Susan, in fact, only once did Cooper ever make notes for a work of fiction. The work was *The Last of the Mohicans*, his sixth novel, and the notes were for its twelfth chapter.

Like all his books, *The Last of the Mohicans* was, Susan tells us, "very rapidly written, yet during its progress—soon after commencing it, indeed—the writer was seized with a serious illness."[27] The trouble was diagnosed as "a form of nervous dyspepsia." During the early 1820s Cooper had recurring digestive complaints, and in the next chapter I shall try to establish the etiology of this nervous disorder. Though he was seldom incapacitated, in this instance a high fever forced him to bed. There, Susan continues, he dictated some notes for the novel in progress, a thing he had never done before. Mrs. Cooper, taking the dictation, thought her husband was delirious, but as soon as Cooper could sit up these notes were translated into Chapter Twelve of *Mohicans*.

The chapter recounts a combat deep in the woods between a party of Hurons in the pay of the French, and Natty Bumppo, Chingachgook, Chingachgook's son Uncas,

[27] *Pages and Pictures*, p. 128.

and an English officer named Duncan Heyward. Its most dramatic episode is the protracted struggle between Chingachgook and Le Renard Subtil, or Magua, the fiercest of the Hurons. Cooper's description of their deadly wrestling match does indeed resemble the chaos of delirium. Mohican's three companions have dispatched their opponents. "Urged by the different motives of filial affection, friendship, and gratitude," Uncas, Natty, and Heyward respectively hurry to the aid of the desperate Chingachgood. They gather around the whirling dust thrown up by the fight, but can do nothing to help. "In vain did Uncas dart around the cloud, with a wish to strike his knife into the heart of his father's foe." Uncas dare not strike, lest he kill his father:

> . . . the swift evolutions of the combatants seemed to incorporate their bodies into one. The death-like looking figure of the Mohican, and the dark form of the Huron, gleamed before their eyes in such quick and confused succession, that the friends of the former knew not where nor when to plant the succoring blow. It is true there were short and fleeting moments, when the fiery eyes of Magua were seen glittering, like the fabled organs of the basilisk, through the dusty wreath by which he was enveloped, and he read by those short and deadly glances the fate of the combat in the presence of his enemies; ere, however, any hostile hand could descend on his devoted head, its place was filled by the scowling visage of Chingachgook.[28]

In the center of this translucent confusion, the father and the father's foe are fighting for their lives; on its edge, the son stands poised with a knife; yet each time he is about to act, the foe becomes the father, the father becomes the foe. "The fiery eyes" of the one merge with "the scowling visage" of the other. Even Cooper's use of the word "devoted"—

28 *The Last of the Mohicans*, pp. 143-44.

which of course means doomed, referring to Magua, but also implies the filial affection Uncas feels for Chingachgook —contributes linguistically to the ambiguity of this scene.

In this scene, I believe, in the heightened state of mind brought on by his fever and through the agency of his imagination, Cooper reveals the most important of his psychic conflicts: his ambivalent unconscious attitude toward the figure of his father. More than the unusual circumstances of its creation draws our attention to this episode. Cooper's father was celebrated for his wrestling, he was in fact murdered by an enemy, and, as we shall see, he represented the most important influence in the novelist's mental life. For this reason I shall be less concerned with Cooper as the founding father of the American novel than with Cooper as a son who was trying to find himself by means of his novels. The son's ambivalence can be simply stated, stated in the terms of the scene just cited: Cooper was variously compelled to perceive his father as friend and as foe. It can be simply stated, but its explication in terms of Cooper's life will take more time. First we must consider the ostensibly accidental moment at which Cooper, by deciding to write a novel, discovered the uses of his imagination.

CHAPTER II

"WHO *I AM*"

THERE IS one story about Cooper that everyone tells, though he himself never did. According to Cooper, he became an author by "accident"—"circumstances of an entirely adventitious nature, induced [him] to publish a novel."[1] Nobody's biographer could easily be satisfied with such an empty explanation, and Cooper's would be especially unhappy with it, for if not entirely adventitious, the novelist's eventual choice of a literary career could not have been predicted. Luckily, the student of Cooper's life has at his disposal a fuller, more attractive account of the circumstances. According to his daughter Susan, the original source of the anecdote, this is how Cooper became a professional storyteller:

> He always read a great deal. . . . He frequently read aloud at that time to my Mother. . . . My Mother was not well; she was lying on the sofa, and he was reading this newly imported novel to her; it must have been very trashy; after a chapter or two he threw it aside, exclaiming, *"I could write you a better book than that myself!"* Our Mother laughed at the idea as the height of absurdity—he who disliked writing even a letter, that he should write a book!! He persisted in his declaration, however, and almost immediately wrote the first pages of a tale.[2]

Like some of Cooper's weaker novels, this story's ending may seem unconvincingly neat, its outline too conventional.

[1] *Precaution*, p. xlv; *The Spy*, p. ix.

[2] Susan Fenimore Cooper, "Small Family Memories," in *Correspondence of James Fenimore-Cooper*, ed. James Fenimore Cooper (grandson) (New Haven: Yale Univ. Press, 1922), I, 38.

A long line of men have claimed that their women somehow talked them into their careers, and we may well be suspicious when someone tries to hand us such a line. Yet I think we can trust Susan's account: she was not only her father's literary executor, but also the self-appointed trustee of his reputation. In this second role she zealously attempted to correct every misrepresentation of his life and character, and I cannot believe she would at the same time have fostered one of her own. A familiar story can still be true.

Cooper surprised his family when he threw aside someone else's novel and picked up a pen to write his own. "Hitherto no man," wrote Susan, "could have shown himself farther from any inclination for authorcraft."[3] Most of Cooper's biographers profess a similar, justifiable amazement: by the time he reaches thirty, the average man has already, irreversibly, and often unhappily committed himself to a lifework. Looking back at his first novel from the middle of his literary career, even Cooper was amazed: "It can scarce be said that the work was commenced with any view to publication; . . . the last thought of the writer was any expectation that it would be followed by a series of similar tales from the same pen."[4] But Cooper's inability to account for his sudden determination to become an author, his reiterated insistence that it was entirely adventitious, does not mean that it is incomprehensible, only that the reasons behind it were inaccessible to him. There is no reason to concede as much as he does to fate. To understand his delayed choice of a career, however, we should first examine its antecedents.

The novelist was the youngest son of Judge William Cooper, the founder of Cooperstown, New York—to us, engaged in the study of the relationship between James Cooper's emotional life and his writing, that is not a simple declarative sentence. William Cooper died in 1809, when James was twenty years old, but the psychic legacy he left

---

[3] *Pages and Pictures*, p. 17.   [4] *Precaution*, p. xlvi.

his son significantly influenced his entire career. For example, almost one half of Cooper's novels are about populating the wilderness, which was the way the Judge gave Cooperstown its name. In one of those novels, *The Pioneers,* his father appears directly, as Judge Marmaduke Temple of Templeton. *The Pioneers* will provide the best context for an analysis of Cooper's childhood; at this point we are concerned with how he became an author, and his father's death, which coincided almost exactly with the official end of his nonage, is the most appropriate place to begin.

Judge Cooper's material legacy to each of his five sons was $50,000 and equal shares in an estate valued at over $700,000. The source of this fortune was William Cooper's shrewdly managed speculations in New York property, a circumstance that would later make James uneasy. At the time, though, having this much wealth at his disposal gave him a novel sense of independence. He was then a midshipman in the United States Navy, a position his father had secured for him. Five months later, on May 3rd, 1810, he wrote the Secretary of the Navy to request a year's furlough, "Owing to the recent Death of my Father and the consequent necessity of my attending, immediately, to my private affairs" (*L/J*, 1, 16). The affairs of the estate he had inherited were extremely complex, but James' oldest brother, Richard, had complete charge of them; the affair James wanted to attend to was more private still. On May 18th, he wrote Richard: "Like all the rest of the sons of Adam, I have bowed to the influence of the charms of [a] fair damsel of eighteen—I loved her like a man and told her of it like a sailor" (*L/J*, 1, 17).

Cooper's proposal of marriage could reasonably be called his first decision as a man—before it, he had always followed his father's instructions, which had sent him to school at Albany, to college at Yale, and to sea; it was among his last as a sailor—the new Mrs. Cooper did not want her husband in the Navy, and at the end of his furlough he sent the Secretary his resignation. Precisely when Cooper first met his future wife is not known, but it was probably just after Judge Cooper's death: writing to Richard about his engagement he said, "The peculiarity of my situation occasion'd me to act with something like precipitancy." James does not elaborate, but one peculiarity of the situation is how closely he appears to have linked his father's death with his own marriage. The way he requested his furlough is one indication of this. Another is the following fragment from an autobiographical sketch he prepared in 1831 for Samuel Carter Hall, who was writing an article on the novelist:

> My father died in 1809. I married the second daughter of John Peter De Lancey of Mamaroneck, Westchester County, N.Y. (*L/J*, II, 59)

Over one year separated these two events, a year that is elided by the juxtaposition of these two sentences. Between these events, these sentences, however, there may be a latent transition. The father's death and the son's marriage may have been psychologically interdependent. Cooper's reference to the first is abrupt and dispassionate, but the death of William Cooper was obviously a significant event in James's life. The fifty thousand dollars he received at the time is symbolic of its deeper meaning: as an inheritance, it represented the past, which had been presided over by the Judge; in itself, it endowed the future, in which he would be responsible for his actions. Marriage would have been a declaration that he was ready to assume that responsibility, to put himself in his father's place with regard to both his own life and the lives of the children he would in his turn father. This is what almost every "son of Adam" or William or John does. But in Cooper's case, as we shall see, he would try too literally to put himself in his father's place.

With his marriage Cooper also declared something else: it indirectly represented an endorsement of his father's social values. As the sketch for Mr. Hall reveals, his wife's background was important to Cooper. To Richard he boasted that "Susan De Lancey is the daughter of a man of very respectable connections and a handsome fortune." More respectable than the Coopers' were the De Lanceys' connections, and if their fortune was not more handsome, it was of much longer standing. The money James inherited was not as old as he, and the connections his father could name, which included some famous ones, were all political cronies. Among his allies, though not a personal friend, was John Peter De Lancey, who, like William Cooper, was a New York Federalist. Here is how Dixon Ryan Fox describes the philosophy of the Federalist Party:

> They believed that government by the wise and good was better than by the ignorant and vicious. But a larger proportion of the wise and good was to be found among the men of property than among society at large. Those who had it by inheritance had therefore more of leisure to acquire wisdom and were immune from the passions of cupidity, while those who earned it did so by the exercise of those abilities which might be serviceable to the state; *ergo*, government by the part was preferable to government by the whole.[5]

Their opponents called them aristocrats, a term that did not, in those early days of the republic, make them wince. John De Lancey had inherited his property, had, in fact, lost much of it through confiscation during the Revolution because he remained loyal to his King. Doubtless when James Cooper, the son of a man who had earned his, asked for Susan's hand, De Lancey did answer him, as Cooper wrote Richard, "in the most gentlemanly manner." One gentleman to another, De Lancey also informed him about a Westchester estate that would soon belong to his daughter, "depending upon the life of an aunt Aetat 72. . . . I write all this for you," Cooper told Richard; "you know *I*

5 *The Decline of Aristocracy in the Politics of New York: 1801-1840* (1919; rpt. New York: Harper Torchbooks, 1965), p. 249.

am indifferent to anything of this nature." And in fairness
to Cooper's passion, it must be noted that he did tell his
brother that Susan De Lancey was "amiable, sweet-tempered
and happy in her disposition," but Cooper was no less
pleased with her social standing. Pleased and impressed—
according to the editor of his letters, "Some years before
his entrance to authorship, Cooper had begun ambitiously
to compile a genealogy of the De Lancey family."[6]

James was writing to his brother because Mr. De Lancey
had attached one condition to his acceptance of James's
proposal: "The approbation of your mother." James was
in New York City, Richard in Cooperstown with the family; the older brother was to secure their mother's approval,
"Then take your pen and write to Mr. De Lancey, stating
the *happiness* and *pleasure* it will give all the family to
have this connection completed." This was of course done,
and on January 1st, 1811, the connection was completed.
Cooper and his family had good reason to be pleased. He
had married into one of the best families in the state, the
bride was amiable and well-to-do, the groom was young and
wealthy. Had William Cooper been alive, he would have
been happy, too.

All this might sound like the final chapter in one of
J. Fenimore Cooper's romances. His novels ordinarily do
end with the marriage of the hero and heroine, who, having
succeeded with each other, are no longer required to succeed in the larger world. Such an ending is labeled a literary
convention because it has nothing in common with the
way people live outside of books. And despite his inheritance and his wife's prospects, which freed him from the
immediate obligations of a provider, Cooper could not have
accepted a similar denouement for his own story. His father
had been singularly successful in his chosen career. The
Judge could proudly and without bravado state in a letter
written a few years before he died that "I began with the
disadvantage of a small capital, and the encumbrance of

[6] Beard, *L/J*, v, 271.

a large family, and yet I have already settled more acres than any man in America. . . . I am now descending into the vale of life, and I must acknowledge that I look with self complacency upon what I have done."[7] As James rhetorically asks in his first novel, "Is not the example of the father as important to the son as that of the mother to the daughter?"[8] In addition to his example, the Judge had undoubtedly provided James with the same advice that he gave his third son, William Junior: "Here is a great country, and no young man has such an opportunity as yourself of being the first man in it. On your industry depends whether you are to be the great good and useful man—or nothing."[9] That James had been promised the same thing as a young man is suggested by a letter he wrote in 1831 to his nephew Richard: "You live in a country in which any man of your capacity and education can make his way honorably and fairly to distinction. . . ." That this same American opportunity also contained a threat, that, as the Judge had said, one could become the great man, "or nothing," James also knew, as the remainder of his counsel to his nephew indicates: ". . . and I sincerely hope, as I believe, that your future career will do no discredit to your early promise" (*L/J*, II, 86).

After his marriage, Cooper's own future career—bright with promise, dark with threat—must have occupied much of his attention. Particularly dark with threat because the son of a famous man is always in an ambiguous position. Unlike his father, Cooper began with a substantial capital and a privileged place in society, but these were advantages that his father had earned for him. To share the Judge's robust self-satisfaction, James would have to succeed equally

[7] William Cooper, *A Guide in the Wilderness; or, The History of the First Settlement in the Western Counties of New York* . . . (1810; rpt. Rochester, N.Y.: George P. Humphrey, 1897), p. 7.

[8] *Precaution*, p. 178.

[9] William Cooper, letter to William Cooper, Jr., at Princeton, 1800; quoted by Beard, *L/J*, I, xx.

by his own efforts. What he wrote his son Paul years later, when Paul was about the same age as he had been at his marriage, we can apply now to himself: ". . . at your time of life, *with the world before you, and your fortunes depending entirely on your own future exertions. . . .*" Those are Cooper's italics. That is how strongly he felt about the individual's personal duty to "succeed in life" (*L/J*, IV, 249). As he considered his chances, however, he knew that his achievements would be measured, by himself and others, against his father's. The world before him had in this way been qualified, made more threatening, for even the favorable circumstances of his young manhood did not preclude the possibility of failure, of discrediting his early promise. "It is not enough simply to be the son of a great man," he said in *Notions of the Americans*, a nonfiction work published in 1828; "in order to render it of essential advantage, some portion of his merit must become hereditary, or the claim had better be suppressed."[10] In 1828, as a world-famous and best-selling author, he could confront that fact without fear. In 1811, it unquestionably inhibited his plans for his own "future exertions."

Another aspect of Cooper's novels helps to provide the perspective from which one can examine the exertions he made before becoming a novelist. According to David Brion Davis, "his narratives were intended to reveal ideal modes of action." "It is only in action," Davis continues, "that Cooper's characters reveal their fundamental differences."[11] Few of Cooper's letters from this period have survived, but what can his actions then reveal about *his* character? For the most part they conform to one ideal mode of behavior —that of the socially responsible man of property, that of the Federalist gentleman. But there was a fundamental difference between the father's and the son's behavior; if the

10 *Notions*, I, 157.

11 David Brion Davis, "The Deerslayer, A Democratic Knight of the Wilderness," in *Twelve Original Essays on Great American Novels*, ed. Charles Shapiro (Detroit: Wayne State Univ. Press, 1958), pp. 2-3.

first was emphatically a Federalist, the second wanted to be decidedly a gentleman. William Cooper had been an active political partisan, serving nine years as the First Judge of Otsego County, two terms as a United States Congressman, and all his adult life as a zealous campaigner and propagandist for the Federalist Party. James Cooper's more passive service was in what could be called the Party's social auxiliaries. For example, from 1814 to 1817 he and his young family lived in Cooperstown. While the Judge was alive he made his house there, in Fox's phrase, "the citadel of Federalism."[12] While the son lived in the village he involved himself with more genteel activities, serving as the Corresponding Secretary of the Otsego County Agricultural Society, the Secretary of the Otsego Bible Society, and a vestryman of the Cooperstown Episcopal Church. Cooper's life there, the first extended period he had spent in his home town in over a decade, represents a disheartening declension: Judge Cooper had founded the village in the midst of a howling wilderness, was almost solely responsible for the existence of its agriculture, had put up the money to build its church; for his part, James seemed content with these minor roles in the continuing process of civilization. He began a new house in which he expected to settle permanently. Had he stayed, his life would probably have been a comparative but significant failure: he was following almost directly in his father's footsteps, but taking much smaller strides. If, as he wrote in 1817 in his official capacity as Secretary of the Agricultural Society, "The county of Otsego has passed its infancy, and is rapidly maturing into manhood" (*L/J*, 1, 37), the same could not be said for the youngest son of the county's founder.

In *Afloat and Ashore*, a novel written late in Cooper's literary career, Miles Wallingford, the first-person narrator, reflects upon the moment at which he left "the paternal roof for the first time, to enter upon the chances of the world"; he felt like all men in that situation "a deep sense

12 Fox, p. 136.

of the dependence in which they had hitherto lived."[13] Miles was sixteen when he left home, but Cooper, who of course had technically left home as well, was at twenty-eight still psychically his father's dependent. Nor did James's four brothers find it any easier to erect separate identities for themselves. All remained near the paternal roof, and instead of entering upon the chances of the great world, settled for living extravagantly off their inheritance. The figure of the great man William Cooper apparently overpowered his sons. Less than ten years after his death, all but James were also dead. Their legacy was a long list of creditors. In 1819 the administration of the Cooper estate devolved on the youngest son; his brothers' prodigality, however, had reduced the Judge's lifework to mortgaged ruin. "Alone as a son, the remains of a large family" is the way Cooper later described his condition (*L/J*, vi, 46). And as a son—not as a man—he had lived. But so little now remained of his family's wealth that he would be forced from the paternal roof into the world.

Between 1817 and 1820 a number of other circumstances conspired to induce Cooper to publish a novel. His wife Susan wanted to be near *her* father, and in 1817 persuaded her husband to take the family for a visit to Westchester. That visit extended itself into a residency, and it was there, three years later, that Cooper became an author. Susan's wishes were the most obvious reason for the move, but Cooper undoubtedly had his own. Soon after he left, his mother died at Cooperstown, abruptly amputating a large part of his psychic attachment to the place. Work was stopped on his house, called Fenimore (his mother's maiden name), and in 1823, never having been occupied, it burned to the ground. After he could no longer return to Cooperstown as his mother's child, Cooper may have felt that he should stay out of his father's shadow. Not till seventeen years had passed did he go home again; then could he con-

13 *Afloat and Ashore*, p. 41.

front his father's achievement with one of his own. Rather, at this time he seems to have tried to transfer his filial allegiance to the De Lancey family. As has been noted, he began to invest much of his energy in the study of their genealogy. The old aunt had conveniently died, and the Angevine farm became Mrs. Cooper's. Into that house the Coopers moved, and James again tried to establish himself as a member of the landed gentry. Though this time the land belonged to his wife, he busily set about improving its grounds. He also joined the local Agricultural and Bible Societies, and acquired the rank of Colonel in the local militia. But his determination to identify with the caste represented by both his father and father-in-law was undermined by his deteriorating finances. To save his father's indebted estate, he began to speculate heavily, but the disappointing results of his efforts must have reinforced his doubts that any portion of his father's merit had accrued to him.

In his attempt to succeed by the same speculative means the Judge had used so well, Cooper mortgaged not only his own but his wife's property, an action which led to a quarrel with his father-in-law. Mr. De Lancey disapproved of Cooper's course—it was not in the most gentlemanly manner —and he assigned one of his sons as trustee for his daughter's property. Resenting this step, Cooper broke off communications with Susan's relatives, and presumably quit researching their family tree.

Now alienated from the De Lanceys' respectable connections and handsome fortune, ineffectually trying to redeem his father's bequest, Cooper yet had one further act of filial obedience to perform before he was psychically ready to abandon the ill-fitting identity of a Federalist gentleman. What he did is revealed in the following letter to a childhood friend, dated April 19th, 1820, written in his official capacity as Secretary to another Westchester County organization—the Federalist Party:

We are all alive here and will do our duty—I never
worked at an election before—but you who know me
so well—know I never do things by halves—for Six
weeks I have given myself up to it—and I sincerely
hope the result will shew not in vain—I find I now
dabble in politics—it is a pleasant thing to find your
old Friends on the same side with you— (*L*/*J*, 1, 41)

In this instance the old friends were his father's: Cooper
was supporting DeWitt Clinton, a candidate for Governor,
and according to Dixon Ryan Fox, "Clintonian and Federalist were often interchangeable terms."[14] And though
Cooper had never worked at it before, electioneering was
his father's forte. As Fox concludes, "no better example
could be found than in the case of Judge William Cooper"
of "how these great Federalist landlords could play an ugly
part in politics if so disposed."[15] The Judge was absolutely
so disposed; about the election of 1791 a friend wrote to
him:

I believe fasting and prayer to be good, but if you had
only fasted and prayed I am sure we should not have
had seven hundred votes from your county—report
says that you was very civil to the young and handsome
of the sex, that you flattered the old and ugly, and
even embraced the toothless and decrepid, in order to
obtain votes. When will you write a treatise on electioneering? Whenever you do, afford only a few copies
to your friends.[16]

Report, however, differed: to the Judge's political enemies,
those same seven hundred votes were grounds for his impeachment. They introduced a memorial in the New York
Legislature charging that he "encouraged illegal voting,"
"knowingly had caused men to vote who were not free-

14 Fox, p. 199.   15 Ibid., p. 140.
16 Quoted by James Fenimore Cooper (grandson), Introduction to
A Guide in the Wilderness, pp. v-vi.

holders," "threatened voters with suits," and "menaced a Mr. Cannon, who came to the polls to challenge illegal voters, that if he challenged any one, he (the judge,) would forthwith commit him to jail."[17] The impeachment was dismissed by the partisan legislature that the Judge had helped to elect, but from other sources we know that this election typified William Cooper's intense participation in politics. Indeed, his death was caused by a blow on the head from a political opponent. Westchester was far more civilized than Otsego, and presumably the son's political efforts were more polite, but his participation was equally intense. It is not hard to understand why, having given himself up to the campaign, he did "sincerely hope the result will shew not in vain"—after so many dutiful failures to match him, he was trying to reproduce one of the father's proudest attainments. It would have been "a pleasant thing" to emulate his father, even to compete with him, but when the votes of the election of 1820 were counted, Clinton failed to carry Westchester County in spite of a statewide victory. Cooper had lost in a winning cause. If he never did things by halves, he also seemed incapable of doing anything well.

Cooper could not have helped comparing the electoral results of 1820 with his father's political successes, could not have helped suffering by the comparison. But Cooper's was not an introspective character, and we have no record of his feelings. Indeed, in all the personal letters and journal pages that have survived, from the whole of his life, Cooper is far more likely to assert than to examine himself. This is a predisposition that both the student of his life and the reader of his fiction must contend with, for the surface of his narratives rarely dissolves to reveal any depth. For Cooper, character is contained in appearance and action, and a character's state of mind is manifested either in what he does or what he says, except in those instances

[17] Jabez D. Hammond, *The History of Political Parties in the State of New-York, From the Ratification of the Federal Constitution to December, 1840* (Buffalo: Phinney & Co., 1850), I, 77.

when his emotions are betrayed by his face—in a blush, a grimace, a tear. And to Cooper, that in 1820 he wrote a book was much more significant than why. If throughout the rest of his career he said almost nothing about the first ten years of his marriage, that was because he sincerely believed they were unimportant, or at least uninteresting. For the same reason he consistently stated that his decision to become a novelist was purely accidental. Yet the events of the decade we have been examining, I believe, made that decision possible and, in a sense, even inevitable.

Behind almost every one of Cooper's actions during this period stands the figure of his father. Consciously he very obviously modeled his life after William Cooper's. Unconsciously he was acting out of a compelling psychic need. In childhood every son first perceives his father as a rival for his mother. To the son's infantile desire to have sole possession of the mother must be traced his desire later in life to identify himself with his father, that is, with the man who enjoyed his mother's love. By becoming his father, by if possible overcoming his father by surpassing his achievements, the son seeks to replace him. In this unconscious drama it does not matter if one or both parents are dead. The unconscious is as timeless as memory—impulses and attitudes that are fixed there in childhood can continue to influence the adult's behavior in spite of changes in the real world. It is this unconscious drama to which Freud refers when he says, "From the time of puberty onward, the human individual must devote himself to the great task of *freeing himself from the parents*," a task that is, as Freud also says, "laid down for every man." Its goal is emotional independence from the attitudes toward the parents which shape the infant's behavior and which are then permanently fixed in the adolescent's unconscious. To become an adult one must outgrow the child within him.

Cooper seems to have had little trouble emotionally in transferring his repressed desire for his mother onto another consenting adult, although later in this chapter I shall have more to say about Cooper's relationship with his mother. When in the next I examine *The Pioneers* I shall discuss his unconscious attitude toward his older sister Hannah, the person whom he first substituted for his mother as a love-object. With his marriage to Susan De Lancey he effectively completed the process of withdrawing his libidinal attachments from Mrs. William Cooper. Just as in every one of his tales the marriage that concludes the novel is considered final, so the novelist's marriage to Susan remained happy and satisfying. There is no substantial reason to contradict, or even to suspect, what Cooper himself said about it to Horatio Greenough in a letter written just after he had learned of his friend's wedding and twenty-seven years after his own: "I am glad you are married. It is the natural condition for both sexes, and it has far more pleasure than pains. Few men know more, or have known more of domestic felicity than myself, or can better speak on the subject of the value of a good wife" (*L/J*, III, 328).

It would be naive to assume that Cooper, any more than any other husband or wife, would have stood behind this opinion at every moment of his marriage, but I think it does sincerely record his fundamental and most prevalent attitude toward that marriage. Several of the critics who have confined themselves largely to the Leather-Stocking Tales, notably D. H. Lawrence and Leslie Fiedler, would protest this conclusion. Natty Bumppo never marries, and in fact feels that it would be "agin' natur' " for him to do so. His explicit preference for remaining a bachelor, it has been argued, reflects Cooper's latent dissatisfaction or impatience with marriage; his celibacy reveals Cooper's unconscious failure to deal with his own sexuality. I intend to examine the reasons that Natty gives for this refusal, as well as the unconscious impulse that it fulfilled for Natty's creator, in my sixth chapter. But I should say here that placing too much emphasis on how Natty's virginal life in the woods represents an evasion of the demands of adult heterosexuality not only limits, but also distorts the implicit meanings embodied in his character. Viewing Cooper's own disposition toward women and marriage solely from the perspective provided by the Tales results in a still more serious distortion. On the whole, the evidence of Cooper's life and of his novels indicates that rather than perceiving the existence of women as unsettling or threatening, Cooper instead was emotionally able to take them for granted. That each of his stories had to contain a romantic subplot was, as I have already noted, for Cooper a fact of literary life, and one would not want to build an argument merely on that fact. But the way in which Cooper treats those ineluctable affairs of the heart does suggest a lot about the facts of Cooper's emotional life. What makes this aspect of his fiction so unsatisfying is that it is, strictly speaking, perfunctory—neither the enamored hero nor the patient reader needs to be in much doubt about whether the heroine will show up for the ceremony in the last chapter; all of Cooper's attempts to keep his characters and his readers in suspense —rivals for her affection, or his; external obstacles of one kind or another—are too transparently fictitious to succeed. In a mediocre novelist this would be much less remarkable, but Cooper can convince us of his ability to depict many other kinds of conflicts with insight, subtlety, and power. If the novelist's psychological investment in the figure of the Leather-stocking were centered in Natty's retreat from womankind, Cooper could hardly be so complacent about the female presence in his other works. Psychically, one is not free to dismiss the things that one feels anxious about; they of course are the very things that one is compelled in various ways to confront. To this rule Cooper is no exception: we shall see how again and again in his fiction he was forced to deal with the conflicts which took dominion over his personality and imagination. But for the most part, as a novelist Cooper could ignore romantic love—by which I mean that he could include it (he always includes it) in a thoroughly conventional manner.

There are few novelists of Cooper's literary stature who

paid as little attention as he did to the characters of his women. Without question, this is a serious artistic deficiency; it led James Russell Lowell, in his *Fable for Critics*, to make his well-known accusation that

. . . the women he draws from one model don't vary,
All sappy as maples and flat as a prairie.

Too many others have already labored at getting Cooper acquitted of this charge for me to bring up its hyperbolic nature again, but the point I wish to make is that Lowell is certainly right to imply that within the pages of Cooper's novels, the women are the people whom both the author and the reader can take most for granted. We would expect to discover a similar attitude in the author's own life, and we do. When he wrote to inform his brother Richard of his engagement to Susan De Lancey, in the letter I have already quoted, James listed briefly for him "the qualities of her *person* and *mind*"—but all he said, besides giving the details of her place in the De Lancey family, was that his fiancée was "amiable, sweet tempered and happy in her disposition." The redundancy of these virtues sufficiently indicates what Cooper considered, to cite his letter to Greenough, "the value of a good wife." In Susan De Lancey's obliging personality he seems to have found, as is often the case, a woman who could fill the role his mother had originally played in his life, and who could fulfill the needs his mother had created in him.

The picture that we have of Elizabeth Fenimore Cooper is little more than an outline, but she was apparently the kind of person who makes sacrifices herself rather than demand them of others, at least where her children were concerned. We do know that she disliked Cooperstown so thoroughly that she persuaded Judge Cooper to buy a house for her to move to in her home town, Burlington, New Jersey. And we know that she gave up the idea and reconciled herself to Otsego County because her sons, especially James, wanted to stay near the forest. Essentially this same pattern was reproduced in the adult Cooper's relationship with his wife. Although, as I have mentioned, in 1817 she seems to have been chiefly responsible for the family's move to Westchester, seventeen years later, when Cooper decided after their travels in Europe to move back to Cooperstown, she seems to have acquiesced without complaint. Her family still lived at a distance, and she could not have anticipated making many friends in the upstate village. A generation had not improved Cooperstown to the point where it could offer a woman, especially one who had lived abroad, very many social resources; in his letters Cooper refers more than once to his daughters' boredom and unhappiness there, but never to his wife's. The Coopers remained in Cooperstown after 1834, but though Cooper occasionally thought of leaving for several reasons, the only familial one involved his children's health. Mrs. Cooper was still amiable. According to Cooper's letters from this period, the only condition she insisted upon was that she not be carried back to Europe. She may have been quite firm about this, but the demand itself is a fairly humble one. And it seems likely that in almost every other aspect of married life she was equally undemanding. There is a surprisingly large number of widowers in her husband's novels. Since Cooper almost invariably provides these wifeless men with at least one daughter, and since they almost invariably dote upon these girls, his widowers cannot be understood as representatives of an unacknowledged desire on Cooper's part to resist "the gentle tyranny," as Fiedler calls it, "of home and woman."[18] Instead, these widowers appear to me to suggest just how comfortable Cooper was within the realm of home and women. Would not a writer with a secret discontent toward conjugality be expected to project that into the plots of his novels? Would it not betray itself at least around the edges of his characterizations? If he did not show his husbands as harried, would he not at least make their wives a

[18] Fiedler, p. 194.

bit insistent or exacting? Is there any man, however, who can take his wife more for granted than a widower?

One place where a tangible sense of the Coopers' marriage survives is on the pages of the novelist's correspondence. "We know of their happiness together," writes James Grossman, "from his letters to her when they were apart. These letters are not great or even good, but they are the letters of a happy man, untroubled, at his ease, and above all never on his guard. Their unaware assumption that he cannot possibly be misunderstood tells us even more of love than do the sweet messages with which they abound."[19] These letters demonstrate how much more Cooper gained emotionally from his marriage than he was ever forced to pay: Grossman here names what was Susan De Lancey's highest value in the scheme of Cooper's interior life. As we shall see, in his public life Cooper often felt acutely ill at ease, often felt compelled to be rigidly on his guard, often felt that he had been viciously misunderstood by the world. In his public stance Cooper became, during the course of his life, increasingly belligerent. Susan, however, remained happy in her disposition, especially toward him, and Cooper could rightly assume that she was one person who understood him.[20] Cooper was unaware of making this assump-

[19] Grossman, *Cooper*, pp. 248-49.

[20] At times she seems, in fact, to understand her husband much better than he himself could: in her letters to her family she can describe his burly anger, his prickly defensiveness, with admirable insight and tact. In 1828, for example, the Coopers visited England. At that time Cooper was working on *Notions of the Americans*, in which he would attack Great Britain for maliciously misrepresenting America in every English account of this country. Whenever he went out into English society, he apparently went expecting to be attacked in his own person. Writing to her sister in America, Mrs. Cooper reveals how well she could read her husband's behavior when she says that, in spite of it, the English "are so very civil to him that I am afraid he will not be able to abuse them, and so the piquancy of his book will be quite spoiled" (quoted by Beard, *L/J*, I, 254). In my fourth chapter I shall discuss further this portion of Cooper's career; as we

tion, because he could feel safe within the realm of his wife's affection, and because unconsciously he counted upon that security. He seems as a child to have felt comparably secure about his mother's affection; I can imagine, though I would not wish to insist upon the point, that Cooper felt he could turn to her for sympathetic understanding. As a father, repeating the pattern at a later stage of his life, he seems to have expected the same amount of affection from his four daughters. Nowhere does he express the slightest surprise that his oldest daughter, Susan, remained unmarried and attached—devoted is probably not too strong a word—to him. When near the end of his life Cooper chose a literary executor, he named Susan, not one of his literary acquaintances; both he and Susan were willing to leave to her the task of handing down to posterity an official version of his character, and so in a sense he was turning to her for sympathetic understanding. What did surprise and even unsettle him, as we can also tell from his letters, was the eventual decision of two of his other daughters to marry and move out of his house; apparently he had taken them for granted as well.

Cooper could resolve the childhood conflicts produced by his mother's existence in a way that brought him sustained "domestic felicity." But that success was by no means sufficient to bring him complete happiness. As we shall see, Cooper never freed himself psychically from William Cooper. His attitude toward his father was complex and ambivalent: in the course of his life Cooper felt compelled variously to reconcile himself with his father and to struggle against him, to gain ascendancy over his father and to submit to him. These unresolved and conflicting feelings dominated his relationship with the rest of the world. At home, with his wife and children, Cooper's life was exceptionally

---

shall see, he could never get far enough back from his actions to be this shrewdly perceptive about them.

calm. But his career as a member of society was incredibly
stormy, at times triumphant, at times anguished. We have
already noted the confusion among the students of Cooper's
life about his public behavior and his literary productions.
The way to account for and explain these perplexities, I
believe, is to trace the novelist's conscious emotions back to
his ambivalent, unconscious attitude toward the figure of
his father.

We have seen how thoroughly he attempted as a young
adult to satisfy his infantile impulse to replace William
Cooper. With one difference, the political, social, and moral
values he embraced were identical to his father's. That difference has been mentioned, but elaborating upon it will
provide additional insight into Cooper's character. Judge
Cooper was a gentleman with ragged edges: he was, as the
Dictionary of American Biography relates, "A curious mix-
ture of silk hose and leather stockings, he made Otsego hall
the finest home west of the Hudson, but he was always
willing to go to any shanty on his settlement to show his
ability as a wrestler."[21] His behavior at the election of 1791
—and one can believe either his friend's or his opponents'
testimony—proves that he did not consider his dignity in-
expendable. Ideally suited for his task in life, the Judge's
personality partook substantially of the rudeness of pioneer
living. His wife, however, aspired to higher standards than
Cooperstown could afford: if he was the well-adjusted "patriarch of the Otsego country,"[22] she was "a patrician who
detested the frontier. With her books, her music, her flow-
ers, and her hospitality to all respectable company, she insisted on the primacy of civilized values."[23] From his mother,
then, did James Cooper acquire his firm belief in the value

[21] James Melvin Lee, "William Cooper," in *Dictionary of American
Biography*, ed. Allen Johnson and Dumas Malone (New York: Charles
Scribner's Sons, 1943), IV, 418.

[22] L. H. Butterfield, "Cooper's Inheritance: The Otsego Country
and Its Founders," *New York History* 35 (1954), 387.

[23] Beard, *L/J*, I, 4.

of civilized manners and respectable company. His choice of a career was strictly limited, as he once wrote his sister, to "some gentlemanly and suitable occupation" (*L/J*, III, 34). No doubt Mrs. Cooper's approbation of James's marriage to a De Lancey, a family that shared her social prejudices, was given wholeheartedly: not all of her children fared so well, and one actually died of injuries sustained in a wrestling match. Until his mother's death, James had planned to live near her in Cooperstown, and his attempt afterwards to involve himself with the patrician De Lancey family can partly be referred to the genteel ideal that his mother represented. But as I have said, Cooper's involvement in financial speculations, in which he clearly modeled his behavior after his father, prompted Mr. De Lancey to disown him; when De Lancey died, he stipulated in his will that the bequest to his daughter was "for her sole and separate use independent of her husband."[24] And this legacy will serve as a symbol of Cooper's inability—despite the Bible and Agricultural Societies—to become the complete gentleman.

For the most part, therefore, the man who became the novelist initially appeared to have inherited William Cooper's identity along with one-fifth of his estate. The foundations of that estate were unsound; a decade after the Judge's death it was bankrupt. Unsound also was the foundation upon which James had tried to rear his identity. Instead of freeing himself from his father, he had remained dominated by him. Although the only indication we have of it is his sincere and modest hope that *his* political exertions "will shew not in vain," James must have begun to grow dismayed with himself. Compared to his father's magnificent accomplishment as a landlord, his secretarial efforts to improve Cooperstown undoubtedly seemed as small to him as they do to us.

When the estate began to fail, and one by one his older

[24] Quoted by Beard, *L/J*, I, 344, n. 1.

brothers died, Cooper was given the perfect opportunity
to gain ascendancy over the Judge. Alone as a son, he would
resurrect the life's work of his father. In 1819, he not only
assumed the administration of the property, but made himself accountable for all his brothers' debts—actions that
were unconsciously designed to turn himself into his father.
It was a grand attempt—had it succeeded, he would never
have written a novel—but it could not have been long before he realized that it would not succeed. By 1823 his
entire inheritance had been sacrificed to creditors, and in
that year even his "household goods," according to James
Franklin Beard, "were seized and inventoried (though not
actually sold) by the sheriff of New York."[25] If he had continued his efforts to succeed in life on his father's terms,
this catastrophe would in all probability have undone him.
It did impair his health: Cooper's digestive disorders began
at exactly this time; it is very likely that they were caused
by the anxiety connected with his disastrous attempt to replace his father. But by 1823 he had found a new identity;
he had become America's first successful novelist. And it
should be noted even this early that his earnings as a novelist eventually enabled him to reclaim a portion of his
father's estate.

Cooper decided to write a novel, and finally found a
viable career, immediately after the election of 1820. In a
letter to Andrew Thompson Goodrich, written May 31st,
1820, Cooper gives this report of that decision:

> The arrangements for the late election and the sub-
> sequent death of the Mother of Mrs. Cooper having
> compelled me to remain at home for the last two or
> three months—For the double purpose of employment
> and the amusement of my wife in her present low spirits
> —I commenced the writing of a moral tale—finding it
> swell to a rather unwieldy size—I destroy'd the manu-
> script and chang'd it to a novel—the persuasions of

25 Beard, *L/J*, 1, 84.

my wife and the opinion of my Friend Mr. Wm. Jay—
have induced me to think of publishing it—it is not
yet completed and the object of this letter is to obtain
some mechanical information that may regulate the
size of my volumes— (*L/J*, I, 41-42)

This is Cooper's first communication with a publisher, and
it immediately reveals his inchoate attitude toward composition: if he began writing as a pastime, he would not finish
the book without seeking to insure its salability; the size
of his volumes will be determined by commercial, not aesthetic, considerations. Was the decision to become an author
made for financial reasons?

In the previous chapter I put this question aside, but it
can be answered now. We know that at just this point in
his life Cooper was suddenly forced to worry about earning
his living. This fact, however, only makes his new-found
inclination for "authorcraft" more incomprehensible. In
1820, almost no one in America was writing novels. A generation earlier, Charles Brockden Brown had deliberately
and energetically tried to establish himself as America's first
professional novelist, but gave up after writing and publishing six long novels in three lean years. Uncopyrighted English novels, less expensive and more attractive to American
readers than any their countrymen could produce, had
spoiled the public Brown had hoped to write for. Among
Cooper's contemporaries, only one man had been able to
turn his pen to profit: over the previous two decades Washington Irving's work had been reaching a larger and larger
audience. *A History of New York*, published in 1809 by
"Diedrich Knickerbocker," was widely read in this country,
and *The Sketch Book*, published in 1820 by "Geoffrey Cray-
on, Gent," was the first American book to find favor with a
British audience. Although in 1820 Irving was living in
England, where he had gone in 1815 and where he remained
for seventeen years, his successes had proven that an American writer could yet be a professional one. But Cooper, who

later developed an antipathy to Irving which may have had
its deepest roots in his envy but which he explained on the
basis of Irving's expatriate apostasy, did not in 1820 seem
even aware of his example. He may not have read *The
Sketch Book*, and in any case, Irving's idiosyncratic collec-
tion of sketches would have offered neither much aid nor
much comfort to a would-be novelist. An avid reader himself, Cooper knew how eagerly Americans received each new
stack of novels from the hold of a London cargo ship, how
thoroughly they had come to think of novels in the same
context as silks or spices—as imported luxuries. The copyright laws had not been changed since Brockden Brown's
time, and British authors were still pirated and published
without domestic competition. To write a salable novel in
1820, Cooper had to overcome not merely his own disin-
clinations but those of the American public. He accomplished the second objective with a ruse: *Precaution* is set
in England, its characters, including lords and ladies, were
exclusively English, and even by English critics it was accepted as one of their own. *Precaution* was at least an intelligent accident.

Yet so slim were the chances for any kind of American
novel that Goodrich would only publish it at Cooper's expense, and though it got fair reviews (better than it deserved) his first literary speculation did not make any
money. In fact, financial considerations almost convinced
Cooper to give up literature in the middle of his second
novel, which was unmistakably American: "So little was expected from the publication of an original work of this
description," he wrote in a revised Preface, "at the time it
was written, that the first volume of 'The Spy' was actually
printed several months, before the author felt a sufficient
inducement to write a line of the second."[26] It was lucky
that he did: *The Spy* was immediately popular both here
and abroad, and its publication launched the American
novel and Cooper the novelist upon their respective careers.

[26] *The Spy*, pp. x-xi.

But the success of his second novel does not explain the existence of his first.

Writing to Goodrich, Cooper himself cites "the late election" (April 20th) and "the subsequent death of the Mother of Mrs. Cooper" (May 7th) as factors that somehow contributed to his decision to produce a novel. We have already discussed his emotional investment in the gubernatorial campaign: any hopes he had of imitating his father's political career—and we cannot know how large were the hopes hidden in his small phrase about "dabbling in politics"—were defeated along with Clinton in Westchester County. We can assume, however, that he did not set down the first words of his literary career until after his mother-in-law's death. According to his daughter Susan's anecdote, his wife appears to have been in mourning: "My mother was not well; she was lying on the sofa." That the death of his mother-in-law induced Cooper to think of his mother is a hypothesis that cannot be directly supported by any physical evidence, but it is consistent with our sense of the mind's emotional economy. Indirectly it is supported by Cooper's startling decision, for his interest in fiction had been inherited from his mother. "She was," writes Susan, "a great reader of romances."[27] When he picked up a pen, Cooper must have felt unconsciously secure about his mother's approbation of his novel occupation: literature had been sanctioned, his literary endeavor made possible, by her preferences.

When, in *Notions of the Americans*, Cooper discussed the particular position of woman in American society, he added this interesting sentence about her role as a mother: "The first impressions of the child are drawn from the purest sources known to our nature; and the son, even long after he has been compelled to enter on the thorny track of the father, preserves the memorial of the pure and unalloyed lessons that he has received from the lips, and, what is far

[27] "Small Family Memories," p. 12.

better, from the example of the mother."[28] This son knew
as well as any how thorny the track of the father could be,
and had learned better than most how valuable the example of the mother could be as an alternative. William
Cooper would definitely have agreed with that old lady in
Cooperstown—"the great good and useful man" did not
write "silly novels"—but James's efforts to be the kind of
man his father represented were collapsing. As the tale that
he wrote reveals, his decision "to remain at home" and
write a novel, a choice he obviously felt he needed to justify
to Goodrich, was a retreat from the demands of manhood.
Precaution's gender is feminine. It may be, as Leslie Fiedler
puts it, "disconcerting to find him impersonating a female,"[29] but since he was working under the psychic aus-
pices of his mother, that inversion is easily explicable.
Cooper was himself apparently disconcerted by the character of his first book: as soon as the manuscript of *Precaution* left his hands he began *The Spy*, and confessed to
some second thoughts about the former: "I wish the work
push'd through the press," he said in a letter to Goodrich;
"It is so—very—very—inferior to the 'Spy' that I have lost
most of my expectations of its success—still, as it is a highly
moral Book— (which bye the bye the 'Spy' is not) I believe
it will sell—" (*L/J*, 1, 48). For Cooper's distinction between
the morality of the two books we must substitute another.
Each has a sufficiently explicit moral, but while *Precaution*
was modeled upon the type of domestic comedy being written by Jane Austen and a long list of lesser English women,
The Spy was inspired by Walter Scott's historical novels.
Precaution is about marriage, *The Spy* about war. Over the
years Cooper gave several reasons for writing *The Spy*. He
told Goodrich at the time that it was "by persuasion of
Mrs. Cooper." Twenty-three years later he told Rufus Gris-
wold that "having accidentally ⟨written⟩ produced an English book, I determined to write one purely American, by

---

[28] *Notions*, I, 106.   [29] Fiedler, p. 186.

way of atonement." By 1843 Cooper's identity as a particularly American author had become a point of pride, to be insisted upon whenever the occasion offered. To write a purely American book was no doubt one conscious motive behind his second novel, but the desire to write an undeniably masculine book "by way of atonement" to his manhood was certainly an unconscious one.

When he set his third novel, *The Pioneers*, in the world of his childhood, Cooper left his mother out. Judge Temple is a widower. Yet if the sensibility of the rest of his novels is masculine, he nonetheless continued to associate his identity as an author with his mother.[30] In 1826, at the zenith of his literary career, he petitioned the New York State Legislature to change his name—to James Cooper Fenimore. His explanation of this action is worth quoting in full:

> My mother had a small property in this county [Otsego], which she had inherited by a transfer of lands in New Jersey from her father, and which she offered to give me, if I would take her family name in lieu of that of Cooper. My father opposed it. The latter died, leaving me an equal portion of his own estate. My mother survived him several years and repeated the offer from time to time. I would not accept the offer of the eight or ten farms she owned, but promised to make the change so far as to add her name to my father's, and to use both as a family name. My mother died several years before the law was passed, the delay arising from the circumstance that I was implicated in many lawsuits and change might produce confusion. In 1826 I got extricated from the law and was going abroad for health and variety. That was the time to redeem the pledge given my mother before her death. The application was, as I have said, to add Fenimore to the old family name, keeping both. The legislators, who

[30] He also impersonated a female again: in 1823 he published two short stories—"Heart" and "Imagination"—as "Jane Morgan."

always know more than their constituents, changed this application by authorizing me to take Fenimore as a middle name, a power I did not ask. As the law authorized me to use Fenimore, and my children were all so young as to render it a matter of indifference as respects them, I did no more in the way of legislation; though I have always used the name of Fenimore as part of my family name, except in discourse. My wife and children do the same, as will probably any descendants I may have hereafter in the male line. Thus the reason I write Fenimore in full, abbreviating the James for shortness. (*L/J*, v, 200-201)

Before introducing this petition, Cooper had tried by other means to perpetuate his mother's name; he called the only house he ever built "Fenimore," and Fenimore was also the name of his first son, who died an infant in 1823, the same year the house was destroyed. But neither these oblique efforts to redeem his pledge nor the lawsuits arising from his administration of the Judge's estate explain why he waited until 1826 to become a Fenimore himself. Cooper denies that his mother's property prompted him to consent to her request, yet denying this motive, he fails to provide any other. His account suggests, however, a particularly significant relationship between the mother and her son. The father left all his sons "an equal portion" of his property; the mother singled out her youngest to be her beneficiary. There is, in fact, reason to suspect this assertion: family tradition states that Mrs. Cooper merely wanted one of her sons, any one, to appropriate the Fenimore name and property. But for our purposes, psychic facts are just as important as real ones —Cooper's distortion of his mother's wishes reveals that he preferred not to share her favors with his brothers, and so he promoted himself to the privileged position of her favorite. Cooper's petition to the legislature doubtless had a similar motive, though it would have been his lingering jealousy over his father's position, not his brothers', that prompted the action. Taking his mother's name, almost a reversal of what normally happens when a man and woman get married, was to some extent Cooper's psychic substitute for the infantile desire to possess her exclusively, as both mother and wife.

Yet saying this, we say little more than that Cooper had to wrestle with the same angel all mankind must wrestle with in his individual struggle to achieve salvation. There was another reason behind the desire to change his name. It was similarly unconscious, it was reinforced by his libidinal desires, nevertheless it testifies to Cooper's progress in that struggle. His father had originally forbidden the change, and his opposition would have been more strenuous at the time it was made, for by then James was an only son. The state legislators had many of them known Judge Cooper, and despite James's annoyance, probably revised his application in honor of his father's memory. Conceivably, they may have intuitively apprehended or dimly sensed the motive behind the son's request—though it does not appear that he ever did. Implied in Cooper's account is the fact that only after the Judge's death did he consider making the application, and even then his subservience to his father, a stance implied by his serious effort to save William Cooper's estate at the expense of his own, led him to postpone it for many years. Concluding that when he finally "got extricated from the law" he also got free from the Judge's domination is much too simplistic—as I have said, Cooper never freed himself psychically from his father—but one may appropriate it as a metaphor. This independence at last made it possible for him to rebel against his father's injunction.

And 1826 was an especially appropriate time for him to satisfy his mother's desire. His new identity as a novelist would never seem more secure; his visit to Europe, where no one had heard of William Cooper, had been preceded by the triumphant reception of his novels there. Since unconsciously Elizabeth Fenimore's patronage had made that new identity possible, she should posthumously share its reward. As Cooper says, he did not use the name Fenimore "in discourse"; instead, he wanted to put it under the titles of his world-famous romances. Upon his return from the continent only eight years later, that identity, for reasons I shall discuss, had apparently become untenable, and in *A Letter to His Countrymen* (1834) Cooper announced that he was laying aside the pen: "I confess I have come to this decision with reluctance, for I had hoped to be useful in my generation, and to have yet done something which might have identified my name with those who are to come after me."[31] William Cooper had taught his son the obligation to be useful, but had somehow failed to equip him to succeed by his example. James could not found a second Cooperstown to perpetuate his original name. But he never did abandon his literary career, and the name that James and "any descendants" of his could identify with consequently had to include his mother's.

Shortly after her name had been added to his, Cooper ended a letter to Robert Campbell in Cooperstown with these words:

> In order that you may know who *I am* I will just add, that my name was altered by a law of the State last session from James Cooper
> to
> J. Fenimore Cooper   (*L/J*, I, 138)

His use of the passive tense in the second half of this sentence is probably attributable to the fact that he was writing an old friend of his father, a man who had worked with James for years in his attempt to salvage his father's property—by invoking "a law of the State" Cooper could dodge some of the responsibility for disobeying the Judge's order. But the sentence's emphatic beginning reveals how completely he embraced his new identity. There was cause

---

[31] *A Letter to His Countrymen* (New York: John Wiley, 1834), p. 99.

for his enthusiasm: no longer merely a son, he had as an author become a member of the community of men in his own right. *He was* J. Fenimore Cooper.

As J. Fenimore Cooper he did gain ascendancy over William, at least in an objective sense, earning a bigger place for himself in history. That was another question put aside in the first chapter: did a desire for fame motivate him to become an author? His letters to Goodrich about the publication of *Precaution* provide ample evidence that it did not. At the head of the earliest one—May 31st, 1820—preceding even the place and date, Cooper wrote *"Most Strictly confidential."* From subsequent letters are the following quotations taken:

[June 12] . . . cannot the thing be done with perfect secrecy as respects me?
[July 2] I would impress on you again my wish to be incog—
[July 12] . . . take care of my *name*, and do not let it appear in any manner.

Several of his letters are even signed like this:

Yours &c —
— —   (*L/J*, 1, 44, 46, 49, 50, 51)

Why did Cooper insist on taking such precautions against letting his name appear? Anonymity was consistent with accepted literary practice; Scott for example had not yet acknowledged authorship of the Waverley Novels. The special case of *Precaution* supplied another reason: "I must be in the dark—the novel being *English*" (*L/J*, 1, 42). But neither of these causes can account for the obvious intensity of Cooper's concern. What he was really anxious about is hinted at in this mispunctuated passage from another letter to Goodrich: "I do not believe my being known as the author will hurt the sale of Precaution, but I believe it will hurt its reputation on the whole I am much more sanguine of its success in England than in this Country and much more in Boston and Philadelphia than in New-York" (*L/J*, I, 64). In his very next letter, perhaps in response to a question from Goodrich, he finally reveals the reason for his "wish to be incog"—"If *I* am supposed the author the book will fail in New-York . . . thank god there are other places and other critics in the world" (*L/J*, I, 66). Here again Cooper does not explain his meaning. It is, in fact, unlikely that he could have: there was no actual reason to worry about New York's reaction to his first novel. A prophet is often honored in his own country, but the son of William Cooper did not want his new attempt to be useful in his generation compared in any way with his father's achievements. New York was where his father had succeeded; where he himself had failed to imitate that success; where, should *he* be supposed its author, *Precaution* would be doomed as well. This syllogism had more psychological than logical force, but Cooper was convinced by it. The name his father had given him must not appear. Cooper wanted something more ambitious than fame: the opportunity to fill in "— —" with a new identity.

That halfway through his life Cooper recognized this opportunity, whether consciously or not, that he took it, that he triumphed as a novelist—these are great achievements for any man. Publishing a novel in Cooper's America was a lot like pioneering a settlement in the wilderness. Had he planned all his life for a literary career, Cooper's decision to become an author would still have surprised his family, would still impress his biographers. If my account of that decision makes it seem purely determined, even overdetermined, that is one of the deficiences of the interpretive process. Let me say as clearly as I can that it is impossible fully to account for the sources of anyone's individual greatness. What Freud suggests about the analysis of a single dream—that it is potentially interminable—is equally and more profoundly true for each psyche. Having said this, however, I would like to continue with my analysis of the circumstances that induced James Cooper to write a novel.

Despite possible appearances to the contrary, that analysis is terminable. All that remains is to examine the particular incident that changed the course of Cooper's life. Our only source for what happened that day at Angevine is his daughter Susan, who was eight years old at the time, and who wrote several descriptions of it in the course of her life. They are essentially similar, but the one given at the start of this chapter provides the most details. Taken from a brief biography she was writing for the family, it strikes one as the most faithful to her memory of the day and the reports she probably heard from her parents later. We may recall that Cooper "was reading this newly imported novel" aloud—

> after a chapter or two he threw it aside, exclaiming, *"I could write you a better book than that myself!"* Our Mother laughed at the idea, as the height of absurdity—he who disliked writing even a letter, that he should write a book!! He persisted in his declaration, however, and almost immediately wrote the first pages of a tale. . . .

In retrospect, Cooper's exclamation no doubt appeared oracular enough to deserve its italics; in fact it was, as James Grossman concludes, a "merely conventional and inherently modest criticism."[32] Yet I share Susan's impulse to underscore the phrase, not, however, as a piece of prophecy, but as evidence of the state of Cooper's mind. Grossman emphasizes the idea that Cooper's wife turned this statement into a challenge. In another record of this moment Susan does say that her father "was playfully challenged to make good his promise,"[33] but he alone could have provided the motivation to persist in his declaration, to make

[32] Grossman, *Cooper*, p. 17. [33] *Pages and Pictures*, p. 17.

the amazing decision to write the first pages of a tale, to find a lifelong career. On the basis of what has been learned about Cooper's adult life, we can easily recognize the source of that motivation. He had, in effect, declared to himself that he could be a better gentleman, run a better campaign, build a better estate than his father. In spite of his persistence, he had in each of these instances failed. The unlikely profession of American novelist offered him the chance to satisfy a growing need to prove his merits, to his wife, to others, and most importantly to himself. Although psychically supported by his mother's values, this new career was very tentative, and Cooper's uncertainty about its fortune in the real world may supply another reason for the perfect secrecy about *Precaution*'s authorship he demanded: he believed that unless some portion of a great man's merit is inherited by the son, "the claim," which is to say the name, "had better be suppressed."

That Mrs. Cooper chose to call Cooper's statement about writing a better book "the height of absurdity" may have been adventitious—perhaps the only thing she wanted was for her husband to continue reading the novel—but her reply should also be taken into account. She knew better than anyone else that Cooper was quick to take offense and equally quick to defend himself, to consider any kind of criticism an injustice that had to be rebuked. As she once wrote her sister, "Mr. Cooper you well know feels deeply and speaks promptly."[34] That his wife's facetious response prompted him to persist was not adventitious. Nor can it properly be traced to the sudden discovery by a born storyteller of his metier. The book he wrote is too imitative, too labored, to represent anything but Cooper's dogged determination "to make good his promise" in the face of his wife's laughter. He never admitted that his first novel was undertaken in this spirit, but he does acknowledge a similar motive for his fourth. The idea for *The Pilot* (1824) was

[34] Quoted by Beard, *L/J*, II, 121.

provoked by a discussion with a friend who had been impressed by the familiarity with the sea manifested in Walter Scott's just-published *Pirate*. Here is how Cooper, the ex-sailor and apprentice novelist, reacted:

> It would have been hypercritical to object to the Pirate, that it was not strictly nautical, or true in its details; but, when the reverse was urged as a proof of what, considering the character of other portions of the work, would have been most extraordinary attainments, it was a sort of provocation to dispute the seamanship of the Pirate. . . . The result of this conversation was a sudden determination to produce a work which, if it had no other merit, might present truer pictures of the ocean and ships than any that are to be found in the Pirate. To this unpremeditated decision, purely an impulse, is not only the Pilot due, but a tolerably numerous school of nautical romances that have succeeded it.[35]

Throughout his life, Cooper found all sorts of provocations to dispute. "Opposition only inflamed him," wrote Lounsbury; "it never daunted him."[36] We shall have a number of occasions to examine this characteristic reflex. His last extant letter, written a month before he died, reveals almost too pathetically that only at the end could Cooper be daunted by opposition: "Here I leave you, for to say the truth, I am not in a condition to carry on any controversy whatever, just now" (*L/J*, vi, 282). Although objective reasons can be found for each of the many controversies that mark Cooper's career, his general enthusiasm for engaging in them can only be attributed to a deep emotional demand. As the passage about *The Pilot* indicates, his need to withstand opposition and his need to prove himself were interrelated. His quarrel with the De Lanceys, which I have already mentioned, provides a clearer example

[35] *The Pilot*, p. viii.   [36] Lounsbury, p. 81.

of this complicated response. When his father-in-law expressed his disapproval of Cooper's financial speculations by removing his daughter's property from Cooper's control —thus both opposing him and questioning his ability— Cooper angrily refused to have anything further to do with his wife's family. A few years later, Mrs. Cooper persuaded him to reopen "the communications between our families," but the conditions under which he agreed to her wishes bristle with the points of this psychic compulsion. Writing to Mr. De Lancey, he insists that "there should be no explanations," that "Concessions, I take to be utterly out of the question, from either party," that "I do and must reserve the right to defend my character from every assult, by all honorable means" (*L/J*, 1, 87, 88). Not surprisingly, relations between Cooper and the De Lanceys remained cool until long after his father-in-law's death.

"Oppression," he told a friend in 1830, "might drive me to resistence, any where" (*L/J*, 11, 23). This sentence closely follows a statement about his "nativity," and his identity as an American, a New Yorker, and "a Cooperstown man." We should be very interested in this suggestive proximity. For it is in Cooperstown, in his childhood, that we must locate the source of the characteristic impulse I have been trying to define. Cooper himself said that "I had somewhat the reputation, when a boy, of effecting my objects, by pure dint of teasing. Many is the shilling I have abstracted, in this way, from my mother's purse, who, constantly affirmed, that it was sore against her will."[37] But it was not his mother's will that ordinarily opposed his. He seems to have been certain of getting those shillings, as he probably got his way with her in more important matters. The relationship between an infant son and the woman who bore him is probably the one in which two human beings feel the least desire to prove anything to each other. James's teasing served to test the limits of his mother's love. Such testing becomes necessary only after the infant realizes that he must share

[37] *Gleanings* [*France*], 11, 214.

his mother, in a sense compete for her, with his father. It was William Cooper who opposed his son, who presented a threat to him; it was the figure of his father that James Cooper needed simultaneously to resist and to convince.

We have in this chapter been concerned with Cooper's adult life before he became an author, in which subservience to his father informed so much of his behavior. In the next two, I will discuss Cooper's attempts, both as a child and an author, to resist.

CHAPTER III

"TO PLEASE MYSELF"

Cooper's third novel, *The Pioneers*, deserves to be closely looked at for several reasons. Many students of Cooper, including myself, consider it his best book, which is perhaps another way of saying that of all his novels, this one can be recommended to an intelligent modern reader with the fewest reservations and explanations. It is the earliest tale about populating the wilderness, an issue Cooper dealt with again and again throughout his career. Six of his subsequent novels were actually sequels to *The Pioneers*. In order of composition, it is the first of the five Leather-Stocking Tales; in it Natty Bumppo, the most famous of Cooper's characters, makes his original appearance. The two Effingham novels, which are no longer read but which were, to Cooper's contemporaries, his most infamous books, depict characters and scenes directly descended from those presented in *The Pioneers*. And most important—at least in the context of our examination of the interrelationship between an author's life and his aesthetic creations—in Cooper's third novel neither the social comedies of Jane Austen nor the historical romances of Walter Scott but rather his personal experience provided the inspiration for and the material of his fiction. *The Pioneers*, as his contemporaries and later critics have uniformly recognized, represents an imaginative re-creation of the circumstances of his early life in Cooperstown. Like his two previous novels, it was published anonymously. Its full title, however, is *The Pioneers; or, The Sources of the Susquehanna.* By giving the actual name of the river Cooper compromises the book's anonymity, by locating its action in Cooperstown he prompts the reader

75

to look for autobiographical elements in it, by using the word "sources" in the title he encourages an analysis of the way in which it was influenced by the unconscious impulses and desires fixed in his childhood. Especially for this reason, I shall look more closely at his third novel than at any of the other thirty-one. At the same time, the novel's other claims to our attention must not be overlooked. Its analysis should also provide a perspective from which to examine the Leather-Stocking and the Effingham novels. These two groups, as we have already noted, affirm antithetical values; the effort to resolve this contradiction must begin with *The Pioneers*. Nor should an explication of the novel's latent meaning ignore its manifest achievement. But I believe that even its artistic success can be discussed in terms of its author's psychic involvement with it.

Cooper's Preface to the original edition of *The Pioneers*, dated January 1st, 1823, indicates his state of mind at the time he wrote it. In the form of a letter to Charles Wiley, his publisher, the Preface begins with an evaluation of his young literary career:

> Every man is, more or less, the sport of accident; nor do I know that authors are at all exempted from this humiliating influence. This is the third of my novels, and it depends on two very uncertain contingencies, whether it will not be the last;—the one being the public opinion, and the other mine own humour. The first book was written, because I was told that I could not write a grave tale; so, to prove that the world did not know me, I wrote one that was so grave nobody would read it; wherein I think that I had much the best of the argument. The second was written to see if I could not overcome this neglect of the reading world. How far I have succeeded, Mr. Charles Wiley, must ever remain a secret between ourselves. The third has been written, exculsively, to please myself: so it would be no wonder if it displeased every body else;

for what two ever thought alike, on a subject of the imagination![1]

Cooper's reference to the power of "accident" repeats a theme we are already familiar with. I have tried to demonstrate that where Cooper says "adventitious" or "accidental" it would usually be more intelligible and appropriate to say "unconscious." In the present instance, Cooper himself empties the word of whatever meaning he intended it to have by offering his reasons for publishing his first three novels. "To prove that the world did not know me" is the motive he cites for *Precaution*, one that reinforces the conclusion that writing a book was for him an attempt to find a new identity. That attempt was specifically provoked by his wife's opposition to an apparently offhand assertion; as I have said, Cooper consistently needed to have "the best of the argument," especially when his own merit was at stake.

One might have thought that the success of his new identity, confirmed by the popularity of his second novel, would have concluded the argument. In fact, Cooper devoted half the Preface of *The Pioneers* to another dispute, this time with literary critics. Thinly disguising his palpable anger behind forced humor, Cooper declares his independence from the reviewers' judgments. He ends the "letter" to Wiley with an echo of his coy allusion, quoted above, to the sales of *The Spy*: "The critics may write as obscurely as they please, and look much wiser than they are; the papers may puff or abuse, as their changeful humours dictate; but if you meet me with a smiling face, I shall at once know that all is essentially well."[2] When *The Pioneers* was placed before the world, it did exceptionally well: eager for the new book by the author of *The Spy*, 3,500 people bought a copy of it within a few hours after publication. The misgivings that Cooper expresses at the end of the first paragraph seem to have been basically rhetorical—they supply the

[1] *The Pioneers*, 1st ed., pp. vii-viii.   [2] Ibid., p. xi.

77

transition to his assault on the reviewers—and the self-confidence that radiates from the remainder of the Preface was certainly justified. But if the popular reception of *The Spy* was the cause of that confidence, Cooper's antagonism to the critics had little relation to their reception of the book. The American reviewers, waiting to see how the English ones would react, were merely, in Grossman's words, "mild in their praise or noncommittal."[3] America's servile deference to English opinion would become the cause of one of Cooper's most persistent complaints against his countrymen. It is not mentioned, however, in this first specimen of his hostility toward the reviewers and the newspapers, a hostility that would culminate fifteen years later in a lengthy series of libel suits. A fuller examination of this attitude must be put off until we have reached that period in Cooper's life, but his contumacious response to their authority is worth noting as another indication of Cooper's compulsion to assert himself over any threat of opposition, even the mild and noncommittal kind represented by the reviewers, who were probably surprised by his strongly worded attack. They had done nothing to deserve it, and besides, new authors do not customarily insult the entire class of men who have the power to pass judgment on their creations. Cooper did so not because they had exercised that power, but solely because they had it.

Instead, Cooper asked to be judged by the public's opinion. To them he apologizes in the Preface for writing a book exclusively to please himself:

> I have already said, that it was mine own humour that suggested this tale; but it is a humour that is deeply connected with feeling. Happier periods, more interesting events, and, possibly, more beauteous scenes, might have been selected, to exemplify my subject; but none of either that would be so dear to me. I wish,

[3] Grossman, *Cooper*, p. 28.

therefore, to be judged more by what I have done, than by my sins of omission.[4]

What he had done is revealed more directly in his letter, written November 29th, 1822, to John Murray, the English publisher of *The Pioneers*. Cooper has an apology to make to him as well:

> I had announced the work as a "descriptive tale" but perhaps have confined myself too much to describing the scenes of my own youth—I know that the present taste is for action and strong excitement, and in this respect am compelled to acknowledge that the two first volumes are deficient, I however am not without hopes that the third will be thought to make some amends If there be any value in truth, the pictures are very faithful, and I can safely challenge a scrutiny in th[is?] particular—But the world must be left to decide for itself, and I believe it is very seldom that it decides wrong— (*L/J*, 1, 85)

The first thing to be said about *The Pioneers*, therefore, is that Cooper's instinct to cater to "present taste" was overridden by his desire to revisit imaginatively the scenes of his youth. In a writer as subservient to literary convention as Cooper, especially the early Cooper, this is an interesting choice. Still more interesting are the older Cooper's efforts in a number of forums to deny both his personal feeling and the novel's fidelity: the world did decide that *The Pioneers* was true to Cooper's life; the world, he would vehemently insist, was wrong. He stated his case for mistaken identity at length in a letter printed in *Brother Jonathan* on March 26th, 1842. Twenty years after his letter to Murray, he reverses the meaning of the novel's subtitle: "The Pioneers is announced, in its title page, as a 'Descriptive Tale'; descriptive, not in [the] sense of a literal account

[4] *The Pioneers*, 1st ed., p. x.

of persons and things; but descriptive as regards general characteristics, usages, and the state of a new country" (L/J, IV, 253; my brackets). In this letter he challenges the world's scrutiny in every particular: "although," he concedes, "a few personal *touches* were occasionally thrown in" (L/J, IV, 255), setting, events, and characters are all, as he pedantically tries to prove, more fictional than real. *The Pioneers* was not meant to be autobiography, nor should it be read as such, but as "a tale descriptive of the progress of society" (L/J, IV, 255).

Cooper's revised version of his motives for writing the novel arouses our curiosity—he does not explain in the *Brother Jonathan* letter why this generally descriptive tale should please himself so exclusively, and his arguments against the received opinion about *The Pioneers* are specious and unconvincing. From what we know about Cooper, the strenuous nature of his resistance suggests that somehow he felt that his own merit was being questioned by the people who found resemblances between his novel and his life. By 1842 he no longer wanted to be judged even by the public on what he had done, and this attempt to renounce the pleasure which the novel afforded him gives additional significance to the question that I want to pose in this chapter: how did it originally please him?

Cooper himself provides the most obvious reason for his pleasure. In 1850 he wrote a new Introduction for *The Pioneers* in which he does not completely discount the influence of his own experience on the novel: "The face of the country, the climate as it was found by the whites, and the manners of the settlers, are described with a minuteness for which the Author has no other apology than the force of his own recollections."[5] The simple use of memory almost always supplies a yield of pleasure. When he wrote the novel, Cooper had not seen Cooperstown at all for five years, and he understandably lingers over the remembered

[5] *The Pioneers*, rev. ed. (New York: W. A. Townsend and Company, 1863), p. x.

details of a landscape, a street, a room. There is no cause for his apology—the reader shares his interest in, if not his feelings about, the descriptions, and the elaborate details give him an enjoyable sense of recognition, even of belonging. One of the novel's greatest virtues is the way its verbal pictures satisfy the reader's wish to participate in the story. But the force of Cooper's recollection did more than inspire the book's marvelous pictures.

At its beginning, two people—a father and his daughter —are travelling through a vast forest toward a pioneer settlement. "Though called Templeton in the book," Cooper wrote in 1827 to his French publisher, "the name of the village is actually *Cooperstown*" (*L/J*, VI, 295). The young woman is being brought home after an absence of five years, and behind her emotions upon returning to "the altered, though still remembered, scenes of her childhood"[6] can be sensed Cooper's own. By means of his imaginative ability to describe it, he gradually reenters the world of *his* childhood. That world unfolds in the novel's leisurely narrative of a full year at Templeton. The date—1794— corresponds to the fourth year of Cooper's life, precisely when the conflicting impulses that constitute what Freud calls "the family romance" began struggling for control of his psyche. It was the force of this repressed struggle—in that sense, his "own humour"—that suggested the tale to Cooper, that prompted him to disregard what he felt were his obligations to the reader. Whatever he may have con-

6 Ibid., p. 47. The text of *The Pioneers* that I use in this chapter includes a number of revisions that Cooper made in 1831 for a new English edition. Although primarily stylistic, some of these revisions are substantive. Since, however, all but one of the editions of the novel presently available are based upon the 1831 text, I shall quote from that version, and point out in footnotes any interesting changes. For example, in the original version the phrase just quoted continues "[childhood] and of joy!" The first edition has never been reprinted, but Leon Howard's edition of *The Pioneers* (New York: Holt, Rinehart and Winston, Inc., 1959) is based on the second (1825) edition, in which only minor corrections of the first edition's text were made.

sciously resolved when he decided to write about Cooperstown, Cooper re-created, along with the countryside, the
climate and the frontier manners, the emotional landscape
of his early life. In that setting personal obligations usurped
professional ones: a large part of the novel's plot, and of the
pleasure he derived from writing it, must be traced to his
unconscious.

Despite Cooper's later attempts to discourage them, readers of the novel have always identified two of its characters
as members of his family. Just as in Cooperstown, there is
one man who presides over Templeton, who owns the patent on which the pioneers buy their farms, who represents
the district in Congress, who sits as First Judge of the
County, and who has bestowed his name upon the settlement. In real life that man was William Cooper; in the
story, Marmaduke Temple. There are many additional
points of identity between the two, and one important
difference. Judge Cooper died before his wife, and seven of
his children lived to become adults; Judge Temple is a
widower with one daughter. This daughter, Elizabeth Temple, is the novel's heroine. The novelist gave his heroine
his mother's name, but her real counterpart was his sister
Hannah. A surprisingly large portion of the novel's action
is concerned with rescuing Elizabeth from a series of improbable dangers—a falling tree, a vicious panther, a forest
fire. James was eleven when Hannah Cooper was fatally
injured in a riding accident. At her death she was about
the same age as Elizabeth Temple, who, however, survives
to marry at the conclusion of the tale.

Marmaduke and Elizabeth Temple are the pair bound
homeward to Templeton. It is Christmas Eve, 1793, and the
slave who is guiding the sleigh over the deep snow has a
smile on his face "that was created by the thoughts of home,
and a Christmas fire-side" (p. 16). A similar sense of happiness, created by the author's thoughts of home, pervades
the opening pages; there is a nostalgic warmth that over-

comes "the depth of a winter in the mountains." Describing the labors of the pioneers, Cooper's tone is unambiguously favorable: "In short, the whole district is hourly exhibiting how much can be done, in even a rugged country, and with a severe climate, under the dominion of mild laws, and where every man feels a direct interest in the prosperity of a commonwealth, of which he knows himself to form a part" (p. 14). When he mentions the way the rude expedients of the first-generation settler are improved by the efforts "of a son, who, born in the land, piously wishes to linger around the grave of his father," Cooper appears almost to suggest that his story is intended as a memorial to the achievement of his father, who, after all, administered the district's "mild laws" and who directed "that magical change in [its] power and condition" produced by the coming of civilization (p. 15). This impression is strengthened by his introductory description of the Judge: although Temple is completely bundled up against the cold, enough can be seen to reveal "a fine manly face, and particularly a pair of expressive, large blue eyes, that promised extraordinary intellect, covert humor, and great benevolence" (p. 17). The filial obedience that characterized Cooper's first decade as an adult seems to predominate over his potential authority as an author—even Temple's "real regard for his child" is cited by the narrator (p. 17). But Cooper's feelings about the real father were mixed. Halfway through the first chapter something happens that abruptly reverses the mood of the narrative.

The silence of the travellers, who are "occupied with their reflections" about their homecoming (p. 17), is interrupted by the baying of hounds chasing a deer through the forest. Temple has the sleigh halted, and readies his rifle to provide some venison for the evening's Christmas feast. A buck bounds onto the road. Temple fires quickly, "with a practised eye and a steady hand" (p. 19), but the deer dashes "forward undaunted, and apparently unhurt."

From the woods, two more shots are fired, killing the deer, and "a couple of men instantly [appear] from behind the trunks of two of the pines."

Seemingly conjured out of the trees in the midst of the wilderness, these two men are, with the Temples, the most important characters in the novel. One of them is Natty Bumppo, also called Leather-stocking, as well known to the Temples as he has become to the world, but to them the other is a stranger. Yet as the three men gather around the carcass no introductions are exchanged. Instead, Temple and Leather-stocking commence an enigmatic debate about who has a right to the buck. It opens amiably, with Temple apologizing for disturbing their ambush and declaring that anyhow his shots had missed. Natty responds "with an inward chuckle, and with that look of exultation that indicates a consciousness of superior skill" (p. 20), followed by a brief homily on the inefficiency of the Judge's fancy rifle, another laugh, and a wipe of his nose. Perhaps annoyed by Natty's familiar condescension, Temple, though still "smiling good-humoredly," suddenly insists that he might actually have hit the deer. Leather-stocking's reaction to this assertion is surprising:

> "Let who will kill him," said the hunter, rather surlily, "I suppose the creature is to be eaten." So saying, he drew a large knife from a leathern sheath, which was stuck through his girdle or sash, and cut the throat of the animal. ". . . although I am a poor man, I can live without the venison, but I don't love to give up my lawful dues in a free country. Though, for the matter of that, might often makes right here."

The conclusion of his speech is muttered inaudibly, but neither his pointed act of violence nor his "air of sullen dissatisfaction" upsets the Judge, who becomes insistent in his claim: " 'Nay, Natty,' rejoined the traveller, with undisturbed good humor, 'it is for the honor that I contend. A few dollars will pay for the venison; but what will requite

me for the lost honor of a buck's tail in my cap?' " (p. 21).
Once again, the Leather-stocking's reply seems slightly out
of context: " 'Ah! the game is becoming hard to find, indeed, Judge, with your clearings and betterments,' said the
old hunter, with a kind of compelled resignation."[7] Natty's
use of the word "your" is not colloquial: he is speaking to
the man responsible for the clearings, the man who owns
the ground on which they stand. Set in that context, their
conversation is at once more important and more puzzling.
They make a strange pair—the sixty-year-old, plainly dressed
hunter and the middle-aged landlord wrapped in a wealth
of furs—arguing over the dead animal at their feet. Even
odder is the juxtaposition of Natty's hostile brooding and
Temple's fixed smile. But still "without heeding the ill-
humor of the hunter's manner" (p. 22), the Judge inex-
orably demands that they determine which man can claim
"the honor of this death." When Natty tells him that "the
cretur came by his end from a younger hand than either
your'n or mine," and that "I'm none of them who'll rob a
man of his rightful dues" (p. 23), the Judge finally turns
to the stranger:

> "You are tenacious of your rights, this cold evening,
> Natty," returned the Judge, with unconquerable good
> nature; "but what say you, young man; will three dol-
> lars pay you for the buck?"
> "First let us determine the question of right to the
> satisfaction of us both," said the youth, firmly but re-
> spectfully, and with a pronunciation and language vast-
> ly superior to his appearance; "with how many shot
> did you load your gun?"
> "With five, sir," said the Judge, a little struck with
> the other's manner; "are they not enough to slay a buck
> like this?"
> "One would do it; but," moving to the tree from be-
> hind which he had appeared, "you know, sir, you fired

[7] "Compelled resignation" is Cooper's revision of "disdainful resignation."

85

in this direction—here are four of the bullets in the tree."

The Judge examined the fresh marks in the bark of the pine, and shaking his head, said, with a laugh—

"You are making out the case against yourself, my young advocate—where is the fifth?"

"Here," said the youth, throwing aside the rough overcoat that he wore, and exhibiting a hole in his under garment, through which large drops of blood were oozing.

"Good God!" exclaimed the Judge with horror; "have I been trifling here about an empty distinction, and a fellow-creature suffering from my hands without a murmur? But hasten—quick—get into my sleigh—it is but a mile to the village, where surgical aid can be obtained;—all shall be done at my expense, and thou shalt live with me until thy wound is healed, aye, and for ever afterwards." (pp. 23-24)

It seems in this passage as though Cooper's creative haste and carelessness have caught up with him. Temple's abrupt shift in pronouns is explained later: like William Cooper, he had been brought up a Quaker, and each man was known, "when much interested or agitated, to speak in the language of his youth" (p. 34). But the young hunter's stiff formality, his melodramatic yet legalistic revelation that he has been shot, that he has been bleeding heavily while the other two deliberated the fate of the dead deer—these details are inexplicable. Both the youth's and the Leather-stocking's behavior are as startling as their sudden appearance. If their actions are not to be merely condemned as very bad art, the episode must be explained. The text, however, can only offer clues to the incident's real meaning, which must be explicated in terms of Cooper's intentions —just as Judge Temple and his daughter had their counterparts in the novelist's mind, so did Natty Bumppo and the young man. But with the first pair, Cooper was consciously

aware of whom his characters stood for; with the second, I
think that he was not.

Perhaps the strangest gesture in the passage quoted above
is Temple's invitation to a nameless young man to live
with him "for ever afterwards." And in spite of the youth's
"unaccountable reluctance" even to enter his sleigh (p. 26),
the Judge renews the invitation: at the very moment when
Templeton "bursts on his sight" he exclaims, "See, Bess,
there is thy resting-place for life!—And thine, too, young
man, if thou wilt consent to dwell with us" (p. 39). Though
Temple seems unaware of one obvious meaning that could
be given to his offer, Elizabeth, a proper young lady, blushes
at it: "the cold expression of her eye, the ambiguous smile
that again played about the lips of the stranger, seemed
equally to deny the probability of his consenting to form
one of this family group,"[8] Yet one day later, the stranger,
who eventually introduces himself as Oliver Edwards, does
move into Temple's house as his personal secretary. Much
of the novel's first half recounts "the incidents that led to
this extraordinary increase in the family of Judge Temple"
(p. 235). It has already been said that two members of this
family group represent William and Hannah Cooper. The
young man who joins it (on Christmas—the day of the Son's
coming) represents Cooper himself; in Edwards' character
does Cooper unconsciously portray his repressed attitudes toward his father and his sister. Only by making this identification can we account for the Judge's impulse to adopt Edwards, which the novelist consistently calls a "family" affair.
Only by making this identification can we explain Edwards'
reaction upon entering Temple's house for the first time.
Even in 1842, when he was trying to disprove all resemblances between *The Pioneers* and his own life, Cooper
admitted that *"one room*, the hall," from his father's house
in Cooperstown "is accurately given" in the novel (*L/J*,
IV, 258). This one room is described at a length that must

[8] "Cold expression" and "ambiguous smile" are Cooper's revisions
of "proud expression" and "scornful but covert smile."

be attributed to the force of his recollection, and Elizabeth Temple's emotions when after five years she sees the hall— "Compared with the chill aspect of the December night without, the warmth and brilliancy of the apartment produced an effect that was not unlike enchantment" (p. 70)— suggest Cooper's own enchantment at imaginatively reconstructing a part of his childhood. Having indulged *her* memory, Elizabeth turns to look at the injured hunter; understandably, she "gazes at him in wonder":

> The contraction of the stranger's brows increased as his eyes moved slowly from one object to another [in the hall]. For moments the expression of his countenance was fierce, and then again it seemed to pass away in some painful emotion. The arm that was extended bent, and brought the hand nigh to his face, when his head dropped upon it, and concealed the wonderfully speaking lineaments. (p. 71)

With his other hand Edwards "grasped the barrel of his long rifle with something like convulsive energy. The act and the attitude were both involuntary, and evidently proceeded from a feeling much deeper than that of vulgar surprise." Fierce, painful, convulsive, involuntary, Edwards' emotions proceed from the depths of Cooper's unconscious reaction upon reentering the world of his childhood. If the novel's opening pages reflect Cooper's subservience to the figure of his father, the rifle in Edwards' hand and the wound in his shoulder graphically indicate the opposite pole of Cooper's attitude toward the Judge. At this end of the psychic axis, the father is perceived not as the infant's protector, but as a threat to him; the son's stance is assumed not out of respect for his father's authority, but out of his need to rebel against it. These contradictory impulses —wonderfully expressed on the young man's face—can be equally present in the unconscious, which ignores the conventional rules of logic. This same polarity is embedded in *The Pioneers*, which, as a work of the imagination, is like the unconscious free from the constraints of reason. On the one hand, the novel treats Judge Temple with great respect (just as Edwards is respectful to the man who has shot him) and endorses his project for settling Templeton; on the other, it sanctions a rebellion against Temple's authority (which partakes of Edwards' fierceness) and repudiates everything that Templeton represents.

What Templeton represents are the claims of civilization, and Temple's authority as landlord and judge is invoked in the cause of social progress. "The enterprise of Judge Temple is taming the very forests!" boasts his daughter; "How rapidly is civilization treading on the footsteps of nature!" (p. 232). For Temple this process is unequivocally good; he would concur fully with William Cooper's statement in *A Guide in the Wilderness*, his one published book, that "if fifty thousand acres be settled, so that there is but one man upon a thousand acres, there can be no one convenience of life attainable; neither roads, school, church, meeting, nor any other of those advantages, without which man's life would resemble that of a wild beast."[9] There is in *The Pioneers* one man who has had none of those advantages—the Leather-stocking. His presence among the characters and scenes of Cooper's childhood is a problem that has interested many of the novel's readers. Almost as soon as it was published attempts were made to identify the prototype of the Leather-stocking. On this topic Cooper, at the end of his career and after the other four Leather-Stocking Tales had been written, said that "in a physical sense, different individuals known to the writer in early life certainly presented themselves as models, through his recollections; but in a moral sense this man of the forest is purely a creation."[10] Physically, Natty Bumppo's gaunt six-foot frame is distinctive, but it is in a moral sense that he is rightly considered one of the most original characters in American literature. Cooper's phrase—a man of the for-

9 William Cooper, *A Guide in the Wilderness*, pp. 11-12.
10 "Preface to the Leather-Stocking Tales," *The Deerslayer*, p. vii.

est—describes his most distinctive moral quality. When Judge Temple, sounding exactly like Judge Cooper, tells Oliver Edwards that "the unsettled life of these hunters . . . totally removes one from the influence of more sacred things," Natty interrupts him:

> "I have lived in the woods for forty long years, and have spent five at a time without seeing the light of a clearing bigger than a wind-row in the trees; . . . and, as for honesty, or doing what's right between man and man, I'll not turn my back to the longest winded deacon on your Patent." (pp. 220-21)

"Thou art an exception, Leather-stocking," replies the Judge, and every reader of the Tales would agree. How did Cooper come to create this exceptional character?

In *Virgin Land*, Henry Nash Smith begins his discussion of Cooper's best-known character by citing the parallels between the Leather-stocking and Daniel Boone, who had died in 1820, three years before Natty was "born" in the pages of *The Pioneers*. A few of the novel's earliest reviewers also made this comparison. As Smith points out, Cooper subsequently borrowed an incident from Boone's adventurous life for an episode in *The Last of the Mohicans*, the second Leather-Stocking Tale, and in *The Prairie*, the third, Cooper refers directly to the "venerable patriarch."[11] And although it was not until much later, until he added a footnote to this passage in a revised edition of *The Prairie*, that Cooper ever mentioned Boone by name (curiously, the name he mentioned him by was "Boon"), it seems very likely that he had Boone in mind at the time he wrote *The Pioneers*. The patriarch of "Kentucke"— like the woodsmen Cooper had known in his youth in Cooperstown—almost certainly served as a figure after which he could model his imaginative creation. Unlike those woodsmen, Boone and Bumppo are also similar "in

---

[11] *The Prairie*, p. 11. Cf. Smith, pp. 59ff.

a moral sense": both, for example, are noted for an un-compromising antipathy to the society of their fellow men. Smith suggests that both the popular conception of Boone and the popularity of Bumppo disclose the extent to which nineteenth century America, busily engaged in civilizing the wilderness, at the same time felt the conflict between the values of civilization and the freedom of the wilderness. That Cooper felt this conflict is clearly revealed in each of the Tales. To a degree he was, as an American author, exploring an issue which he shared with his culture. But at least to an equal degree, this was for Cooper a particu-larly personal issue. Saying that the story of Daniel Boone provided Cooper with a source for Natty's character does not account for Cooper's initial interest in the figure of the radically asocial man of the woods, an interest which eventually resulted in the five Leather-Stocking Tales. Natty Bumppo seems, indeed, to have supplanted Boone in the American mind as the archetypical backwoodsman. And I think that the best way to explain not only Cooper's intense imaginative involvement with this figure, but also his literary success with him, is to look closely at Natty's role in *The Pioneers*, to see what role he played for Cooper.

In this first Leather-Stocking Tale the history of Natty's life is materially different from the one provided by the series as a whole. Although he has fought alongside the Delaware Indians, especially his friend Chingachgook, he has not spent his life among them. Instead, he has been alone most of the time he has lived in the woods, alone in his cabin on the shore of Lake Otsego. He is a man of the particular forest around Cooperstown; in this wilderness —which he calls "a second paradise" (p. 320)—has Natty learned the moral lessons embodied in his character. "I never read a book in my life," he explains to Edwards, "and how should a man who has lived in towns and schools know anything about the wonders of the woods?" (pp. 322-23). Natty represents the claims of the wilderness: the land around Templeton "was a comfortable hunting ground,"

91

he says, "and would have been so to this day, but for the
money of Marmaduke Temple, and the twisty ways of the
law" (p. 320). Law and property are both the basis of
Temple's authority and the benefits of the civilization that
he is actively trying to establish. For his part, Leather-stocking spurns as "wicked" and "wasty" what he calls "the
carryings on of the world" (p. 321), which are nothing less
than all the institutions, forms, and rules of society. Natty
cites an asocial authority for his renunciations: "none know
how often the hand of God is seen in the wilderness, but
them that rove it for a man's life" (p. 323). The confrontation between these two men and their respective values is
at the center of *The Pioneers*; at stake is the moral right
to possess Templeton. Every episode in the novel's loose
narrative is informed by this conflict, which had its source
in the novelist's psyche. If the novel's deference to Judge
Temple (whose name suggests that he should be wor-
shipped) reflects Cooper's unconscious submission to his
father, his unconscious need to resist him was responsible
for the creation of the Leather-stocking. Natty's morality
must be understood in terms of Temple's; Natty's opposition to the values of civilization must be set in the particular
context of Temple's efforts to promote them. Each man asserts a right to his beliefs—Temple on the basis of his seven
years as a landlord, Leather-stocking on the basis of his forty
years in the wilderness—and the novel supports both of
them. But so far from making his man of the forest resemble
a wild beast, the author of *The Pioneers*, the son of "Judge
Temple," shaped the plot of his imaginary account of the
founding of "Templeton" to demonstrate Natty's moral su-
periority to the Judge's society. Creating the Leather-stocking undoubtedly provided Cooper's greatest pleasure in
writing the novel. He would devote four more novels to
him. But Natty was not conceived as the heroic figure of
the Tales; he was conceived as an antithesis to the Judge,
as a psychic alternative to Cooper's father. The sayings of
Natty I have quoted in his paragraph are taken from the

twenty-sixth chapter of *The Pioneers*. The convention of placing an epigraph at the head of each chapter was another that Cooper subscribed to, and for Chapter Twenty-Six he chose these two lines of poetry: "Speak on, my dearest father!/Thy words are like the breezes of the west."

The person to whom Natty recounts his solitary life beside Otsego is Oliver Edwards, and the epigraph refers specifically to their conversation. I have already said that Edwards stands for Cooper in the imaginary world of the novel. His real father is dead, but both Marmaduke Temple and Natty Bumppo serve as father-figures to him. During the course of the story he lives both in Natty's hut and in Marmaduke's mansion, and the novel variously implies that he belongs to each man's family. After Edwards' wound has been dressed and he has left Temple's house, the Judge asks if anyone can "inform me of anything concerning the youth whom I so unfortunately wounded? I found him on the mountain, hunting in company with the Leather-stocking, as if they were of the same family" (p. 118). Some of the townspeople assume that Edwards is actually Natty's son (cf. 163-65). Temple has several reasons for wanting the young stranger to live in his house as his secretary. Not the least interesting is that he seeks "one who might greatly aid me with his pen" (p. 219)—an unusual way to describe the duties of a secretary, and a suggestive request for the man who represents Cooper's father to make to the man who represents Cooper in the middle of Cooper's novel about his father's village. But the primary reason is Temple's guilt for having injured Edwards coupled with his feeling that, as he tells Natty, "this youth is made of materials too precious to be wasted in the forest" (p. 221). Temple is anxious to remove Edwards from Natty's care: "I entreat thee to join my family." When, despite "the reluctance, amounting nearly to loathing" (p. 220) with which Edwards entertains the invitation, he does accept it, Natty is in turn "mistrustful" of the change (p. 225). And though Natty never visits the Mansion-house, "Edwards

[seeks] every leisure moment to visit his former abode"
(p. 236). In the conflicting claims that each man makes
upon the youth's allegiance, in the many trips he makes
between their separate homes, is represented the ambivalence of Cooper's attitude toward these two "fathers"—the
one who created him and the one he created himself.

In addition to Cooper's admitted haste, expressed in the
letter to his publisher quoted in my first chapter, in com-
posing *The Pioneers*, the text itself suggests that, as James
Grossman writes, "the story's major interest," that is, in the
character of Natty Bumppo, grew disproportionately as
Cooper filled up manuscript pages, "as if by itself and
without the storyteller's conscious will."[12] Natty begins to
usurp the place Marmaduke Temple might have been expected to occupy in the narrative as well as in Cooper's unconscious; there is not enough psychic room in Templeton
for both of them. From their opening clash in the forest
over the buck's carcass, the two men move toward a cli-
mactic confrontation in the courtroom. Once again, a dead
deer precipitates the conflict: Natty kills a buck out of season. The legal issues involved, however, are eclipsed by the
moral ones. On trial is the right of Templeton, of Judge
Temple in particular, to pass judgment on the Leather-
stocking. We may remember that a major topic of Cooper's
original Preface to the novel was the right of the literary
critics to pass judgment on his work—this thematic rever-
beration underscores the significance of Natty's day in
Judge Temple's court. To understand the verdicts—Temple's decision in Natty's case and the novel's decision in
Temple's—we must examine the way in which the action of
the story progresses inevitably toward its judgment day.

Of course, a confrontation between these two men, described by one of the characters as "Judge Temple, the
landlord and owner of a township, [and] Nathaniel Bumppo, a lawless squatter" (p. 292), is historically as well as

[12] "James Fenimore Cooper: An Uneasy American," *Yale Review*
40 (1951), 696.

psychologically inevitable. Natty's hunting ground is daily being cleared by Temple's settlers, and his forty long years in the wilderness have unfitted him for life in the "clearin's." Temple represents the future, Natty, the past. The Judge believes that "the laws alone remove us from the condition of the savages" (p. 422), and, as George Dekker points out, "he is anxious to establish a more permanent authority [in Templeton], of which he will be both creator and instrument—the Law."[13] Telling the Judge that "one old law is worth two new ones" (p. 175), Natty believes that the ultimate arbiter of "what's right between man and man" is not law, but conscience, conscience opened to God by communion with nature, conscience humbled by awe of His works in the wilderness. Temple's perception of nature is more secular: "To his eye, where others saw nothing but a wilderness, towns, manufactories, bridges, canals, mines, and all the other resources of an old country, were constantly presenting themselves" (p. 353). History, the progress of society, is on Temple's side. "Heaven knows I would set out six trees afore I would cut down one" (p. 368), declares Natty, but the sound of the axe and the hammer "in incessant motion in the village" (p. 317) signal the doom of his way of life. As Natty himself laments, "They say that there's new laws in the land, and I am sartain that there's new ways in the mountains" (p. 225). In this sense, Francis Parkman, the historian, had a right to say, in the first review of the collected edition of Cooper's novels, that civilization must "eventually sweep from before it a class of men, its own precursors and pioneers, so remarkable both in their virtues and their faults, that few will see their extinction without regret. Of these men Leatherstocking is the representative."[14] Yet regret is not the dominant tone of Cooper's treatment of the historical plight of the Leather-stock-

13 *James Fenimore Cooper the Novelist* (London: Routledge & Kegan Paul, 1967), p. 56.

14 Francis Parkman, "The Works of James Fenimore Cooper," *North American Review* 74 (1852), 151.

ing—defiance is. And the essentially impersonal conflict between two stages of civilization is transposed into a very personal one between two patriarchs.

Natty breaks two of Templeton's laws. The first, prohibiting the killing of a deer between January and August, has been but recently introduced into the settlement. "The Judge," as a villager informs Natty, "had a great hand in getting the law through" (p. 342). Concern about the wants of posterity is the Judge's philanthropic motive for desiring to have that statute on the books, and because he helped to place it there he is "determined to see the law executed to the letter" (p. 361). But his moral authority to enforce it is repeatedly undermined throughout Cooper's book. There is more than the simple justice of Natty's assertion, made in the first chapter to the Judge's face, that his "right to shoot on these hills is of older date than Marmaduke Temple's right to forbid him" (p. 24); there is also the testimony of each man's behavior. Among the most memorable scenes in *The Pioneers* are the pigeon shooting and the bass fishing. In these episodes, the assorted pioneers of Templeton wantonly destroy thousands of the animals, most of which are left to rot uneaten. The scenes are worthy of D. H. Lawrence's praise as two of "the loveliest, most glamorous pictures in all literature,"[15] but it is as tests of Natty's and Temple's characters that they are made meaningful. Twice Temple fails. The standard by which Cooper would have the reader judge him is set by the Leather-stocking, who reacts to the destruction with righteous indignation at the waste of God's creatures. Instead of the indiscriminate slaughter wreaked by the settlers, who fire even a cannon at the pigeons and who take the fish in a huge seine, the hunter's skillful deeds—shooting one pigeon on the wing with a single ball, taking one bass with a fourteen-foot spear—invest his indignation with authority. After his "wonderful exploit" at hitting the bird, Natty announces

[15] *Studies in Classic American Literature* (1923; rpt. New York: Viking Press, 1961), p. 55.

to the admiring crowd that "now I have got one I will go home, for I don't relish to see these wasty ways that you are all practysing as if the least thing wasn't made for use, and not to destroy" (p. 272). In the exchange that follows his pronouncement, Temple professes to agree with him, but Natty's reply is returned across the full moral distance that separates them:

> "Thou sayest well, Leather-stocking," cried Marmaduke, "and I begin to think it time to put an end to this work of destruction."
> "Put an ind, Judge, to your clearings. An't the woods his work as well as the pigeons? Use, but don't waste. . . ."

Having delivered this exhortation, Natty leaves. Temple, however, remains, and as the largest flock of pigeons approaches, as the cannon is readied, "Even Marmaduke forgot the morality of Leather-stocking . . . and, in common with the rest, brought his musket to a poise" (p. 273).

Exactly the same thing happens with the bass: Temple is implicated in the settlers' "wasty ways" both as their landlord and by the work of his own hands. In both instances the Judge repents of his actions, but in neither is he punished for them. He has no response to Natty's accusation that "you fish and hunt out of rule" (p. 291). That is his crime, but he has his turn as accuser when Natty is arrested for hunting out of season. Natty does kill a deer on the lake. But the legitimacy of the indictment against him is compromised further by the fact that one of Temple's legal subordinates, Hiram Doolittle, justice of the peace, actually entraps Natty. Doolittle and several others, including Richard Jones, County Sheriff and Temple's cousin, absurdly suspect that Natty, Edwards, and Mohegan (Chingachgook) are mining silver out of the Judge's ground. In order to break into Natty's hut, which is of course illegal, Doolittle lets the hunter's dogs loose, which is also illegal, and it is the dogs who drive the deer into the lake where the three friends are peacefully fishing, tempting Natty beyond his power to resist. Like Temple, he gets carried away by an impulse which he immediately regrets —not, however, before he exclaims, "So much for Marmaduke Temple's law!" (p. 328); unlike Temple, he gets punished.

By far the most serious charge against Leather-stocking in the court is that he threatened a sworn officer of the law in the pursuit of his lawful duty—what he does is point his rifle at Doolittle, who again wants to search his hut. The first time Doolittle was defeated by Natty's locks, but this time he has a search warrant signed by Judge Temple. And although he is there under false pretences—not to find evidence of the slain deer, but of the imaginary silver—Natty's refusal to admit him incurs the wrath of "Marmaduke Temple's law." Temple himself makes a large issue out of Natty's defiant gesture, asking Edwards, who has come to plead with one of his "fathers" on the other's behalf, "Would any society be tolerable, young man, where the ministers of justice are to be opposed by men armed with rifles? Is it for this that I have tamed the wilderness?" (p. 379). The Judge asks this second question rhetorically. Ignorant of Doolittle's ulterior motives, he feels certain of the values of his society. But in the context of the novel, as the "king" of Templeton (p. 42), he is unquestionably to blame for the patent assault on Leather-stocking's dignity and rights. In view of the behavior of the citizens of Templeton, especially its ministers of justice, his question echoes in the reader's mind. When he appeals "to Heaven for a testimony of the uses" he has put his wealth and power to (p. 380), one seriously wonders what Heaven's reply would be. Neither God nor "chance," however, has arranged the plot of *The Pioneers* to cast these doubts upon Temple's project for taming the wilderness. When Edwards, realizing that the Judge is deaf to his appeal for mercy, abruptly ceases to be respectful, it seems as though James Cooper has finally worked up the psychic courage to defy William:

"Crime!" echoed Edwards; "is it a crime to drive a prying miscreant from his door? Crime! Oh, no, sir; if there be a criminal involved in this affair, it is not he."

"And who may it be, sir?" asked Judge Temple, facing the agitated youth, his features[16] settled to their usual composure.

This appeal was more than the young man could bear. Hitherto he had been deeply agitated by his emotions; but now the volcano burst its boundaries.

"Who! and this to me!" he cried: "ask your own conscience, Judge Temple. Walk to that door, sir, and look out upon the valley, that placid lake, and those dusky mountains, and say to your own heart, if heart you have, Whence came these riches, this vale, those hills, and why am I their owner? I should think, sir, that the appearance of Mohegan and the Leather-stocking, stalking through the country, impoverished and forlorn, would wither your sight." (p. 380)

And in turn, Temple's response to this emotional eruption suggests nothing so much as a father finally losing patience with an intractable son: "After this language, we must separate. I have too long sheltered thee in my dwelling; but the time has arrived when thou must quit it."

Edwards is not the only one of Temple's "children" who revolts against him by enlisting in Natty's cause. Natty is nominally tried by a jury, but it is Judge Temple, "interposing his authority" (p. 406), who dictates their verdict, and Judge Temple, citing "the dignity of the law" (p. 408), who sentences the old hunter to an hour's humiliation in the stocks and a month's confinement in the jail. Natty also pleads eloquently for mercy, with more than poetic justice in his plea:

"Hear me, Marmaduke Temple. . . . Have you forgot the time that you [first] come on to the lake-shore,

---

16 "His features" is Cooper's revision of "his fine, manly features."

when there wasn't even a jail to lodge in; and didn't
I give you my own bear-skin to sleep on, and the fat
of a noble buck to satisfy the cravings of your hunger?
Yes, yes—you thought it no sin then to kill a deer! . . .
No, no—there's them that says hard things of you,
Marmaduke Temple, but you an't so bad as to wish
to see an old man die in prison, because he stood up
for the right." (p. 409)

This appeal is not acknowledged by the Judge. But if Natty
must bow "his head with submission to a power that he
was unable to oppose" (p. 411)—the power of Judge Temple, not of social progress—other characters in the novel
stand up defiantly for him. Temple's steward and household favorite, Ben Pump, whose life Natty had saved earlier
in the story, insists on being placed in the stocks with him;
by brutally assaulting Doolittle, Ben avenges his preserver
and gets himself sentenced to jail as well.

The most significant defector from Temple's rule is his
daughter. Elizabeth had also been rescued by the Leather-
stocking—at the very moment he kills the panther that
threatens her, her father is off trying to locate Natty's silver
mine—and she is not convinced that the law's dignity requires an old man's humiliation. After the trial she almost
works up the courage to defy her father's judgment: "In
appreciating the offence of poor Natty, I cannot separate
the minister of the law from the man" (p. 421). Her father's
efforts to defend his actions are unsuccessful:

"I know Natty to be innocent, and, thinking so, I
must think all wrong who oppress him."
"His judge among the number! thy father, Elizabeth?"
"Nay, nay, nay; do not put such questions to me. . . ."
(p. 422)

Yet the question cannot be ducked: Natty's innocence
impeaches Temple's authority and the values of the civiliza-

tion over which he presides. The rebellion against him escalates that night when Edwards breaks Natty and Ben out of jail—"Judge Temple may sintence, but he can't keep" (p. 429). Forced to choose between the novel's two father-figures, Elizabeth, by actively helping the prisoners to escape, commits herself to that rebellion.

At this point in the narrative Cooper appears to have unconsciously made any peaceful reconciliation between the two fathers impossible. Indeed, the psychic conflicts represented in *The Pioneers* have continually threatened to become physical ones. As Thomas Philbrick has noted, "the progression of the novel as a whole" is a "movement from suppressed enmity to the verge of violence."[17] Usually directed toward the Judge, this repressed violence corresponds to the son's ultimate solution to the problem of the father who stands in his way—parricide. As we have seen, at the very beginning Leather-stocking is unaccountably hostile to Temple. Throughout the novel, beneath Edwards' polite deference to the Judge lurks an ambiguous resentment for some darkly hinted injury more serious than even the gunshot wound, a resentment which, according to the Reverend Mr. Grant, "[borders] on one of the worst of human passions" (p. 150); without elaborating, Grant warns the young man that "these angry passions must be subdued" (p. 154). Only once is Temple's life actually in danger, but the circumstances are extremely suggestive. During the Christmas Eve festivities in Templeton's tavern, the drunken Chingachgook, brooding on the wrongs Temple has done his people, suddenly turns on him; for one ferocious moment, "with an expression of wild resentment" on his face (p. 181), he tries to free his tomahawk to bury it in Temple's head. "Shed not blood!" cries Natty, but only Mohegan's drunkenness saves the Judge. Judge Cooper was not so fortunate: as he was leaving an Albany tavern in December 1809, he was fatally wounded by a blow on the

---

[17] Thomas Philbrick, "Cooper's *The Pioneers*: Origins and Structure," *PMLA* 79 (1964), 589.

head—he died three days before Christmas. Cooper spares his father in the comparable scene, but after the "break-jail," as the escaped prisoners fortify themselves in a cave and the Templeton militia mobilizes for "an attempt . . . to punish the offenders" (p. 470), it appears that his need to resist his father will demand a blood sacrifice.

Instead, the battle between the irregular forces of civilization and its malcontents is turned into a farce—the only casualty is Doolittle, who suffers a direct hit on the "postee-rum" from Natty's rifle. Unaccountably absent as both sides prepared for the battle, Judge Temple shows up just as it becomes earnest, bringing an anticlimactic end to Templeton's "rebellion and war" by commanding the peace (p. 480). Suddenly there is no one who defies him: "the habitual respect with which all the commands of the Judge were received, induced a prompt compliance" (p. 485). In the novel's penultimate chapter, in fact, Cooper himself tries to undo almost all the work of his imagined defiance, bringing *The Pioneers* close to an anticlimax. Explanation, not violence, concludes the conflict. Edwards, also a peacemaker on this occasion, announces that he is really Oliver Effingham, the son of Judge Temple's former friend and business partner, Edward Effingham, and this announcement explains the source of Oliver's hostility. The land at Otsego had belonged to the Effinghams, who had received it originally from the Indians but who had lost it during the Revolution because the family remained loyal to the King; after it had been confiscated, Marmaduke Temple, who while "serving his country during the struggle, . . . never seemed to lose sight of his own interests" (p. 36), purchased the land with Effingham's money and proceeded to found his own village on the lake.

The reader has been prepared for this revelation by Cooper's account in Chapter Two of the friendship and respective fortunes of the two men—how the aristocratic Effingham had entrusted all his property secretly to the management of the impoverished Temple, how they had divided over the cause of the colonies, how Temple had become wealthy by "purchasing estates that had been wrestled by violence from others." Nevertheless, the painless way in which Temple acquits himself of any misconduct is astonishing. When Edwards, "fixing a piercing eye on the other" (p. 484), reveals himself as the dispossessed heir, there is a moment of "deep anxiety."

> But the moment of agitation soon passed. Marmaduke raised his head from his bosom, where it had sunk, not in shame, but in devout mental thanksgivings, and, as large tears fell over his fine manly face, he grasped the hand of the youth warmly, and said—
> "Oliver, I forgive thee all thy harshness—all thy suspicions. I now see it all. I forgive thee everything. . . ."

One might have expected Temple to ask for forgiveness, not to bestow it. As it happens, however, the Judge is able to prove that he had already set aside one-half of his wealth for the son of his friend; the heir was never dispossessed at all.

As young Effingham and Temple continue to talk—"each moment clearing up some doubtful action, and lessening the antipathy of the youth to Marmaduke" (p. 488)—Cooper psychically retreats from a confrontation with the fine manly face of his father. The alter-father that he had created and onto whom he had projected so much of his own antagonism toward the real father does not say a word during this scene; conscious that "heavier interests than those which affected himself were to be decided" (p. 482), Natty effaces himself out of sight. The chapter's most amazing revelation could also be considered as Cooper's most abject attempt to reconcile himself with his father by denying the novel's moral indictment of the Judge: Leatherstocking's antagonism toward Temple and his existence on the shores of Lake Otsego are explained away when Oliver tells Marmaduke that Natty had been a servant of the Effinghams, "left here as a kind of locum tenens on the

lands" (p. 487). After learning this, the reader is not surprised to learn that Natty returns peaceably to jail, or even
to hear "Edwards" fervently declare "God bless him!" the
next time Temple's name is mentioned (p. 490). "I thank
thee, my son," is the Judge's response.

For very good reasons, this denouement bothers most
critics of the novel. "The return of the lost heir," concludes
Donald A. Ringe, "to claim the inheritance that he mis-
takenly believes Judge Temple has wrongfully appropriated is obviously a stock element and may be dismissed as
a concession to the popular taste of the times."[18] The theme
of the lost heir was an overworked literary convention, and
Cooper was obviously following what Walter Scott calls
"the custom of story-tellers" by keeping Edwards' identity
a poorly concealed secret "for the purpose of exciting the
reader's curiosity." It would be a mistake, however, to dismiss the reconciliation of the penultimate chapter either,
as Ringe and others do, as a stock element, or, as we might
be tempted to do, as evidence of Cooper's ultimate failure
to overthrow his father's domination. It is both of these
things, but more.

"All that related to the Effinghams," Cooper insisted in
1842, "is pure fiction; no persons or events ever existing in
real life, to give rise to either their history, or their experience" (*L/J*, IV, 254-55). Despite this assertion, which
should be classed with Cooper's other disclaimers about
The Pioneers, Andrew Nelson, in his article "James Cooper
and George Croghan,"[19] demonstrates convincingly that
much of what Oliver Effingham reveals about himself in
this chapter describes a real Cooperstown family, the Prevosts. They were the descendants of George Croghan, the
man who, like Oliver's grandfather, had acquired the land
at Otsego from the Indians only to lose it during the Revo-

[18] *James Fenimore Cooper* (New York: Twayne Publishers, Inc.,
1962), p. 33.
[19] Andrew Nelson, "James Cooper and George Croghan," *Philo-
logical Quarterly* 20 (1941), 69-73.

lution; after confiscation it was bought by William Cooper.
The real and the fictional cases are not exactly similar:
Cooper had never known Croghan. But he did know the
Prevosts—like Oliver Effingham, they returned to Otsego
and tried to reclaim the land. Less generous than Judge
Temple, Judge Cooper refused to restore any of their property, though it was clear that he had appropriated the
Croghan Patent by "questionable methods."[20] The issue
went to court, where it was never decided. In the lengthy
legal proceedings James Cooper consistently defended his
father's title to Cooperstown. In *The Pioneers* the Judge's
right to the possession of Templeton is more often attacked
than defended. Unless one is aware of the resemblances
between the Effinghams and the Prevosts, it would appear
that the novel concludes with an affirmation of that right.
But if that conclusion clears up "some doubtful actions"
on Marmaduke Temple's part, it also, by merging the Prevosts' claims with the Effinghams', raises the real issue of
William Cooper's questionable methods.

I believe that Cooper's decision to introduce the Prevosts
into his novel was made unconsciously and spontaneously
at the moment he was writing Chapter Forty.[21] His reasons

[20] Albert T. Volwiler, *George Croghan and the Westward Movement: 1741-1782* (Cleveland: The Arthur H. Clark Company, 1926),
p. 330. Volwiler mentions, for example, the fact that William Cooper
arranged to have the forced sale of the lands held "in the middle of
the winter in a remote place," and in spite of an injunction obtained
by Croghan's heirs and creditors.

[21] An assertion like this is based as much upon intuition as upon
reason. Obviously it cannot be rigorously proved, but since I shall
make similar assertions several more times in this study, perhaps I
should in this instance explain my reasons for making it at some
length. Nelson's most persuasive textual evidence for his identification
of the Effinghams with the Prevosts comes from this chapter—particularly Temple's reference there to the sinking of "the packet," which
claimed the life of Oliver's father. Nelson points out that George
Croghan's grandson went down with the *Albion*, a packet that sank
off Ireland on April 22nd, 1822. Report of this catastrophe reached
America that summer, six months after Cooper had started the

for doing so are not transparent. One of them undoubtedly was that it allowed him imaginatively to challenge his father's authority even while he seemed to be upholding it. But more significant, and still more complex, is the suspicion that he chose to give Oliver someone else's identity in order to put some psychic ground between that character and himself. To do that it was not enough simply to make him a "lost heir"—after all, Cooper was writing the novel in 1822, the year in which his inheritance was being lost to his family's creditors. But if Oliver Effingham were Augustin Prevost (the grandson of Croghan) he could not be James Cooper. And he could not be James Cooper because he had just proposed marriage to Elizabeth Temple.

Cooper repeatedly denied that the Judge's daughter represented his sister Hannah. For example, he wrote in the 1850 Introduction to *The Pioneers*:

> Circumstances rendered this sister singularly dear to the author. After a lapse of half a centry [Hannah died in 1800], he is writing this paragraph with a pain that would induce him to cancel it, were it not still more painful to have it believed that one whom he regarded with a reverence that surpassed the love of a brother, was converted by him into the heroine of a work of fiction. (p. xv)

That Cooper should consider the immortalization of a loved one in a work of fiction sacrilegious is perhaps not unusual. That he should be so pained by the thought,

---

novel (cf. Nelson, pp. 71-72). Clearly this detail could not have occurred to Cooper much before he reached Chapter Forty; that he should have incorporated what he had just learned into his text is entirely consistent with his methods of composition. One of Cooper's most attractive traits is precisely the way he confidently, naively, left such details to take care of themselves as he wrote. For all his complaints about the tedium of telling a tale, he genuinely enjoyed the working of his imagination. Even in his didactic novels, he always left room for the tale to tell itself.

however, indicates that he was unconsciously troubled about a more unthinkable sin than sacrilege.

Some of his pain can be attributed to his enduring grief at his sister's early death. The intensity of his sense of loss makes itself felt in the novel by the way the preservation of Elizabeth's life becomes a major element in the plot. Near its end she, Edwards, and Mohegan are trapped by a forest fire. Escape appears impossible, and Elizabeth, with Christian fortitude, resolves that they must submit to "the will of God . . . like his own children" (p. 452). Behind Edwards' hysterical reply one senses the novelist's need to reject the idea of her death: " 'Die!' the youth rather shrieked than exclaimed, 'No—no—no—there must yet be hope—you at least must not, shall not die.' "[22] Hannah died after being thrown by a spirited horse. Judge Temple is determined that the same fate shall not befall his daughter. When Elizabeth "fearlessly" rides her horse over a dangerous bridge, Temple begs her to be more careful: "if thou venturest again, as in crossing this bridge, old age will never overtake thee, but I shall be left to mourn thee, cut off in thy pride, my Elizabeth" (p. 254). That Cooper's Hannah is actually meant is revealed in a footnote he added in 1831:

> In reviewing his work, after so many years, [the author] is compelled to confess it is injured by too many allusions to incidents that are not at all suited to satisfy the just expectations of the general reader. . . .
>
> More than thirty years since, a very near and dear relative of the writer, an elder sister and a second mother, was killed by a fall from a horse, in a ride among the very mountains mentioned in this tale. (p. 255)

It is in those same mountains that the forest fire and, in another episode, a panther threaten to prevent Elizabeth

[22] The words "at least" were added by Cooper in 1831; in the original text the phrase reads: "you must not, shall not die."

from reaching old age. But in every case Cooper does in his fiction what he could not do in life—Elizabeth *must not* die, and she does not.

Cooper does something else in his fiction that he could not do, could not even contemplate doing, in life. Elizabeth marries Oliver Edwards at the novel's conclusion; by that time he is known as Effingham, but by either name he stands for the novelist. Attempting to disprove the identification of Elizabeth as Hannah, Cooper wrote in the *Brother Jonathan* letter that "the difference in our years, made this sister a sort of second mother to me" (*L/J*, IV, 256), a description which repeats what he had said in the footnote quoted above. Also mentioned is Cooper's discomfort at having to discuss the similarities between the two women: "A lapse of forty years has not removed the pain with which I allude to this subject at all." The source of this pain is the same as the source of one cause of his pleasure in writing *The Pioneers*—almost all his novels conventionally end with a marriage, but in this one the marriage unconsciously fulfills Cooper's repressed infantile desires for both his mother and his sister, that is, his second mother.[23] The two are fused together in the character of Elizabeth. Although he left Elizabeth Fenimore Cooper out of the emotional landscape of his childhood by making the Judge a widower, he did give her name to his heroine. In almost all Cooper's novels, the hero must compete for the love of the heroine with another young man; in this one, as in Cooper's childhood, it is the Judge with whom Oliver competes for Elizabeth's affection, the Judge who stands in his

[23] The following passage from a letter Cooper wrote in 1849 to a family friend, about his daughter Susan and his sister Hannah, needs no interpretation—"How I love that child! Her countenance is that of a sister I lost, ⟨from⟩ by a fall from a horse, half a century since, and her character is very much the same. They were, and are, as perfect as it falls to the lot of humanity to be. I am in love with Sue, and have told her so, fifty times. She refuses me, but promises to live on in gentle friendship, and, my passion not being at all turbulent, I do not see but this may do" (*L/J*, VI, 99).

way with her. Only in the midst of a raging forest fire, when both of them seem doomed, does Oliver finally, almost against his will, declare his passion. Elizabeth orders him to escape without her:

"Fly! leave me—but stay! You will see my father. . . . Tell him that I died happy and collected; that I have gone to my beloved mother. . . . And say," she continued, dropping her voice . . . as if conscious of her worldly weaknesses, "how dear, how very dear, was my love for him; that it was near, too near, to my love for God."

The youth listened to her touching accents, but moved not. In a moment he found utterance, and replied:—

"And is it me that you command to leave you! to leave you on the edge of the grave! Oh! Miss Temple, how little have you known me! . . . No—no—dearest Elizabeth, I may die with you, but I can never leave you!"

Elizabeth moved not, nor answered. It was plain that her thoughts had been raised from the earth. The recollection of her father, and her regrets at their separation, had been mellowed by a holy sentiment, that lifted her above the level of earthly things, and she was fast losing the weakness of her sex in the near view of eternity. But as she listened to these words she became once more woman. She struggled against these feelings. . . . (p. 454)

In this strangely worded love scene are represented all the conflicts of the family romance—the intensely ambivalent configuration of the father, the mother, the daughter, and the son. Just before, Oliver and Elizabeth had noticed the Judge, the third member of the novel's emotional triangle, "standing in his own grounds, and apparently contemplating, in perfect unconsciousness of the danger of his child, the mountain in flames" (p. 453). Under his unseeing eye the young lovers reveal themselves to each other, though Oliver is reluctant to speak, though Elizabeth tries not to listen. In the text, of course, her struggle is against earthly feelings; but I believe that in the context of Cooper's emotional involvement with the novel, her struggle, like his, is against incestuous ones. At the last minute, Natty rescues the couple, making the consummation of their love possible, which in turn unconsciously necessitated Cooper's last-minute decision a few pages later to identify Edwards-Effingham as a Prevost. But he could not really disassociate himself from his hero. Temple, now Oliver's father-in-law, does not appear in the novel's final chapter. As Mr. and Mrs. Effingham, now happily married, discuss *their* plans regarding *their* property at Templeton, it is as though the Judge did not exist. Oliver's sudden freedom from Judge Temple's authority, his uncontested possession of Elizabeth and the Judge's estate, fulfill Cooper's most heartfelt wishes. He could not have conceived a happier ending.

With this conclusion, Oliver chooses the values of civilization over those of the wilderness. As he passionately tells Elizabeth during the fiery scene on the mountain, "I have been driven to the woods in despair; but your society has tamed the lion within me" (p. 454). His rebellion has ended bloodlessly, but none the less the king has been overthrown and the prince has succeeded him, has even succeeded with the king's consort. The son has promoted himself to manhood. Yet a portion of Cooper's psyche remained defiant. Out of his resistance to his father had the Leather-stocking been formed. During the reconciliation between the novel's son and one of his fathers, Natty, as we have noted, silently capitulated. But in this final chapter he is given back his voice and his antagonism to the Judge. He is not about to choose civilization. "I have took but little comfort," he informs Elizabeth, "sin' your father come on with his settlers" (p. 502). To the newlyweds, who had planned to use part of their wealth to make the old man domestically comfortable, he replies: "I know you mean all for the best, but our ways doesn't agree. I love the woods, and ye relish the face of man; . . . The meanest of God's creaters be made for some use, and I'm formed for the wilderness" (pp. 502-03). Again and again throughout the novel Natty has left the other characters standing in a clearing to disappear in the shadows of the forest; at its end he leaves Otsego, his home for forty years, to find happiness once more in the wilderness. Natty's withdrawal from the community of men to commune with nature is repeated in each of the other Leather-Stocking Tales. In the last-written novel of the series, *The Deerslayer* (1841), it is again Lake Otsego that he leaves. I want to postpone a further examination of Cooper's greatest character until this other story set on the scene of Cooper's childhood can provide the context for an analysis of the series as a whole. But it should be noted here that Natty's first retreat from society is the direct re-sult of Judge Temple's oppression. These are his last words to Oliver and Elizabeth: "I pray that the Lord will keep you in mind—the Lord that lives in clearings as well as in the wilderness—and bless you, and all that belongs to you, from this time till the great day when the whites shall meet the red-skins in judgment, and justice shall be the law, and not power" (p. 504). Natty is content to appeal Judge Tem-ple's ruling to the highest court at the end of time, and having delivered this subversive benediction, he exiles him-self from mankind. The novel's final moral victory belongs to him: "This was the last that they ever saw of the Leather-stocking, whose rapid movements preceded the pursuit which Judge Temple both ordered and conducted" (p. 505).

This is not, however, the novel's last word. Cooper added one more sentence: "He had gone far towards the setting sun,—the foremost in that band of pioneers who are opening the way for the march of the nation across the continent." Cooper's undoubtedly deliberate use of the word "pioneers" in his orotund conclusion is equivocal: Natty escapes from the Judge only to be subsumed under the Judge's project for settling the continent. Marmaduke Temple, created in the image of William Cooper, and Natty Bumppo, created as his antithesis, represent the poles of Cooper's imagination, and the contradictory impulses fixed in these two sentences—to free himself from his father, to submit to him—continued to struggle in Cooper's psyche for the rest of his life. His failure as the administrator of Judge Cooper's estate, which finally went bankrupt as he was writing *The Pioneers*, had two effects on James Cooper's literary career. Writing was now his sole means of support. Writing was now the only means by which he could gain ascendancy over his father. To please himself, he said, he had written *The Pioneers*. After his failure in the real world, he could in the novel award himself the inheritance he had lost—no creditors could contest him there. But his imagination was not similarly free to ignore his father's claims upon him. In childhood, every son identifies himself with his father, and the unconscious force of this identification continues to influence the child even after he becomes an adult, a parent himself. We have already seen how completely William Cooper's identity dominated his son until he was inspired to publish a novel. The success of his second novel insured his success as a novelist. It was, I believe, Cooper's confidence in his new identity, coinciding as it did with the bankruptcy of his old one, that prompted him to reassess his childhood by imaginatively revisiting it.

Like Oliver Effingham, he returned resentful of the man who had appropriated what he felt belonged to him and determined to force a confrontation in which he could reveal his true self. One of the fictional ways he tried to assert that self was by inciting a rebellion against the figure of his father, another was by controverting his father's values, and another was by debunking his father's greatest accomplishment—the founding of "Templeton." Yet in the novel each of these psychic assertions is qualified by Cooper's additional need to obey the dictates of that element in his psyche that had internalized his father's authority. When, in fact, he next returned to the imagined world of Templeton, it was to put down a rebellion against his father, to affirm his father's values, and to uphold his father's position as "Templeton's" founder: fifteen years after *The Pioneers* he wrote the Effingham Novels exclusively, as we shall see, to please William Cooper, and it was then that he attempted, by publicly denying the affinities between *The Pioneers* and his own life, tacitly to disclaim the filial disloyalty he had shown in the tale. When he wrote *The Pioneers*, however, Cooper's psychic needs were more complex. What makes this novel so good is precisely that its thematic conflicts—between civilization and nature, between law and conscience, between authority and freedom—reproduce the most important conflict in Cooper's mind. His forceful and arresting treatment of these issues is commensurate with the power they exercised in his interior life. To free himself from his father a son must be able to assert his own manhood without measuring it against his father's, without needing to rebel against it or submit to it. Cooper never attained that independence—probably no one wholly does —but *The Pioneers* is the record of his struggle.

< no>
CHAPTER IV

⬤⬤

"MENTAL INDEPENDENCE"

⬤⬤

"NOT an incident of the Pioneers, that I can recall, ever occurred," wrote Cooper in *Brother Jonathan* (*L/J*, IV, 254). But his recollection, coerced by his desire to repudiate the novel's latent meaning, was faulty—many specific episodes, including important ones like the forest fire and minor ones like the arrest of a gang of counterfeiters, were part of Cooperstown's history before they became part of Templeton's. The two most important events in the novel, in terms of both its plot and Cooper's psychic involvement with it, are the fictional rebellion against the Judge's rule and the imaginative creation of the Leather-stocking as an alternative father-figure. These also correspond to real occurrences, this time in Cooper's personal history. Writing *The Pioneers* was not his only attempt to free himself from his father.

Very little is reliably known about Cooper's childhood; even family tradition seems on the whole to respect his demand for biographical silence. Only a handful of his letters from the period before his father died have survived. One of them, written to his brother Richard and dated December 19th, 1808, suggests that this lack of evidence was deliberate.

> Family dissensions are ever to me disagreeable—If any have or should take place in which I should be unfortunate enough to participate—it would always be my ardent wish to bury them in oblivion—could it be done consistent with my own honor, and that of my family —The ebullitions of *my* youth, will I hope be forgotten. They have afforded me a lesson by which I may

hereafter profit—I flatter myself your caution on this subject was unnecessary. *Nature* will *predominate*— I am convinced that no connection will ever break the ties of blood—I write freely for I am writing to a *Brother*— (*L/J*, i, 12)

No doubt Cooper wrote freely enough for Richard to understand him, but whatever provoked this carefully worded yet deeply felt declaration of the intensity of the family bond has been, as Cooper must have wanted it to be, buried in oblivion. That he needed to assert "the ties of blood," however, is significant; in his first novel he concluded that they were not indissoluble: "It is a dreadful truth, that the bonds of natural affection can be broken by injustice and contumely."[1] Almost certainly this is a dreadful truth that Cooper had learned for himself. As his relationship with the De Lancey family reveals, the mere thought of injustice or contumely assaulted the tenderest part of his personality, and even with his brother he reserves the right to defend his honor apart from his family's.

In December 1808 Cooper was a nineteen-year-old Midshipman in the United States Navy, stationed on Lake Oswego. At nineteen, he apparently believes, his youth is over. Yet eighteen years later, addressing a farewell party of friends before leaving for Europe, Cooper said that "I am always ready to declare that not only the earliest, but many of the happiest days of my youth" had been spent in the Navy, where he served between 1808 and 1810.[2] Implicit in this autobiographical evaluation is a wish to forget the *earlier* days of his youth. The wish is a common one: Herman Melville, for example, once wrote Nathaniel Hawthorne, "Until I was twenty-five, I had no development at all. From my twenty-fifth year I date my life." When he turned twenty-five Melville was also in the Navy. For both men, their experience at sea was the first instance they had

[1] *Precaution*, p. 426.
[2] From the *New-York American*, May 30, 1826; quoted by Beard, *L/J*, i, 140.

to depend on themselves. Both, in fact, first shipped from New York for England, Cooper in 1806 on the merchantman *Sterling*, Melville in 1837 on the packet *St. Lawrence*. But while Melville went before the mast for a number of reasons, Cooper went for one—his father the Judge ordered him to go. Writing to the Navy Commissioner in 1841 to request a berth for his nephew William, the middle-aged novelist said, "Morally there is no cause to complain of him, for he has not been sent to sea to tame" (*L/J*, IV, 186). To tame James had been his father's motive in 1806, and he had good grounds for complaint.

That James may have required taming at ten is suggested by his sister Hannah, who wrote in 1798 that her brothers "are very wild, and show plainly they have been bred in the Woods."[3] But judging from Elizabeth Temple's character, Hannah's standards of behavior were probably over-refined, and the testimony of Cooper's own conduct a few years later is much less impeachable. William Cooper first sent his youngest son to Albany to learn from the Reverend Thomas Ellison, the Rector of St. Peter's Episcopal Church. An unreconstructed Tory, Ellison had even more faith than the Federalist Judge in the social and moral virtues of property. There Cooper was taught Latin and decorum, but according to Mary E. Phillips, who cites family tradition, he was also "often a ringleader" in the pupils' insurrections against the Rector's authority.[4] After Ellison's death in 1803, William Cooper sent his son to Yale, where, according to James Franklin Beard, "he neglected his studies and achieved notoriety for a series of escapades which could only end in his dismissal."[5] Escapades is perhaps too light a word for a student career that climaxed when Cooper used gunpowder to blow up the door to another student's room.

[3] Quoted by Beard, *L/J*, I, 4.
[4] *James Fenimore Cooper* (New York: John Lane Company, 1913), p. 31.
[5] Beard, *L/J*, I, 5.

With this action he earned his expulsion. It is commonly acknowledged that school authorities function *in loco parentis*; William Cooper had sent his son to Albany and New Haven, and James Cooper's consistent rebellion against his teachers can easily be understood as a defiance of his father's dominion. Cooper was twenty years older when he wrote a letter to Professor Benjamin Silliman, one of his instructors at Yale, in which he asked to be remembered to two other professors, "both of whom I doubt not will be willing to receive such a mark of respect from a *Prodigal Son*" (*L/J*, I, 217).

In addition, like the biblical prodigal the young Cooper spent his father's wealth lavishly. Of the five extant personal letters from his nonage, two—one from Albany, one from Yale—mention his need for more money, and when he was sent back to Cooperstown in the summer of 1805 he left debts in New Haven "whose full extent could not be determined for some months."[6] The undergraduate is always allowed, even expected, to test the limits of his freedom and to try the patience of his elders; college provides a transition from the dependency of the paternal roof to the responsibilities of the adult world. But Cooper, just thirteen when he entered Yale, did not want to be graduated. Filled with adolescent rage against the claims of authority, he seems to have deliberately sought dismissal. Destroying a door was an appropriate expression of his urge for freedom,

[6] Ibid. When Cooper's only son, Paul, was growing up, Cooper repeatedly warned him against contracting debts: "I wish you never to have a debt if possible," he wrote on one occasion; "it is an evil of a magnitude of which you can have no idea" (*L/J*, IV, 467; cf. also IV, 451 and 468). Of course Cooper's fear of indebtedness was probably due in the main to his experience with his father's estate, but his experience as a student must have been in his mind when he wrote to Paul, who was away at school, "I hear the best accounts of you, my son, and your mother and myself feel a gratification in it, that you will never understand, until you become a parent yourself" (*L/J*, IV, 192). That gratification he never allowed his father to feel.

but it worked both for and against him—it liberated him from the faculty at Yale only to restore him to his father's house.

He remained at home for one year. Unfortunately, almost all we know about this period is that fourteen months later he was bound for England on the *Sterling*. It is unlikely either that the Judge killed a fatted calf for his return or that James came home with the chastised prodigal's humility. His brother William Junior had earlier been expelled from Princeton for setting fire to Nassau Hall. Apparently the two children for whom Judge Cooper tried to provide the education he had lacked both used the opportunity to violently assert their independence, but in William's case the Judge did not think it necessary to send his son to sea. There is thus every reason to suspect that James continued his active defiance of authority in the Mansion House, transferring his anger toward his teachers back to the man they represented. Oppression, he later wrote, would drive him to resistance anywhere: that it did so in Cooperstown is beyond question. Despite William Cooper's statement in his *Guide* that none of his many tenants "can justly impute to me any act resembling oppression,"[7] he was, as Dixon Ryan Fox describes him, "a testy and choleric gentleman easily wrought into passion."[8] He presided sternly over his estate, using his wealth and his judgeship to enforce his power. During his impeachment trial in 1792, one of his tenants testified that their landlord "had been round to the people and told them that they owed him, and that unless they voted for Mr. Jay, he would ruin them." Another quoted him as saying, "what, then, young man, you will not vote as I would have you—you are a fool, young man, for you cannot know how to vote as well as I can direct you, for I am in public office."[9] He liked to settle certain disputes with wrestling matches, but on occasion he also used the threat of the County Jail to silence opposition.

[7] *A Guide in the Wilderness*, p. 7.
[8] Fox, p. 141.   [9] Ibid., pp. 140-41.

On at least one notorious occasion he actually did imprison a man who pushed his short-tempered patience too far. Judge Jedediah Peck was an elderly Revolutionary War veteran, a settler at Cooperstown and a steadfast anti-Federalist. Over the years he unceasingly tried to convince the other settlers to reject their landlord's politics, and in 1799 he aroused Judge Cooper's anger by circulating a petition among them for the repeal of the Sedition Laws. Cooper reacted by having him indicted for violating those very laws. According to Jabez Hammond, who cites this incident as a factor in the popular decline of Federalism in New York, Cooper's act of oppression miscarried:

> A bench warrant was issued and Judge Peck was taken from his family by an officer, to the city of New-York. A hundred missionaries in the cause of democracy, stationed between New-York and Cooperstown, could not have done so much for the republican cause as this journey of Judge Peck, as a prisoner, from Otsego to the capital of the state. It was nothing less than the public exhibition of a suffering martyr for the freedom of speech and the press and the right of petitioning, to the view of the citizens of the various places through which the marshall travelled with his prisoner.[10]

To the reader of *The Pioneers*, Jedediah Peck in chains may recall the figure of Natty Bumppo in the stocks: and likewise, Judge Temple's attempt to assert the authority of the law by "an open exhibition of the consequences" of Natty's defiance of it has just the opposite effect, both on many of the Judge's villagers and on the novelist's audience.

Within his own family Judge Cooper could be similarly autocratic: according to family tradition, when his wife refused to quit her house in Burlington in 1790 to move to the wilds of Lake Otsego, William picked up the chair she was sitting in and loaded it and her onto a wagon. Tradition also says that the thirteen-month-old James was on his

10 *History of the Political Parties in the State of New-York*, p. 132.

mother's lap—if so, this was not the last time that the Judge would compel his son's obedience. Such a father could quickly force his son into subjugation or revolt, and Cooper's fearful hostility toward any kind of opposition began at home. Somehow, sometime during 1806, he pushed his resistance too far. There may have been, as in the scene between Oliver and Temple in *The Pioneers*, a bitter emotional eruption. Cooper probably did hear his father say "I have too long sheltered thee in my dwelling; but the time has arrived when thou must quit it." At any rate, he gained his freedom again: between 1806 and his father's death in 1809 he only went home to visit.

We cannot tell precisely what "family dissensions" took place between Cooper and his father, or how seriously "the bonds of natural affection" were threatened, although, as indicated by his letter to Richard, it must have seemed possible that nature would not predominate. The boy who was fond of teasing had grown considerably more aggressive. His adolescence was a sustained revolt against the figure of his father, a revolt which was unconsciously incited by his fixed infantile antagonism, but a revolt which was also an attempt to preserve his selfhood. There is only a superficial contradiction between the pattern of his adolescent behavior and that of his first decade as an adult. Guilt would have been part of his psychic reaction to his father's murder; guilt prompted his haste to marry and to emulate his father's role. If the intensity of his remorse was commensurate with the devotion he showed at adopting his father's identity, he must have felt guilty indeed. To atone for the ebullitions of his youth he would even assume the financial burden of his brothers' prodigality. In this sense he did (unconsciously) learn a lesson from those ebullitions, but it was, as we have seen, one from which he could not profit. By the time he determined to write a novel he was acutely uncomfortable with his father's identity. In *The Pioneers*, his attitude toward the Judge was at once respectful and rebellious. In the decade that followed, he was simply rebellious.

Between *The Pioneers* (1823) and the Effingham Novels (1838), Cooper wrote ten romances. Not all these books were popular, but Cooper's audience and earnings were large, he was translated into most continental languages, and he could safely have been ranked among the world's most successful authors. He had every cause to be pleased with himself: in letters to his publishers he almost invariably proclaims that the new book is better than the last. Shortly after his third novel was published he had decided to go to Europe; he left America in 1826 and remained abroad seven years, travelling and writing. The first American novelist was also the first to expatriate himself, but he had as yet no quarrel with his country. Cooper always felt that Irving, who had gone abroad for financial reasons, had abandoned republican principles, his identity as an American, on the other side of the Atlantic. Cooper went to Europe with different intentions. Before leaving he had acquired the purely honorary post of United States Consul at Lyons as a symbol of his citizenship, and in a letter from Europe in 1831 he declared to an American friend that "I was born and will live and die a Yankee" (*L/J*, II, 75). He could have added, he would write as one. To a sympathetic English critic's comments about his work he replied: "You have appreciated my motives, in regard to my own country. . . . Her mental independence is my object, and if I can go down to the grave with the reflection that I have done a little towards it, I shall have the consolation of knowing that I have not been useless in my generation" (*L/J*, II, 84). American independence—mental and political—is the major theme of his writing during this period. Political independence had been won in the Revolutionary War, but, he believed, the country still had to fight for its mental freedom. According to Cooper, the enemy was still England, yet it is not hard for one to take the interpretative step from his struggle against British domination to his older struggle against the rule of the Federalist Squire at Cooperstown.

Three of Cooper's first five novels are set during the Revolution. Obviously the scenes of such a conflict would be attractive to an American writer of romances, especially one influenced by the work of Walter Scott. But as Frank M. Collins, referring to these and the first three Leather-Stocking Tales, points out, Cooper's "basic concern in both sets [is] with the two ultimately related types of freedom, national and individual."[11] If we exclude *Precaution*, the heroes of every novel Cooper wrote before 1838 are, to use Collins' phrase, "rebels against authority." For these characters, the instinctive response to oppression is defiance, and in each instance their rebellions are sanctioned by the novelist. In *The Pilot*, his fourth novel, a female proponent of the colonies' cause asks her guardian during a heated debate on the morality of the Revolution: "In what behalf would a just Providence sooner exercise its merciful power, than to protect the daring children of an oppressed country, while contending against tyranny and countless wrongs?" To this the man, a Tory, can only reply that the war "is something shockingly unnatural . . . 'tis the child inflicting a blow on the parent."[12] But tyranny and countless wrongs have forced the child to predominate over nature; they justify his blow. *The Pilot* (1823) is one of three sea novels from this decade. The other two—*The Red Rover* (1827) and *The Water Witch* (1830)—are pre-Revolutionary, but the hero of each is an American rebel, who has suffered some wrong from England, who fights for freedom and manhood both for himself and for his country. Thomas Philbrick, whose interest is in Cooper's aesthetic use of the sea, concludes that "in their common celebration of national independence Cooper's first three nautical romances gain a kind of epic unity. In each the free and daring life of the sea becomes equated with the promise of political identity

[11] "Cooper and the American Dream," *PMLA* 81 (1966), 80.
[12] *The Pilot*, pp. 126 and 128.

and liberty."[13] Neither Collins nor Philbrick is much concerned with the interrelationship of Cooper's life and the novels under discussion. But in the context of Cooper's juvenile struggle for identity and liberty, the sea had meant not the promise but the actuality of independence; he had sailed for England rather than submit to the rule of his father. It is in that context that his rebels against authority should be understood.

In Cooper's mind, national and individual freedom were intimately related—political identity was not less precious than personal. As America's first popular novelist, he felt during this decade that he had a particular obligation to his country. He extended the limits of his sympathies and desires to include what he believed were those of his countrymen: "with me," he wrote his English publisher in 1831, "it is a point of honor to continue rigidly an American author" (L/J, II, 61). In 1824 he had even planned an ambitious series that he called "Legends of the Thirteen Republics," thirteen novels about each of the original states during the Revolutionary War. When the first of these, *Lionel Lincoln*, was unfavorably received, he abandoned the idea, but not the intention of identifying his work with his nation. In *The Heidenmauer* (1832), he interrupts the narrative to assert that

> we profess to write only for the amusement—fortunate shall we be if instruction may be added—of our own countrymen: should others be pleased to read these crude pages, we shall be flattered and, of course, grateful; but with this distinct avowal of our object in holding the pen, we trust they will read with the necessary amount of indulgence.[14]

In return for his patriotism Cooper expected the ideological and pecuniary endorsement of his fellow Americans. How much he needed their moral support was revealed in

13 *James Fenimore Cooper and the Development of American Sea Fiction* (Cambridge, Mass.: Harvard Univ. Press, 1961), p. 58.
14 *The Heidenmauer*, p. 90.

1834 when, convinced that he had lost it, he retired from the literary profession. This decision will be discussed later; it is mentioned now to show that Cooper appropriated America's interests and principles in his own behalf. He built up his identity on the broad base of his national popularity, and his doctrinal adherence to "distinctive American thought"[15] was the prop that sustained his image of himself. "Mental independence" was the object of his writing. The struggle to achieve it was waged on two fronts: America's best interests, Cooper believed, were antithetical to England's; its best principles, he also felt, were antithetical to William Cooper's. Actually, the tenets of the Judge's Federalist philosophy merged these two aspects of the struggle. Most New York men of property were not only potential aristocrats, but very pronounced Anglophiles. As the novelist himself said in the book about his visit to England, "I had been born, and had hitherto lived, among those who looked up to England as to the idol of their political, moral and literary adoration."[16] The fight for him was against inherited ideals, and for his country, against imported ones; and the fight, so he thought at the time, was for survival.

Cooper's most explicit declaration of American independence from English influence was made in *Notions of the Americans* (1828), a nonfictional work purporting to be the account of a European's visit to America in the mid-1820s. Cooper had two reasons for writing the book. One was to provide an antidote to the numerous contemporary accounts of the country published by English travellers. From the majority of these reports it seems that England reconciled itself to the loss of its colonies by deciding that there was nothing in them worth keeping. Determined to disabuse the world of this idea, Cooper wrote a belligerent encomium upon politics and morals in the United States,

[15] *Letter to His Countrymen*, p. 99.
[16] *England: with Sketches of Society in the Metropolis* (London: Richard Bentley, 1837), I, 19.

and aimed it primarily at British readers. His traveller is a sympathetic Belgian, and Cooper provided him with an American companion—John Cadwallader, of Cadwallader, New York—to explain the more intricate blessings of the American system. In the persona of Cadwallader, Cooper inserted a long essay on intellectual relations between the two countries; this polemical treatise, appended to the first volume of *Notions*, was specifically provoked by the English descriptions of America, but "Cadwallader" cites them only as the most obvious, as well as the most odious, English attempt to suppress distinctive American thought. At the conclusion, "Cadwallader" admits that he has "treated this matter more gravely than the security and indifference of most Americans would induce them to believe necessary."[17] Indeed, four times does he warn that it might someday mean war, an outcome he appears almost to desire: "nature and self-preservation point to only one course when the appeal is seriously made to the patriot" (I, 327).

Cooper had more reason than most to be upset by the influence of English opinion in America: his pioneering effort to become an American novelist was often demeaned by the cowardly diffidence of American reviewers, who merely echoed the judgment of their British counterparts. But his struggle for mental independence predated his career as an author, just as his antagonism toward literary critics preceded any bad notices. In 1844, he wrote an editor: "God be thanked! I am not yet a slave, though many have endeavored to hold me in mental bondage" (*L/J*, IV, 461). The first man who tried to do that was William Cooper. About Judge Temple, Cooper said that in Templeton "his influence was too powerful to be opposed."[18] Inside the Mansion House, however, and at school, the young Cooper's opposition was strenuous. He was an adult when he visited England at the time he was working on *Notions*,

17 *Notions of the Americans*, I, 331.
18 *The Pioneers*, p. 126.

but his behavior in English society then suggests what had driven the Judge to send him to sea. According to James Franklin Beard,

> The polite attentions he began to receive soon after his arrival were somewhat disconcerting. The "Johnny Bulls," remarked Mrs. Cooper, "are so very civil to him that I am afraid he will not be able to abuse them, and so the piquancy of his book will be quite spoiled." There was slight cause for alarm. . . . Sydney Smith jokingly advised Thomas Moore to call Cooper out "the first thing I did, for, as it must come to that, I might as well begin with it." Barry Cornwall reported that on being told his books had pleased the English Cooper replied, "It wasn't what I intended then." Cooper seemed, Cornwall added, "to have 'meant nothing but fighting,' as they say in the ring."[19]

While these Englishmen's accounts may of course have been colored by the "prejudice against Americans" that Cooper insisted was part of every Englishman's character, there is reason to accept them as accurate. In his account of his visit to London, Cooper nowhere describes himself as this disputatious; after reporting on one conversation, however, he does caution his American reader that "I would strenuously urge on every American who really loves the institutions of his country, never to make any concessions to mere politeness, on these topics, when actually required to say anything in England."[20] On these topics Cooper seems to have said much more than he was required to. In this fighting spirit he wrote *Notions of the Americans*.

The fiercest part of *Notions* is Cadwallader's essay, and throughout it Cooper treats the relationship between England and America as a family drama. In this tragedy England is assigned the villainous role of the tyrannical father, who should be blamed for not following a just course "which would have secured a devoted friend in every de-

[19] Beard, *L/J*, I, 253-54.   [20] *England*, I, 159-60.

pendant as it was released from the dominion of the parent" (I, 321). America's heroic part is that of the son, who looks to his English heritage as "the glory of our fathers" (I, 312), who has no desire to imitate "the example of the prodigal son" (I, 318), but who is forced to revolt by the actions of England—forced, in fact, to revolt twice. The pattern which Cooper traces in the history of the two countries—oppression, rebellion, subjugation, independence—repeats the one which we have traced in his own life. Oppression: England "banished our ancestors from her bosom, because they would not submit to an oppression against which she herself has since revolted" (I, 320). Rebellion: England "cumbered our infant efforts with her vicious legislation, and drove us to a premature majority" (I, 320). Subjugation: "There was so much that was true, blended with a great deal that was ideal in our admiration of English character, and, more than all, there was so much which, admirable or not, resembled ourselves, that it was not easy to depreciate its merits. . . . This extraordinary mental bondage continued . . . during the first ten years of the present century" (I, 313). Independence: "While the American was fondly, and, one might say, blindly clinging to his ancient attachments, his advances were met by jealousy, or repelled by contempt. Whatever may be the future consequences of this unnatural repulse, America has no reason to lament its occurrence. It has already relieved her from the thraldom of mental bondage. So generally and so forcibly is this truth felt, that while the war of '76 is called the war of the revolution, that of '12 is emphatically termed the war of independence" (I, 315).

At the end of the essay, Cooper himself merges the nation's situation with an individual's, and the person he has in mind is himself.

I think our people have been wrong: they have often met calumny with deprecation, when they would have better shut its mouth by exhibiting spirit. We never got any thing from England in the way of petition or remonstrance; but we have obtained a glorious empire by resolution. . . . I think the nation or the individual who would maintain his proper position, must take justice and self-respect for his guides, and care as little as possible for others. (I, 326)

The deepest source of Cooper's touchy animosity toward England was his perception of it as a fatherland. He urges his countrymen to assert their manhood, to overthrow their ideal faith in the opinions of their national parent. No longer threatened with political oppression, America must yet free itself from the remnants of its psychological en-slavement. In 1828, Cooper was confident that America would.

Probably his own progress toward mental independence inspired his optimism. During the preceding decade he had allied himself, tacitly and overtly, with the set of political and social beliefs espoused by his father. By 1828, however, he had had a change of heart. What he said in *Notions* about the Federalists' sons—"It is worthy of remark, that the children of these men are almost always decided demo-crats" (II, 168)—applied directly to himself. To quote from Dixon Ryan Fox, "William Cooper was the mirror of parti-san perfection as a Federalist squire . . . he rode far and wide in the cause of Jay and later Aaron Burr, always preaching the old and musty doctrine that government had better be left to gentlemen, and that simple folk should vote as they were told."[21] In *Notions*, again using the per-sona of John Cadwallader, James Cooper sharply refuted his father's contention:

"If men, when a little better than common, were any thing like perfect, we might hope to see power lodged with safety in the hands of a reasonable portion of the enlightened, without any danger of its abuse. But the experience of the world goes to prove . . . that [most of

[21] Fox, pp. 136-37.

this minority] would pervert their philosophy to selfish-
ness. This was at least our political creed. . . . Since
the hour of the revolution, the habits, opinions, laws,
and I may say principles of the Americans, are getting
daily to be more democratic." (I, 265)

The result of which is, as Cooper's imagined visitor notes
with approval, that "that high and manly principle of fear-
less independence," which "makes men truly noble," is "a
conspicuous feature" in the American character (II, 296).
It is this new breed of man, falsely maligned by European
aristocrats seeking to preserve their inherited privileges
from the universal rise of democratic notions, that Cooper
seeks to introduce properly to the world.

However, Cooper originally decided to write *Notions* for
another reason. He explains in a letter dated early in 1828:

> . . . it is now more than a year since La Fayette mani-
> fested a strong desire that I should write some account
> of his reception in America. The good old man was so
> frank, and showed, mingled with his acknowledged
> personal interest, so strong a desire to do credit to the
> country, that I scarcely knew how to resist him. I am
> perhaps foolishly romantic enough to think that he has
> almost the right to command the services of an Ameri-
> can author. At all events, be the motive what it might,
> I finally consented. (*L/J,* I, 242)

Cooper's motive for serving Lafayette was in fact similar
to Oliver Effingham's for helping the Leather-stocking—
like his character, the novelist had psychically adopted the
good old man as an alter-father. Cooper had seen the
Frenchman during the latter's visit to America in 1824;
he met him soon after his arrival in Europe; but his emotional investment in him was of longer standing. "Though
personally unknown to La Fayette," he wrote in 1825, "I
never felt so much interest, when a boy, in any foreigner
as I did in him—It is a wonderful feeling, that binds us

all, so strongly to that old man" (*L/J*, I, 126). "Cadwallader" elaborates on this childhood interest in a way that reminds one of Natty's plight in *The Pioneers*: "I remember the deep, reverential, I might almost say awful, attention, with which a school of some sixty children, on a remote frontier, listened to the tale of [Lafayette's] sufferings in the castle of Olmutz, as it was recounted to us by the instructor. . . . We plotted among ourselves, the means of his deliverance" (I, 38-39). I am not suggesting that Natty Bumppo was in any sense modeled after the Marquis de Lafayette, only that they have several things in common. Lafayette's imprisonment and oppression appealed strongly to the boy whose greatest wish was for freedom and independence, the two gifts that, after delivering Natty from jail, the novelist grants him at the story's conclusion. Only after Cooper met Lafayette did the bond he felt assume a filial character. This seems to have happened immediately: almost seventy, Lafayette possessed a fatherly air, and the American responded to it enthusiastically. About a year later, Cooper wrote him to arrange an interview for himself and another American in Paris to discuss "a subject of great personal interest to yourself; for like dutiful children we occu[py] ourselves, impertinent as it may be, with all matters that we think likely to have an effect on [your][22] position or happiness" (*L/J*, VI, 297).

Also like a dutiful child, he did in *Notions* describe Lafayette's return to the United States, where the General, as Cooper indicates several times, "was literally like a father among his children."[23] Yet according to Fred Somkin's well-documented analysis of Lafayette's thirteen months as "the nation's guest," the majority of Cooper's countrymen received the Frenchman in a more complex way: these second-generation republicans sought not simply to honor

[22] The manuscript of this letter is damaged, and Beard restores the missing portions in brackets. However, he gives "our" for this word, a choice I do not understand. The context seems to require "your."

[23] *Notions*, I, 184; cf. also I, 178 and 202; II, 145 and 215.

this representative of the Founding Fathers, but ritually to promote themselves by means of their homage to the Fathers' rank. Cooper, however, unequivocally assumed that Lafayette was the father and America the land of his children. Somkin concludes that "it sometimes happened that the living Lafayette disappeared entirely behind the multiple facade of his social meanings,"[24] but Cooper never took his eyes off the patriarch, whose significance to him was entirely personal. Cooper himself conceded in 1836 that "I may have imbibed notions peculiar to myself" regarding an American's relationship with the General (*L/J*, III, 246). Swayed by those notions he gave in to Lafayette's request and undertook his first nonfiction work. And to account for at least part of Cooper's extraordinarily warm praise of democratic equality in *Notions of the Americans* we must cite Lafayette's "desire to do credit to the country" he had helped at its birth. Cooper's renunciation of his father's aristocratic political philosophy was carried out under the psychic aegis of Europe's greatest republican.

Throughout his life Cooper had an intense unconscious need for a father with whom he could identify, although it was often in conflict with his equally compelling need to resist domination by his real father. Lafayette was not the only alternative father-figure he offered to his unconscious as a way of resolving this conflict. I have already tried to define how the Leather-stocking was created to fill that psychic role. Cooper's earliest extant letter, from March 3rd, 1800, was written to the Judge; it is signed "Your / affectionate / son / James K Cooper" (*L/J*, I, 7). The novelist's grandson explains that Cooper "had a boyish admiration for Moss Kent [his father's law clerk and secretary] and for a time called himself James Kent Cooper."[25] A quarter century later he would again change the name his father had given him, this time permanently—both actions are

---

[24] *Unquiet Eagle: Memory and Desire in the Idea of American Freedom, 1815-1860* (Ithaca: Cornell Univ. Press, 1967), pp. 144-45.
[25] James Fenimore Cooper (grandson), *Correspondence*, I, 77.

emblematic of his filial disaffection. George Dekker concludes that John Jay, the Revolutionary patriot and Federalist Governor of New York, also belongs on the list of Cooper's substitute fathers; as Dekker points out, after the Judge's death Cooper became very close to the Jay family, "the Governor told Cooper the story which was to form the basis of his second novel, *The Spy*. And it was to John Jay and his family that he read the manuscript of his first novel, *Precaution*, before seeking a publisher."[26] Cooper certainly seems to have responded to Jay as a dutiful child: an entire chapter in *Notions* is a eulogy to him.

But John Jay, like John Peter De Lancey, had much in common with William Cooper; all three agreed that, in the Governor's words, "those who own the country are the most fit persons to participate in the government of it."[27] Lafayette, I believe, claimed so much of Fenimore Cooper's interest at this time basically because of his differences. For example, until the Revolution William Cooper was almost destitute, although immediately afterwards he was rich enough to purchase Croghan's Patent and begin his rise to social preeminence. The sources of his sudden wealth are unknown, but there is, as Dekker suggests, a possibility that he was "a war-time profiteer who used his Quakerism as a cloak whilst others hazarded their lives and fortunes for the sake of liberty or loyalty."[28] Among those others was General Lafayette, whose exceptional sacrifices during the

[26] Dekker, p. 13.   [27] Quoted by Fox, p. 9.

[28] Dekker, p. 3. To me, this is more probable than merely possible. It would help to explain James Cooper's creation of Harvey Birch, the hero of his second novel, a man who sacrifices his reputation and income to serve Washington as a spy, repeatedly refusing to accept a cent for his patriotism. About *The Spy*, Cooper wrote his publisher in 1820: "I confess I am more partial to this new work myself as being a Country-man and perhaps a younger child" (*L/J*, 1, 44). The confused syntax of this sentence suggests that Cooper might unconsciously have meant to suggest that *he* was the younger child. In *The Pioneers* Judge Temple is credited with aiding his country as well as himself during the Revolution, but absolutely no record of Judge Cooper's revolutionary services has survived.

Revolution were described by Cooper, in a letter to the *Evening Post,* in this way:

> He owed us no allegiance, no duty, not one drop of his blood. In possession of all that commonly renders life desirable, he abandoned his pleasures to risk life itself, in our behalf. . . . In the darkest period of our distress, he joined us, not an adventurer in quest of preferment, but one who had all to bestow and little to receive. (*L/J,* III, 246)

One reward that Lafayette was now entitled to, Cooper steadfastly insisted, was the devotion and respect of every American. For his part, Cooper was prepared to go further, to use even his status as a writer in Lafayette's behalf. This sense of obligation was his conscious motive for publishing *Notions,* and a few years later, as we shall see, he would again put his pen at Lafayette's disposal.

Of course, the most relevant difference between Judge Cooper and General Lafayette was their respective political philosophies. By 1831, James Cooper, the son of the American equivalent of an aristocrat, had become so decidedly democratic that he could write to a friend at home in the middle of the Presidency of General Jackson, the "common man's President," "If you should come to Europe and live three years, you would go back, with the best possible opinions not only of our institutions but of the men who are in power. Both are so much better than what one sees here . . . that it puts an American in perfect good humour with himself" (*L/J,* II, 76). What he had seen were the stirrings of egalitarian impulses in Europe—the Polish and Dutch insurrections, and especially the July Revolution in France—being effectively suppressed by the minorities of privileged men in power. In 1830 he settled down in Paris, where Lafayette was at the center of the French Revolution, got active in support of the republican cause, and wrote his first explicitly political novels. If *Notions of the Americans* was written to acquaint Europe with the virtues of democracy, Cooper's "European trilogy"—*The Bravo* (1831), *The Heidenmauer* (1832), and *The Headsman* (1833)—was written to instruct America on the evils of aristocracy.

By publishing these three novels, Cooper was at the end of his first and most successful decade as an author significantly changing the terms of his relationship with his audience. Before, he had written primarily to amuse his readers. While his earlier novels do have more or less clearly defined themes, meaning in them is subordinated to movement. *Notions* was a serious attempt to explicate social issues; that it was advertised as nonfiction sufficiently warned the reader who sought the diversion of a tale's romantic and adventurous incidents not to sit down with it, a fire, and an empty evening. The reader who picked up *The Bravo* in this mood, having noted its subtitle, *A Tale*, could justly have claimed that he had been misled. For despite Cooper's effort to supply both adventure and romance, he was clearly more interested in instructing his audience than in entertaining it. *The Bravo* marks the beginning of Cooper's habit of setting aside long passages within the narrative for explicit social comment, comment less on the characters of the story than on the race of men in general. This is a bad habit for a storyteller to indulge, and despite the fact that in *The Bravo* he often manages the instruction with great subtlety and insight, the book, like the other two works of this trilogy, was unpopular.

Cooper and his reading public tended to blame each other for the trilogy's failure, but the problem was chiefly a misunderstanding—the first serious one of his career—between them. Much could be said for both sides: for the reader's desire vicariously to escape the real world in the pages of a romance and for Cooper's to use those pages as a blackboard on which he could illustrate a point about that world. One may feel that the novelist's disposition to educate his listeners politically was a trait he had inherited from his father, the outspoken Federalist Squire, even though the son was now registered in a contrary school of thought. Yet this trait is also one which the first American novelist shared with a great many of his literary descendants, and the predisposition may be as much national as individual. A European writer whose predominant interest is in social characteristics rather than individual characters, in political affairs rather than emotional ones, in assuming a moral stance rather than exploring a moral question, would be far more likely to write a satire than a novel. In America, such a generic division is harder to make. How much of *Huckleberry Finn* was written by a novelist, how much by a satirist? How much of *The Confidence-Man*? How much of *Invisible Man*?

At the time he decided to write the first book of his trilogy, Cooper was in fact working on a satire with a similar theme. Five years later he published it as *The Monikins* (the only book he published without a subtitle), but in 1830 he put the manuscript aside to write *The Bravo*, feeling that the form of a novel could equally serve a didactic purpose. With this belief would William Dean Howells, Frank Norris, Sinclair Lewis, and a large number of later American novelists agree. Certainly almost every novelist, regardless of nationality, is to a considerable extent preoccupied with the relationship between a character and his society—that preoccupation seems to be one of the definitions of the genre. But American novelists especially seem to feel that in portraying that relationship they have both an aesthetic and a moral responsibility: an aesthetic responsibility to the character; a moral one to the society. Norman Mailer, for a contemporary example, pauses halfway through his account of the March on the Pentagon in *Armies of the Night* to consider this issue, which he sees as a conflict:

> how much guilt lay on the back of a good writer— it grew worse and worse. As the power of communication grew larger, so the responsibility to educate a nation lapped at the feet, new tide of a new responsibility, and one had become a writer after all to find a

warm place where one was safe—responsibility was for the pompous, and the public servants; writers were born to discover wine.

America, of course, is the nation that once prohibited wine, and I believe there is something representatively American about Mailer's reluctant conclusion that if the writer's wine yields up no social lesson, it is a guilty pleasure, one he ought not to enjoy. Writing is intoxicating; responsibility has the bitter taste of salt water; but if an author wants to escape the easy American judgment—so foreign to European opinions—that a hangover implies something about a person's moral nature, he must accept his responsibility as a kind of public servant.

I suspect that this opinion, which Mailer in 1968 shared with Cooper in 1830, is something both owe to the men who founded this country in the 1620s. The most direct testimony to this historical source is provided by Nathaniel Hawthorne, an American writer whose relationship to the Puritans was hereditary as well as cultural, in his "Custom-House—Introductory" to *The Scarlet Letter*. There he deprecates his own success as an artist by viewing it through the sombre eyes of his ancestors: " 'What is he?' murmurs one gray shadow of my forefathers to the other. 'A writer of story-books! What kind of business in life,—what mode of glorifying God, or being serviceable to mankind in his day and generation,—may that be?' " This often-cited passage should remind us of another that I have already quoted: Cooper's father was being thoroughly American when he told his son William that the only kind of man that mattered in this country was great, good—and useful. To the American mind, which still owes many of its most deeply held assumptions to its New England forefathers, the likelihood that something which is neither serviceable nor useful must therefore be immoral is very great. Of course, the Puritan notion that art is somehow immoral is as old as Plato's *Republic*. But while Plato would have prohibited art from his state, to a great degree the Puritans did succeed in prohibiting it from theirs. Their state became our republic, and it may be the cultural remnants of their distrust for story-books which has led subsequent Americans to compensate for the potentially damnable act of using the imagination by using it ostensibly to educate the nation.

To assert that more than any other country America demands that all its public men be not merely useful, but moral as well, is to iterate a cliché, a cliché that recent political events have reinvigorated, may perhaps have redeemed. Americans have lately shown that they are capable of acting upon that cultural demand, and I want to suggest that American writers have traditionally felt its force. In Cooper's case, however, he was responding to a demand that the majority of his public apparently did not feel. This may have been because during the period when he was writing, the novel was considered the least serious of the arts, with the possible exception of the play. Reading a tale, investing all those hours in someone else's artificial problems, was supposed to be slightly wicked, and thoroughly self-indulgent. Of course, in spite of themselves these readers were learning a great deal about themselves and their world, and in spite of its avowed intentions, every novel had something to teach them. But it is understandable that they preferred a novel that did not invite them into its story as a teacher summons his children to class, a novel that accepted *their* fiction that this was merely entertainment. Nor, on the other hand, is it surprising that the first American novelist was one of the very first novelists who refused to accept that limitation. By denying his readers the chance to feel guilty about enjoying his novels, he made it difficult for them to enjoy them at all, but he may also have made himself feel less guilty about writing them. Whatever Cooper's readers wished for, what they got in the European trilogy was an earnest and well-meant lesson in politics, and Cooper did his best to make it useful to them.

137

These novels are set in Europe and in the past, but Cooper's perspective includes contemporary America: in the first two he defines a class of men, a combination of office-holders and landlords (in this regard at least men very like his father), who present the greatest threat to individual liberty. To underscore his lesson he set *The Bravo* in the Republic of Venice and *The Heidenmauer* in Germany during the revolutionary period of the Reformation. Neither republic nor revolution can safeguard an unfranchised society against Senator Gradenigo, who uses his office as an extension of his own power, or the Count of Hartenburg, who uses a revolution to further his own interests. Cooper's definition of an aristocrat fits a Federalist perfectly:

> To [Gradenigo] Venice seemed a free state, because he partook so largely of the benefits of her social system; . . . As a Venetian he was equally opposed to the domination of one, or of the whole; being, as respects the first, a furious republican, and, in reference to the last, leaning to that singular sophism which calls the dominion of the majority the rule of many tyrants! In short, he was an aristocrat; and no man had more industriously or more successfully persuaded himself into the belief of all the dogmas that were favorable to his caste.[29]

That such men existed in America Cooper well knew. That they were capable of trying to subvert the American system he firmly believed.[30] That the only just government is "the dominion of the majority" he offered without reservations as the moral of both tales.

[29] *The Bravo*, pp. 98-99.

[30] Cf. *Sketches of Switzerland* [*Part First*] (Philadelphia: Carey, Lea & Blanchard, 1836), II, 158. There Cooper declares that some Federalist leaders "aimed at a return . . . to the old system" of monarchical government. As he says, "I was educated in the particular opinions of this political sect; . . . I had every opportunity of ascertaining their real sentiments."

The meaning of *The Headsman* is more complex. Toward the end Cooper interrupts the narrative with a digression for which there is no contextual justification:

> The nation which, by the adverse circumstances of numerical inferiority, poverty of means, failure of enterprise, or want of opinion, cannot sustain its own citizens in the acquisition of a just renown, is deficient in one of the first and most indispensable elements of greatness; . . . We see, in this fact, among other conclusions, the importance of an acquisition of such habits of manliness of thought, as will enable us to decide the merits and demerits of what is done among ourselves, and of shaking off that dependence on others which it is too much the custom of some among us to dignify with the pretending title of deference to knowledge and taste, but which, in truth, possesses some such share of true modesty and diffidence, as the footman is apt to exhibit when exulting in the renown of his master.[31]

"We" of course refers to the Americans. The passage refers to James Fenimore Cooper. Cooper himself provides a gloss in a letter written for publication in 1841:

> This country requires to be made independent of England. . . . As things now are, England holds the character of almost every man in the nation at her mercy. . . . Look at my own case—I had exceeding popularity in this country, until I wrote The Travelling Bachelor [the subtitle of *Notions*]—This book displeased the English; they abused me, and even those who had known me from childhood began to look on me with distrustful eyes. (*L/J*, IV, 203)

The passage from *The Headsman* marks the literary beginning of Cooper's quarrel with his countrymen. His anger had been aroused by the failure of American re-

---

[31] *The Headsman*, pp. 326-27.

viewers to endorse his vindication of democratic principles by sufficiently praising his books or American readers to do so by eagerly buying them. He was prepared for the British reaction—indeed, he had intentionally provoked it—but not, after his strident assertion of America's unshackled thought, for any criticism from America. In August 1831 his wife warily wrote her sister that "Mr. Cooper you well know feels deeply and speaks promptly—and should he meet with injustice from his Countrymen—whom he has supported with so much ardour and so much ability abroad —his feelings will I know burst forth."[32] A few months later the storm broke.

The precipitating factor was the publication in November of *A Letter of J. Fenimore Cooper, to Gen. Lafayette.* There is nothing in the *Letter* itself to indicate the importance it would have in Cooper's life: it is a competent, dryly written rebuttal of a French writer's claim that a monarchy was less expensive to administer than a republic. Lafayette, who had publicly asserted the contrary, asked Cooper, as an American and a republican, to reply. Against his will, according to Cooper, he agreed; this is how he describes his entrance into the dispute:

> The vindication of the country already published [i.e. *Notions*], had occasioned a heavy pecuniary loss; it had even lost me the favor of a large party at home. I had many demands on my limited means, and was unable to make further sacrifices of this nature, to any abstract notions of patriotism or of truth. It was some months [later] . . . that I was told the principal object of the article in question. It was to injure Gen. Lafayette. . . . This fact presented the affair in an entirely new aspect. I determined to furnish the answer that was requested.[33]

32 Quoted by Beard, *L/J*, ii, 121.
33 *Letter to His Countrymen*, p. 9.

No longer willing to defend his country, he defended the General, he said, to avoid "a lasting stain upon the national character" (*L/J*, II, 346) and "to secure my own self-approbation."[34] The second motive was the one that mattered: it was his filial duty to protect his adopted father. Even though he had begun to regret giving in to Lafayette's previous request, he was psychically unable to resist him this time either. Undoubtedly Cooper believed that "the deep and nearly filial interest that is taken in [Lafayette's] comfort, by all classes of the citizens" of the United States,[35] insured their support in 1831. At first he was probably shocked when the American press severely censured him for interfering in the internal affairs of another nation. But his response quickly turned to outraged indignation and chagrin.

In measuring Cooper's reaction to this injustice it is necessary to keep in mind his unconscious involvement in the issues jointly at stake—America's obligation to respect Lafayette and to maintain its own self-respect. Any equivocation on these points threatened the hallowed ground on which he had staked out his identity, and to be abused, and by America, for protecting them literally took that ground out from under him. In addition, as Lounsbury notes, "the attacks in the American newspapers made a painful impression upon a mind that was morbidly sensitive to criticism even from the most insignificant of men."[36] The letters of 1832 are full of Cooper's anguished sense of betrayal. "The humiliation comes from home," he wrote one close friend. "It is biting to find that accident has given me a country which has not manliness and pride to maintain its own opinions" (*L/J*, II, 310). To another old friend he said that he was considering a trip to the States "to ascertain whether for the rest of my life I am to have a country or not. . . . I am tired of wasting life, means, and comfort in behalf of those who return abuse for services" (*L/J*, II,

<hr>

34 Ibid., p. 10.   35 *Notions*, I, 178.   36 Lounsbury, p. 115.

268). Early in 1833 he characterized the whole affair in these words:

> I have seen many extraordinary and some impudent transactions in my time, but I can recall none more flagrant than this of putting an American on his trial, at the bar of public opinion, and that, too, in his own country, for having told the truth in defence of Gen. Lafayette, at a great pecuniary loss to himself, and without the smallest possibility of personal advantage. Every hour convinces me, more and more, that we are a nation in name only. . . . (*L/J*, II, 380)

There is much self-pity and a great deal of overreaction in these comments, but much also that is genuinely sad. Perhaps the saddest moment in all the letters is found in one dated November 14th, 1832, replying to a friend who had expressed the hope that "I may go on & prosper"—after referring to the "abandonment of public favour," Cooper went on to tell him that he had decided to quit: "The next book will probably be published like the others, sneer'd at like the others, and forgotten like the others, and the world may ask a year or two after what has become of our annual novel" (*L/J*, II, 360-61).

The next book was *The Headsman*; when Cooper sent the final portion of manuscript to his American publishers in April 1833, he told them it would be his last: "I do not wish to retire with any *parade*, like that of a petted author, for I feel as if I had been any thing but petted at home at least" (*L/J*, VI, 319). Yet so strongly did he feel about the circumstances that had forced him to retire that he did, a year later and after his return to America, make a parade of his grievances in a pamphlet titled *A Letter to His Countrymen*, a title that appropriately echoes his *Letter* of 1831. The 1834 *Letter* was meant to be a farewell address:

> The American who wishes to illustrate and enforce the peculiar principles of his own country, by the agency

of polite literature, will, for a long time to come, I fear, find that *his* constituency, as to all purposes of distinctive thought, is still too much under the influence of foreign theories, to receive him with favor. It is under this conviction that I lay aside the pen.

Almost the last sentence that he planned to write with that pen recapitulates his experience of the preceding ten years: "I am not ashamed to avow, that I have felt a severe mortification that I am to break down [i.e. to come to grief] on the question of distinctive American thought."[37] In his mind he had equated the peculiar principles of America with his particular calling as a novelist, independence from England with independence from Judge Cooper, the denunciation of aristocratic ideals with the renunciation of his own background—no wonder he felt mortified, and he probably was ashamed. By 1820 he had realized that his effort to embrace his father's identity had failed; by 1834, that his effort to appropriate an identity antithetical to his father's in so many respects had also become unviable.

It was during this period of his greatest disillusionment that Cooper conceived the idea for *The Headsman*, "an idea," he wrote his publisher, "that has seized me with such force, that there is no resisting it." Travelling through Switzerland in mid-1832, he had likewise been unable to resist the beauties of Lake Leman. Having no particular destination, the Cooper family impulsively moved into a house in Vevay, where the novelist "determined now I am here to commence a Swiss tale."[38] He divided his days between boating on the lake and working on the novel. It is apparent from his letters that Leman reminded him of Otsego, the first water he had ever navigated, and I believe that his Swiss tale can only be understood by looking beyond the text at the author's life. Like the two previous novels, it is an analysis of aristocratic society, except that, in

37 *Letter to His Countrymen*, pp. 98-99.
38 From Cooper's Journal for September 6, 1832; *L/J*, II, 330.

Grossman's words, "this time in terms of hereditary liabilities instead of hereditary rights."[39] Its hero is the son of a headsman, "the highest executioner of the law,"[40] a position which under the strict aristocratic rules of descent will soon be his. Understandably the son feels ambivalent toward his father: when the heroine insists that he cannot actually dislike his parent, he replies, "Heaven forbid that I should be wanting in natural feeling of this sort, and yet . . . it is horrible not to be able to respect, to love profoundly, those to whom we owe our existence!"[41]

This conflict has emotionally crippled him, and for very good reasons Cooper's artistic treatment of the young man's existential dilemma is profoundly acute. Cooper was himself caught up by a similar problem, which, if not strictly hereditary, did involve the legacy from his childhood. In Cooper's psyche, the child was too well preserved. His failure to digest the emotional conflicts of his early life forced him to make unreal claims upon the world. To assign blame in such a situation is useless; perhaps the worst thing his father did was to die before Cooper had reached a manhood in which he could confidently assert his own identity, could quit wrestling with the contradictory impulses to submit to and to rebel against his father. But the fact remains that Cooper had not gained that autonomous identity when the Judge died, and it was forever forbidden him. During the period we have been considering he went as far as he would ever go toward mental independence from his father's authority. Despite his immense popular success as an author, however, this progress was only made in the patriarchal presence of Lafayette and under the conviction that he was in sympathy with the majority of his countrymen: on them he depended to supply and sanction his identity.

When both Lafayette and his countrymen unwittingly and innocently conspired against him, Cooper felt psychically dislocated. All that had really happened was that a

---

[39] Grossman, *Cooper*, p. 81.   [40] *The Headsman*, p. 24.
[41] Ibid., p. 249.

small group of spineless men had truckled to foreign opinion, and a larger group of his readers had decided that
his most recent books lacked the interest of his earlier ones.
The first were unmistakably wrong, the second, just as
right, and Cooper's friends and publishers repeatedly tried
to make him ignore those and write to please these. But
it was an issue he could not examine rationally. He had
tried to achieve manhood, and his country had not the
manliness to support him. He had placed his self in the
keeping of his countrymen, and they had betrayed him.

The first evidence of what seems to have been a mild
form of paranoia in Cooper's personality appears at this
time. In August 1832 he wrote his friend Samuel Morse to
say that a recent vituperative review of *The Bravo* was "a
design to frighten me into silence" (*L/J*, II, 303); for at
least several years he seriously believed it had been prepared
by the French government and published by an international conspiracy. In September he again wrote Morse to
advise him on where to exhibit his painting, "Gallery of
the Louvre," in America: "I doubt your success in New-
York. . . . Your intimacy with me has become known, and
such is the virulence of my enemies in New-York, that I
have no sort of doubt, of their attacking your picture in
consequence" (*L/J*, II, 336). This feeling of persecution
may have been induced by Cooper's guilt over his second
revolt against the Judge; that cause is suggested by his incredible assertion that "even those who had known me
from childhood began to look on me with distrustful eyes"
after he wrote *Notions of the Americans*. The name we use
to define Cooper's state of mind is not very important.
What matters is that he had been overcome by this imagined
betrayal.

Not, however, before finishing *The Headsman*. This was
not accomplished easily; at the beginning of 1834 he wrote
in a letter.:

My pen is used up—or rather it is thrown away. . . .
The amount of this . . . is a disgust in myself, that is

far stronger than any of the expedients of my enemies.
I never ⟨wrote⟩ did anything with the disgust and reluctance that I felt while at work on the Headsman,
and I can not conceive of a consideration that would
induce me to tax my feelings in the same way again.
(*L*/*J*, III, 28)

Yet the conclusion of this novel actually points to the new
way which Cooper would take toward salvation. It has a
surprise ending, one which the text plainly indicates was
unplanned, one which occurred to Cooper only at what he
thought was the conclusion of his literary career. In the
novel's thirtieth chapter the hero, who had never been able
to acknowledge his father without disgust and reluctance,
suddenly learns that the dreaded headsman of Berne is not
his father after all. His father is the noble, generous, and
wise Doge of Genoa. Of course, this discovery completely
jumbles the novel's meaning. As Grossman says, "Cooper
unforgivably ruins his story by its solution."[42] At that
moment, however, Cooper was not concerned about the
story.

[42] Grossman, *Cooper*, p. 84.

CHAPTER V

"AT HOME"

COOPER left Europe in September 1833. Forty-four years old, he had never been more doubtful about his future. As an author he did not think of himself as a craftsman religiously dedicated to aesthetic perfection, for whom solitude or exile were favorable, in a sense requisite, to his task, but as a storyteller whose first need was an audience to listen to his stories. During the 1820s Cooper was perfectly content with his role; his sense of himself coincided with that of his readers—he wanted to be an American novelist, to represent America in the world, wanted especially to write for Americans. More than a goal, popularity was his means: he wanted to write popular novels and, by and large, he did. When after seven years abroad he decided to return to the United States his situation had changed radically. Of only one fact was he certain: "I am not with my own country," he wrote in 1832; "the void between us is immense" (*L/J*, II, 237). Fronting that void Cooper dismissed any attempt to communicate across it. Retirement was the most honorable alternative. Shortly before leaving Europe he wrote to a friend: "The quill and I are divorced, and you cannot conceive the degree of freedom I could almost say of happiness I feel, at having got my neck out of the halter. I could write forever—or as long as God pleased—for a *nation* that was a *nation*—but Heaven help us!" (*L/J*, II, 384).

Such a reproach was not altogether fair to his nation. Although one can understand the causes, conscious and unconscious, of Cooper's complaints against his countrymen, can to an extent empathize with them, it is less easy

147

to endorse them. For a man who refused to concede that his motives could be misunderstood except by someone with bad intentions, Cooper was at times almost perversely unwilling to understand those of others. For a social critic, he was at times uncharitably insensitive to the legitimate anxieties of his society. Throughout the Jacksonian period, America was having as much trouble as Cooper in fixing its identity. Exactly what principles, since changing economic conditions forced both neo-Federalist and neo-Republican into new postures, the nation would believe in; who, since the generation of the Founders had finally died out, would be allowed to affirm those principles; how forcefully, since rhetoric is the means by which a democratic electorate is rallied to a cause, those affirmations would be worded—the debate over questions like these stirred up so much enthusiasm and anger, unsettled so many tentative certainties, that not even the country's leading novelist was above the dispute. Once he espoused an interest in politics, not even the Atlantic Ocean could put Cooper beyond the reach of the flailing partisans at home. Yet why did he confuse partisan attacks with public opinion? That was a logical error that General Lafayette never made, but the sources of Cooper's initial sympathy with and final antipathy toward the mood of Jacksonian America were basically psychological. In his own eyes Cooper felt he had been unjustly tried and condemned by his country, tried by the reviewers and condemned by the public, and as he wrote two months after his arrived in New York, "God has so constituted my mind that it never recovers from a disgust of this nature" (*L/J*, III, 29). Though few of us would agree with the cause Cooper cites, he was right about the way his mind was constituted: he would never forgive his nation for betraying the trust he had depended upon, the bond between the particularly American novelist and his audience at home which had sanctioned his identity.

Cooper had probably not realized how much he did depend upon that bond until it was broken. In *A Letter to*

His Countrymen he describes the break as a clean one: "As between me and my country, the amount current of both profit and honor exhibits a blank sheet. I have never laid any claim to having conferred either, and I do not feel disposed to admit that I have received either."[1] His audi-ence lost, he resolved to write no more novels. But if he ever really felt free and happy with this choice, he soon had second thoughts about it. Three years later, in 1837, he wrote his English publisher, Bentley, that "a freak has got into my head to write a novel, again" (*L/J*, III, 269). As he told Bentley, "I have some disgust to overcome," but as we shall see, events had compelled him to swallow his reluctance in order to deal with a psychically more pressing problem. Yet the rupture with his audience did provide a new kind of freedom: as an unpopular novelist he could use his imagination with fewer restraints for his own pur-poses, both conscious and unconscious. In this chapter I shall be concerned with the first freak that got into Coop-er's head after his premature retirement. It produced the Effingham Novels, *Homeward Bound* and *Home As Found*, two of the most personal books Cooper ever published. But before we can examine them, we must follow Cooper him-self homeward, and try to explain what he was looking for at home.

So apprehensive was Cooper about his reception in New York, the town he had triumphantly sailed from in 1826, that he initially planned to take his family directly from the ship to Newburgh without spending a single night among his "enemies." When he actually arrived he decided to rent a house in the city after all, but his anxiety on this point typifies the way the ex-novelist regarded his future in America; "indeed," he wrote in January 1834, "but for my family, I do not think I should ever have returned" (*L/J*, III, 29). Both how and where he would live were un-certain. A year earlier he wrote to a friend: "We are coming

[1] *Letter to His Countrymen*, p. 45.

home next season. . . . What we shall do with ourselves it
is hard to say. . . . I shall probably be driven into the interior, but where, Heaven only knows" (*L/J*, ii, 360). In
1831, writing to his nephew Richard Cooper, who remained
at Cooperstown, he had been more specific about his desires: "Now my longing is for a Wilderness—Cooperstown
is far too populous and artificial for me and it is my intention to plunge somewhere into the forest, for six months
in the year, at my return. I will not quit my own state, but
I shall seek some unsettled part of that" (*L/J*, ii, 89).
Referring to this passage, Henry Walcott Boynton appropriately describes it as a "Leatherstocking mood."[2] Natty also
plunges into the forest whenever the society of men becomes
oppressive and unbearable. The disappointments and in-
justices he had suffered forced Cooper to retreat from the
demands of the world. It is hard to imagine him setting
up a homestead in a clearing, even hard to believe that he
ever seriously considered doing so, but his subsequent actions prove that he was in earnest. Cooper did retreat inward—not to the pathless wilderness, however. Instead, he
fell back on his own past: from the independent identity
he had tried to achieve as an author he regressed to the
role of being his father's son.

"Now for a little *private* business"—with these words in
a letter to nephew Richard, Cooper opened up the subject
of his new plans for a place to live. He was at Vevay, working on *The Headsman*; he had made up his mind about
returning to the States and begun to think that this novel
would be his last. Under these circumstances he no longer
felt that Cooperstown was either too artificial or too populous:

> I wish you to write to me the exact condition of the
> Mansion House—if it is to be bought—whether it is
> capable of being repaired. . . . I am not rich, but
> your aunt and myself possess together what would

2 Boynton, p. 236.

be an easy property at Cooperstown, and my annual receipts are large. If an arrangement can be made with Mr. Averill amicably, at a moderate price, I may be induced to take the old house, fix it up, and spend six months of each year in it—My habits and pursuits require town for the rest of the year. (L/J, ii, 296)

Averill was the present owner of Judge Cooper's house, which had been sold for debts against the estate a decade earlier, and which had been empty even longer. The house was for sale, but the price that Richard reported was higher than Cooper wanted to pay, and he decided to wait until he was on the scene before committing himself. In June 1834 he visited Cooperstown, and although Averill's price was in fact twice what Richard had quoted, although the Mansion House was more dilapidated than Cooper had expected, he determined to buy it. This he did in August 1834, and several months later he moved into the house.

There Cooper would live until his death in 1851, the planned six months in town reduced to several yearly visits. His decision to go home again so emphatically must have surprised his family. Imaginatively he had revisited Cooperstown when he wrote *The Pioneers*, but in person he had not been back since 1817, the year his mother died. And in the novel that followed *The Pioneers* he included the following exchange between John Paul Jones, "the pilot," who was English by birth, and the woman he had courted in his youth, who had remained in England: "And will they," she asks Jones,

"who know so well how to love home, sing the praises of him, who has turned his ruthless hand against the land of his fathers?"

"For ever harping on that word home!" said the Pilot. . . . "Is a man a stick or a stone, that he must be cast into the fire, or buried in a wall, wherever his fate may have doomed him to appear on the earth?"[3]

3 *The Pilot*, p. 415.

Yet in Switzerland, in 1832, the idea of home suddenly exercised a powerful influence on Cooper. He had no intention of returning to the site of his boyhood to surround himself with old friends; in 1831 he had learned from Richard that there were few old friends left. "I am unable," Richard wrote, "to point out every chasm that death has made in the living circle with which you were acquainted. Some that you desired to be remembered to I never heard of, and some are in their graves."[4] Of his family, only his sister, Mrs. George Pomeroy, and his nephew still lived there.

Cooper himself underscored how private the decision was, and I doubt that he could have fully articulated his motives even to himself. To Richard, in the letter from Vevay, he gave this explanation: "If we can succeed in this purchase, the Jews shall be driven from the Temple, dear Dick, and your name will occupy its old station in Otsego." This reason suggests that Cooper, who only recently had finished paying the creditors, was ready to apply some of his literary profits to a renewed effort to preserve the Judge's estate. His use of the word Temple both reminds one of *The Pioneers*, and indicates that for the son there was now something sacred about restoring his father's image to a high place in Cooperstown. I shall discuss Cooper's conception of his duty to his father in a moment—it was certainly one of the unconscious ways by which he sought at this time to find his place in the world—but I want first to examine what Cooper called "my pilgrimage to the scene[s?] of my youth and childhood" (*L/J*, III, 12).

That phrase occurs in a letter to Jacob Morris, a man Cooper had known all his life, an ardent Federalist and a close friend of William Cooper. Fenimore Cooper was writing from New York in November 1833 about his anticipated visit to Cooperstown in the spring. General Morris lived in Butternuts, and Cooper assured him that he would call upon his father's friend "as a part of my pilgrimage." Alone, Cooper set out on this journey into his past the next June.

[4] Quoted by Beard, *L/J*, II, 92, n. 25.

Along the way he stopped overnight at Canajoharie, where he wrote to his wife:

> This place is redolent of youth. It is now sixteen years since I was here. . . . I have been up the ravine to the old Frey house. . . . I enjoyed this walk exceedingly. It recalled my noble looking, warm-hearted, witty father, with his deep laugh, sweet voice and fine rich eye, as he used to lighten the way, with his anecdote and fun. (*L/J*, III, 41)

This is the earliest intimate reference to the Judge in all of Cooper's surviving letters. But it is more than intimate; it is such a catalogue of merits that I suspect he was introducing his wife to his father in this character for the first time. He may even have been remembering his father in these unequivocally favorable terms for the first time. Less than two years before, he had allowed the hero of *The Headsman* to discover that his father was really noble-looking, warm-hearted, and good—he seems here to make the same discovery for himself. And it is safe to say that the spirit of this thoroughly benevolent father, summoned up on the walk, accompanied him to Cooperstown and psychically oversaw and approved the purchase of the Mansion House.

In that same letter Cooper tells his wife about meeting an aged Dutchman on his walk: ·

> I asked him about the Freys. . . . You are a relation probably?—No; only a very old friend. Are you of these parts?—No. I am from Otsego—a Cooper of Cooperstown. The old Dutchman bowed, eyed me sharply, and muttered—"Ah—you are a Cooper!" I thought he spoke respectfully as if he remembered the time when the name had influence in this region.

The pilgrim did not choose to call himself Fenimore Cooper, the name by which he was known on two continents, but "a Cooper of Cooperstown," which was merely, as his remark about the name's influence reveals, another way of calling himself a descendant of Judge William Cooper. Eight years earlier he had tried to renounce the name, but at the end of his pilgrimage he would become a Cooper of Cooperstown legally, and on this day in Canajoharie he announces that he had already become one psychologically. It was also in June 1834 that J. Fenimore Cooper the novelist painfully announced his retirement in the *Letter to His Countrymen*. This juncture in Cooper's life was an identity crisis similar to the one that immediately preceded his decision to write a novel. Then he had failed precisely as a Cooper of Cooperstown, and he vigorously insisted that his name be kept separate from his new attempt to define himself. Now that new identity, betrayed and traduced, had become a source of mortification, and the older one offered itself as an alternative. On June 30th he wrote Lafayette's son to express his grief at the Marquis' death, his love for the old man, and his conviction that "he has left you a glorious inheritance in his name, as you will soon see" (*L/J*, III, 49). It had taken Cooper nearly a quarter century to reach the same conclusion about *his* father, but thenceforth he never forgot it. The Dutchman's respectful reply obviously flattered him, and after reaching Cooperstown he could happily inform Mrs. Cooper that although "the faces of the people are mostly strangers to me . . . The older inhabitants seem glad to see me" (*L/J*, III, 43). As a Cooper of Cooperstown he had a place. As I have said, this pilgrimage was a direct retreat from his ambitions in the larger community of men, but like any form of regression it had its compensations: if he could not be useful in his generation as an American novelist, he could at least be master in his father's house.

"J. Fenimore Cooper" was still the name with which he signed his letters, but his unvarying superscription became "The Hall, Cooperstown." The Hall itself, which Cooper made even more imposing by remodeling its exterior (the interior he would not change) and raising its roof three

feet, became a sanctuary—associations and memories con-
secrated it, and behind the formal tower that Cooper built
at the gate to its grounds he found refuge. As he wrote Mrs.
Cooper on one of his trips to town, "I am no-where so
happy, as under my own roof" (*L/J*, III, 334); as he wrote
Horatio Greenough in Italy, "Our family circle is our
world" (*L/J*, III, 328). Twice during these years he went on
pilgrimages to other family shrines. In 1836 he visited Burlington to look at the house where he was born, and in
1837, Camden, where a different branch of the Cooper
family was located. In both places he eagerly traces the
lingering presence of his father. "In my wanderings" at
Burlington, he wrote his wife, "I asked an old man who was
blind, eighty years old, and who was seated on the stoop
of an old fashioned brick-house, if he had ever known William Cooper?" (*L/J*, III, 225). At Camden he called on Richard Matlack Cooper, who supplied a trivial episode from
the Judge's past that the son considered worth recording:
"He said my father had come into a counting house in
Philadelphia, when he was a boy, and when he was a clerk,
to purchase something, and for which he signed the receipt.
Seeing the name he introduced himself to him, as a cousin"
(*L/J*, III, 255).

Cooper might have been trying to consolidate his past
because the future remained problematic. Buying the Hall
and some adjoining properties had used up much of his
savings. In 1834 he wrote to his sister, "Thank God, I am
still young, and in the full vigor of both mind and body,
and I do not see but some gentlemanly and suitable occupation may yet offer to take the place of that from which
I am driven by my own country" (*L/J*, III, 34). Soon after
his return from Europe he began once again to speculate,
notably in Michigan land, the contemporary equivalent of
the means by which Judge Cooper had gotten rich, and in
cotton futures. But the early returns were not promising,
and almost immediately Cooper tried to retract the Michigan investment. Ownership of the Judge's house did not

furnish him with the Judge's financial acumen. Cooper's only success had been with his pen. From France in 1833 he had written Greenough: "The tales are done. There are a few half finished manuscripts on other subjects to finish, and I turn sailor again—or something else" (*L/J*, ii, 384). Cooper never threw away a manuscript, and his repudiation of the novel did not mean he could not publish. To America he brought the nearly completed manuscript of the satire on which he had been working since about 1830, and extensive notes on his travels in Europe. *The Monikins* was rapidly concluded; published in 1835, it received, and deserved, very bad reviews and had almost no sale at all. The journals he had kept while living in and travelling through Switzerland, France, Belgium, Germany, England, and Italy were hastily reworked and published as five books between 1836 and 1838; there are many good moments in each of them, but these also failed to find a public. His annual receipts had all but disappeared, and no other occupation had yet offered. His publishers, who had grown restless with the long string of travel books, kept prompting him to return to fiction, but Cooper reiterated his determination not to write for a country that repaid him so badly. It was perhaps fortunate that his countrymen soon inflicted a new injustice on him, one that made it impossible for him to remain silent.

The trouble started in Cooperstown, in July 1837. Three years earlier Cooper had officially become the executor of Judge William Cooper's will. One of its devises left an acre of land on Lake Otsego, called the Three Mile Point or Myrtle Grove, in common to all of the Judge's descendants until 1850, when it would belong to the youngest William Cooper alive. That Cooper's father would seek, by means of this kind of economic coercion, to secure for as long as it was feasible such a firm place in the minds of his posterity adds to our sense of his character, and adds still more to our understanding of Cooper's attempt, in 1826, to change his name, and of course the name of *his* descendants, to

Fenimore—it emphasizes the extent to which, as Cooper would have realized at the time, he was rebelling against his father's stated wishes.

During his life the Judge had reserved this part of his patent as a picnic and fishing spot for his family. A number of parties had been held on the Three Mile Point during James's youth, but the founder of Cooperstown had also allowed his villagers to use the spot freely, and thirty years after his death many assumed that he had somehow given it to the community. Upon his return to Cooperstown, Cooper later said, he took pains to correct this error:

> and this so much the more, because my recollection carried me back to a time when this very acre of land, next to the paternal dwelling, and the enclosure in which we buried our dead, was considered *family property*; sacred to the feelings which such associations and uses would be likely to generate. My father's will showed that he so esteemed it also. (*L/J*, IV, 270-71)

This passage is from another of the *Brother Jonathan* letters, published on April 9th, 1842. Attempting to explain the true relationship between himself and the Effingham Novels, Cooper gives the most explicit account of his motives and actions in what became known as the Point controversy. According to him, the quarrel began with an act almost of sacrilege: in 1837 some people "went upon this Point, and cut down a tree that had a *peculiar association with my father*" (*L/J*, IV, 271).[5] Cooper's first response was to send a mildly worded notice to the local paper, "cautioning the public against injuring the trees." The public,

[5] Nowhere does Cooper explain the association, but Susan mentions a beech tree on the Point with "the initials of my Grandfather and Grandmother, W-C. and E-C., cut in the bark" (*Correspondence*, I, 18). Susan does not say if this beech was the tree that the villagers cut down, only that "it has long since vanished," but at this point in his life Cooper could very well have associated such a tree exclusively with his father—it was not his mother's will that he had committed himself to execute.

however, heard of the notice before it could be printed, and according to Cooper's account, "this was followed by menaces and messages that induced me to withdraw the first card, and to publish *a simple, ordinary notice of a warning against trespassing.*"

Here we have another example of Cooper's psychic reflex to opposition: the threats only strengthened his need to resist. I have said that this behavioral characteristic was formed at home in the son's reaction to a domineering father. But in this case, Cooper was not trying to preserve his selfhood in the face of his father's will, but to defend his father's will in the face of the public. Self, he repeatedly maintained, formed no part of his motive: "I acted, principally, in all I did, as the executor of an estate" (*L/J*, IV, 85). In a letter to James Kirke Paulding, Cooper amplified this construction of his actions: "The affair of the 'Point' has been generally misconceived. . . . the real question has been for the ownership. It is not *mine*, but I am appointed by my father, to protect it for a descendant who will inherit it in 1850" (*L/J*, III, 379-80). Now, Cooper became the executor of his father's estate only because his four older brothers were dead, and in no legitimate sense was he appointed by Judge Cooper to protect the Three Mile Point. But in just this exaggerated way did Cooper view the quarrel. When the villagers, on the basis of their belief that the Judge had left them the land, called upon Fenimore Cooper to honor the bequest, he bought several columns in the Cooperstown *Freeman's Journal* to make known the facts. On one point he did agree with his neighbors: "It *is* proper that the son should carry out the *intention* of the father, and it is precisely for this reason that I am determined that these persons shall not possess Myrtle Grove" (*L/J*, III, 283). Without ever acknowledging the contradiction, Cooper here affirms a new doctrine. Earlier it would have been more proper for the son to stand up for himself.

As we shall see, this complex reorientation of his unconscious attitudes and impulses is the latent theme of the Effingham Novels. On July 6th, in the midst of the Point controversy, Cooper wrote Bentley about the freak idea that had suddenly seized him, and in *Brother Jonathan* he said that "it was precisely on account of this affair that Homeward Bound and Home As Found were written, at all" (*L/J*, IV, 269).

Not until September, however, did he begin writing. The people of Cooperstown, or at least a portion of them, responded more quickly. The day Cooper's notice appeared they called a public meeting to declare that they owned the Point and they would visit it whenever they wanted. A set of resolutions was duly passed to proclaim these spurious rights. One ordered the trustees of the village library "to remove all books of which Cooper is the author, from said Library."[6] Many at the meeting, it seems, were in favor of burning the books. They might have done better to read them, especially *The Pioneers*. Natty Bumppo's case against the private ownership of land is poetically just and convincing, and Cooper's representation of the Prevosts' claims in the person of Oliver Effingham throws a legal doubt on the right of Judge Temple-Cooper to any of the property at Otsego. In *Notions of the Americans* the villagers could have found additional support for their cause: Cooper's European traveller spends a night in Cooperstown, and after naming *The Pioneers* as a faithful description of the early life of the settlement, goes on to state that the vicinity's "academies, churches, towns, and, in short, most things which an advanced state of civilization can produce" are not as in Europe the work of one autocrat, but rather "the spontaneous work of the population."[7] Had they bothered to read this passage, the population at Cooperstown could have cited it to Cooper and asked for the Point as the fruit of their own labor.

But Cooper had already decided to issue a revised version of his father's accomplishments. Even before the quarrel,

[6] Quoted by Beard, *L/J*, III, 285.   [7] *Notions*, I, 256.

he had commenced a pamphlet titled *Chronicles of Coop-erstown*, which was printed in Cooperstown in 1838. In the Introduction he gives his love for the place as his reason for compiling its history, but Otsego's physical features are barely noticed—the descriptions in *The Pioneers* are much more loving. Instead, Cooper seems chiefly concerned with setting his record straight. He minutely recounts the trans-actions by which William Cooper acquired George Cro-ghan's patent; missing from his account are all the ambi-guities that make "Cooper's acquisition of this tract," as L. H. Butterfield notes, "a labyrinthine chapter of land and legal history" that is unclear even today.[8] Cooper mentions the Prevosts' claims against the estate only to dismiss them: "The proceedings connected with this law suit, lasted sev-eral years, when they were discontinued in consequence of the statute of limitations . . . [but] there can be no doubt that had the issue been tried on its merits, the defendants would have prevailed."[9]

Nor does he have any doubts about William Cooper's share in the history of the region: "To the enterprise, energy and capacity of this gentleman, the county of Otsego is more indebted for its rapid settlement, than to those of any other person" (p. 59). The spontaneous work of the popu-lation is unchronicled, the population itself referred to spe-cifically only once: "John Miller is now . . . the oldest liv-ing settler. . . . James White a carpenter, . . . is the next oldest settler, and Joseph Baldwin, cooper, is the third; the fourth male is James Fenimore Cooper, Esquire" (p. 72). About his neighbors in general, Cooper has this to say:

Few persons visit [Cooperstown] without acknowledg-ing the beauties of its natural scenery and the general

[8] L. H. Butterfield, "Judge William Cooper (1754-1809): A Sketch of His Character and Accomplishment," *New York History* 30 (1949), 389. Albert T. Volwiler gives the Prevosts' side of the case in *George Croghan and the Westward Movement*, pp. 328-32.

[9] *Chronicles of Cooperstown* (1838); rpt. in *A Condensed History of Cooperstown*, by Rev. S. T. Livermore (Albany: J. Munsell, 1862), p. 62.

neatness and decency of the place itself. The floating
population, it is true, has brought in some of that rudeness and troublesome interference which characterizes
the migrating and looser portion of the American people; but a feeling has been awakened among the old
inhabitants that is beginning to repel this innovation,
and we already, in this class, see signs of a return to
the ancient deportment, which was singularly respectable, having been equally free from servile meanness
and obtrusive vulgarity. One or two instances of audacious assumptions of a knowledge of facts and of a right
to dictate, on the part of strangers, have recently met
with rebukes that will probably teach others caution,
if they do not teach them modesty. (pp. 80-81)

This is the sole reference in the pamphlet to the Point controversy, the major instance of such audacity, which Cooper
blamed entirely on the newcomers. "I have inquired," he
later wrote in reference to the public meeting assembled
to defy him, "and I cannot find that a single person was
present . . . who ever saw Judge Cooper!" (L/J, IV, 272).
Never having seen Judge Cooper put these immigrants outside the pale of that special community who had directly
communicated with the founder. The original settlers and
their children, Cooper suggests, form the real Cooperstown,
and for them the *Chronicles* was written (p. 10). Behind the
impersonal prose of that pamphlet can be sensed Cooper's
attempt to trace the true apostolic succession, the men, including James Fenimore Cooper, Esquire, who had inherited the founder's mission, men who would recognize an
appeal on behalf of "the ancient deportment." Of course,
one attribute of that deportment was respect for the per-
quisites of the Mansion House. Now that the founder's
house is reoccupied, Cooper seems to be saying, the traditional values will reassert themselves: "On the whole, the
feeling of the community is sound, and is little disposed to
tolerate this interference with the privileges of those who

have acquired rights by time and a long connection with the place" (p. 81). So he believed at the time he wrote the *Chronicles.* It was only a matter of months, however, before he realized that he was wrong—that a further rebuke would be necessary, and that he could depend on no one but himself to deliver it.

Unlike his father, the landlord, judge, and congressman, the retired novelist had no real power, no social authority, and certainly no disposition for physical violence. In a similar position, the Judge would have confronted his opponents directly: for example, when William Cooper once quarreled with another Federalist who had won his seat in Congress, the two men decided the personal issue with a wrestling match in the street. On the issue raised by the Point controversy, Fenimore Cooper felt that he was compelled to fight "since, to my sailor-like notions, it is defending liberty, to resist ag[g]ression any where, and most of all aggression, in a republic, that assumes to come from the community" (*L/J*, IV, 85). But the weapons he was capable of using were more sophisticated, and less manly, than either the sailor's or the Judge's. Cooper could have attended that public meeting to face his accusers and perhaps settle the matter on the spot, but the two ways by which he chose to act both distanced him from the enemy and prolonged the quarrel for a number of years. It seems that he preferred to sacrifice the time to gain the distance.

One of Cooper's responses was new. In August he decided to bring libel suits against three New York editors—Elias Porter Pellet, Thurlow Weed, and Andrew Barber—who had misrepresented the facts and slandered Cooper in their coverage of the dispute. These would be the first of many such suits, and the actions were not completed until the mid-1840s. For this reason I shall postpone an analysis of Cooper's motives in initiating and prosecuting these trials, but it is worth noting that by moving this part of his battle into court Cooper was arming himself with, and at the same time shielding himself behind, the law. Both the Three

162

Mile Point and the courtroom were properly speaking his father's territory.

Writing was the territory that Cooper had staked out for himself. Consistently, as in the French finance controversy or the circumstances of his retirement, he had recourse to the written word to explain and defend his behavior; he employed his pen as his means of acting upon the world. Cooper was a tireless, if tiresome, polemicist, another way of saying that he felt more comfortable in his library than in public. After his return from Europe he spent as little time as possible in the presence of people, declining even a proposal by some of his friends for a homecoming dinner to match the farewell affair. Along with Irving, also lately back from the continent, and William Cullen Bryant, Cooper made the third in the triumvirate of leading American literary figures at this period. But the novelist played his part in the life of American letters *in absentia*, from the study of "The Hall, Cooperstown." During the several years of his career that preceded his expatriation, he had enthusiastically and gregariously participated in whatever of cultural and intellectual society New York City could provide, and had himself founded "The Bread and Cheese Club" in 1823 to give the city's artists, thinkers, and high-toned businessmen a table around which they could assemble once a week to argue over matters of the moment. Bryant, five years younger than Cooper and new at the time to the city, first met him at one of these lunches, and remembered "being struck with the inexhaustible vivacity of his conversation."[10] All such gatherings, however, all the social life of America's minds, Cooper now shunned. So exclusively did he limit his contacts to relatives and very old friends that among other litterateurs he acquired the reputation of a recluse.

In a letter dated November 15th, 1833, he indicates one reason for this withdrawal: "I have been but once in what

10 Bryant, "Discourse," *Precaution*, p. xvii.

may be called society since my return, and then I was attacked by a man young enough to be my son and who was never out of sight of the smoke of his father's chimney for thinking like an American" (*L/J*, III, 11). To spare himself such attacks he retreated to Cooperstown, making his family circle his world. But the Point controversy was an assault by Cooperstown upon himself and his family. In response Cooper wielded the written word: a notice in the paper was replaced by a stronger notice; the facts were made public in print. At the end of his first column in the *Freeman's Journal* Cooper boldly proclaimed, "So far as my means allow, insult shall be avenged by the law, violence repelled by the strong hand, falsehood put to shame by truth, and sophistry exposed by reason" (*L/J*, III, 282). The strong hand, however, held only a pen.

Cooper decided to expose the sophistry of his opponents, and all other Americans who felt as they did, by publishing *The American Democrat* (1838). Besides its title, the book is in many respects similar to Tocqueville's *Democracy in America* (the publication of Tocqueville's two volumes bracketed Cooper's work), although *The American Democrat*, strongly spiced with Cooper's indignation about events at home, is less analytical and more hortatory. Like Tocqueville, Cooper reports that just because a republic is free from a monarchical ruler does not mean it is free from tyrannical rule; it simply means that "tyranny can only come from the publick, in a democracy."[11] But the American, for obvious reasons of his own, is insistent where the Frenchman is incisive: "It ought to be impressed on every man's mind," urged Cooper, "in letters of brass, '*That, in a democracy, the publick has no power that is not expressly conceded by the institutions. . . . All beyond this, is oppression, when it takes the character of acts, and not unfrequently when it is confined to opinion*'" (pp. 139-

[11] *The American Democrat* (1838; rpt. New York: Minerva Press, 1969), p. 138.

40). And when he focuses on religion in America, Cooper abandons any pretense of disinterested social analysis. Though he omits the italics and letters of brass, he closes the article "On Religion" with words carved by the Almighty on stone: "Thou shalt not covet thy neighbor's house; thou shalt not covet thy neighbor's wife; nor his man-servant, nor his maid-servant, nor his ox, nor his ass, nor any thing that is thy neighbor's" (pp. 180-81). Including, of course, his land on Lake Otsego.

"Carper" may be more accurate than "critic" as a description of the way in which Cooper responded to contemporary American society; much of *The American Democrat* is the product of his spleen. Nonetheless, the points at which Cooper's analysis of the social forces within a democracy accords with Tocqueville's are extremely suggestive and insightful. Though it appears doubtful, it is possible that Cooper had read at least part of the Frenchman's study. He knew French very well, and in any case Volume One of *Democracy in America* had been translated into English in 1835. No one, however, has made this connection, and certainly Cooper could have earned all of his insights from his own experience. Perhaps the most important, beyond question the most heartfelt, of the Frenchman's indictments of American life in that first volume is contained in the chapter titled "Unlimited power of the majority in the United States, and its consequences." Tocqueville's conclusions there are as ominous as this title indicates they would be. One of his most arresting phrases refers to "the tyranny of the majority," and the combined testimony of Tocqueville's book, and Cooper's, and Cooper's life on this subject reinforces the validity of each man's argument. From all the sources, one learns that power in the hands of the public is potentially much more omnipotent than any other kind of political authority. If a monarch can only compel physical obedience, a majority can additionally compel intellectual subservience, can not merely insist that individuals submit to its laws, but can also drive them by main force into the camp of its opinions. "The constant appeals to public opinion in a democracy," wrote Cooper,

> though excellent as a corrective of public vices, induce private hypocrisy, causing men to conceal their own convictions when opposed to those of the mass. . . . A want of national manliness is a vice to be guarded against, for the man who would dare to resist a monarch, shrinks from opposing an entire community. (p. 63)

When we call this public pressure by a more familiar name —for example, the passion for conformity—we can immediately see how well the charge brought by these two men stands up against the course of America's cultural history. This is an indictment against democracy that none of America's defenders have been able to dismiss.

One paragraph in Tocqueville's analysis specifically applies his conclusion to the lot of an American author, and though he seems to mean particularly a *philosophe* (an understandable emphasis in a Frenchman), what he says is worth quoting in the context of Cooper's career as a *romancier*:

> In America, the majority raises very formidable barriers to the liberty of opinion: within these barriers an author may write whatever he pleases, but he will repent it if he ever step beyond them. Not that he is exposed to the terrors of an auto-da-fé, but he is tormented by the slights and persecutions of daily obloquy. His political career is closed for ever, since he has offended the only authority which is able to promote his success. Every sort of compensation, even that of celebrity, is refused to him. Before he published his opinions, he imagined he held them in common with others; but no sooner has he declared them openly, than he is loudly censured by his over-bearing opponents, whilst those who think, without having the cour-

age to speak, like him, abandon him in silence. He
yields at length, oppressed by the daily efforts he has
been making, and he subsides into silence, as if he was
tormented by remorse for having spoken the truth.

This account is hypothetical, and not all its hypotheses apply equally well to Cooper. Having realized that he had run
up against the kind of barriers here described, Cooper refused to back off in silence—instead he picked up his pen
and began writing all over the walls. But the problem he
confronted at this time seems to me a representatively American one. We need not take Tocqueville's speculative word
for its existence, nor Cooper's busy actions; we also have the
evidence of the lives of other American authors.

Common sense indicates that a writer depends particularly upon the support of public opinion: unless opinion
decides that he is a good writer, or an entertaining one, his
work will be denied a public. Of course every writer, except
a solipsist with independent means of support, is in this
position. But the situation of the nineteenth century American writer was significantly different from, for example, his
counterpart in England. If he chose, a British writer could
address his work to a specific class within his country. That
choice was unavailable to an American: opinion belonged
to the vast, classless majority. In addition, since Americans
generally subscribed to the democratic belief that the majority was not just the most equitable body for determining
political questions, but the final arbiter of all moral, cultural, and even aesthetic ones—since, in short, the majority
was not just rightly absolute, but absolutely right—the
American writer was especially vulnerable to its verdicts.
The most facile but effective way for a nineteenth century
American literary critic to make an adverse case against an
author was simply to say that his books did not sell. It
would have required the most strenuous intellectual effort
on the part of a writer to emancipate himself from the rea-
soning behind this kind of belief. To the extent that he
called himself a democrat, he had to be prepared to accept

the public's judgment of his work. And almost to the extent that he called himself an American at all, he had to call himself a democrat.

Walt Whitman was a writer who defined himself by his Americanness and his faith in democracy, and the last sentence of the Preface to his first edition of *Leaves of Grass* (1855) shows the extreme of an American author's dependency upon his readers. "The proof of a poet," Whitman wrote, "is that his country absorbs him as affectionately as he has absorbed it." Confident was he in 1855 that his country would embrace his verses. When, despite his best efforts to promote its sale, *Leaves of Grass* was initially ignored and eventually condemned as "immoral," Whitman had to work very hard to reconcile this reception with his democratic creed. He did manage to overcome this rebuff from his contemporaries—but how many American writers did not! The literary history of the last century is littered with names, which we now pronounce respectfully, that belong however to men whose careers suffered drastically from their failure to reach or to keep an audience. Brockden Brown, Herman Melville, Nathaniel Hawthorne, Mark Twain, Henry James—these are all different men, who wrote in response to different needs and events; but one thing they all have in common is that when certain of their works failed to find their countrymen's favor, they found it incredibly difficult to keep writing. Some even, as Tocqueville had prophesied, subsided into silence. Simply because he did not capitulate, we should admire Cooper's dogged courage to write in the face of what he considered a similar repulse—admire it even while we try to understand its causes.

As Tocqueville looked about him at America's institutionalized equality of conditions, he concluded that "a new science of politics is indispensable to a new world." For his part, Cooper was not prepared to undertake the same reevaluation of his beliefs: familiar words in his vocabulary, words like tyranny and oppression, are simply redirected at an unfamiliar enemy, from the class of rulers to the people themselves. Defining his stance in a letter to a newspaper, Cooper said, "I resist the tyranny I find in the country: not that which exists in distant lands" (*L/J*, IV, 202). What mattered was resisting. Lounsbury succinctly describes the state of Cooper's mind: "The people were the source of power; and it was his cardinal principle that power ought always to be censured rather than flattered."[12] And though its source was different, the threat to Cooper was the same one he had struggled against in adolescence and in the 1820s—that by failing to resist domination he would lose his identity. In *The American Democrat* he asserts the dogma that "individuality is the aim of political liberty" (p. 174). To preserve his individuality he had actually and ideologically quarreled with an overbearing father and he was equally ready to quarrel with every one of his country-men.

Because it did not have the interest of a tale, *The American Democrat* was neither published in Europe nor purchased in America. Still committed to the written word, Cooper felt that he had to carry his struggle to the wider audience that only fiction would command. *The American Democrat* would be rewritten as a novel about democracy in America, with particular emphasis on demagoguery in Cooperstown. "Templeton in 1837" was his working title: "This may not be the name," he told Bentley, "but it gives the idea" (*L/J*, III, 269). The idea was basically to use the international constituency formed by his readers to give the world the true version of the Three Mile Point affair. Having been slandered by the newspaper reports,

> I determined to use such means to defend myself, as chance put in my power. . . . It was not easy, however, to make a book out of this one transaction, but it could be introduced as an incident of an ordinary tale, so as to answer all my purposes. The necessary machinery

12 Lounsbury, p. 162.

stood ready made to my hands, in the Pioneers, that
book having the *real scene* [i.e. Cooperstown], with fictitious characters [the Effinghams]; and all I had to do,
was to connect the characters and scenes of the two
works, in a way to meet the probabilities of a fiction.
. . . This is the simple history of the conception of the
two novels. *(L/J,* IV, 274)

According to this account, from a *Brother Jonathan* letter,
Cooper repopulated Templeton and created a contemporary
generation of Oliver Effingham and Elizabeth Temple's descendants as an economy measure. Connecting the characters and scenes of the earlier novel to the new one, however,
did not prove as easy as he had anticipated, and the history
of the conception of the Effingham Novels is not that simple.

In place of the one tale that Cooper had planned and
contracted for, he wrote two. As he said in the Preface to
Homeward Bound, that novel actually ends where it was
supposed to begin:

> It was commenced with a sole view to exhibit the pres-
> ent state of society in the United States, through the
> agency, in part, of a set of characters with different pe-
> culiarities, who had freshly arrived from Europe, and
> to whom the distinctive features of the country would
> be apt to present themselves with greater force.[13]

Instead, it takes the travellers the whole novel to cross the
Atlantic, and American society is deferred to a sequel. Sequels did not usually sell well, and neither Cooper nor his
publishers were happy about this change: Bentley reduced
his payment for *Home As Found,* and in the Preface to the
second book Cooper conceded, "We are fully aware of the
disadvantage of dividing the interest of a tale in this manner; but in the present instance, the separation has been

[13] *Homeward Bound,* p. v. When additional references to the Effingham Novels are cited in my text, *Homeward Bound* will be abbreviated as *"HB"* and *Home As Found* as *"HAF."*

produced by circumstances over which the writer had very little control" (*HAF*, p. v.). This is an unusual admission, and it is difficult to understand what circumstances Cooper had in mind. In February 1837 Bentley had written him to "indulge the hope" that the novelist would shortly begin a new "Work of Fiction"—"either a story of the Sea, or of the Back Woods,"[14] but Cooper's letters from the period he was working on *Homeward Bound* (September to December 1837) indicate that he alone was responsible for its contents. Perhaps to please Bentley, his original intention was to make the novel "half sea half shore": "One volume on board a London Packet, another at *Templeton*" (*L/J*, III, 295). While he was writing, however, he decided it should be two-thirds sea, and finally, that it would be "all sea": "I found it impossible," he apologized to Bentley in January 1838, "to do my plot justice in the narrow limits I had left myself" (*L/J*, III, 305). Therefore the first novel Cooper published after his retirement somehow wrote itself, and we have already learned to look closely whenever Cooper explains his actions as adventitious or beyond his control.

Another passage from the section "On Individuality" in *The American Democrat* provides an epigraph for my analysis of this unplanned novel. There is one qualification that Cooper attaches to his concept of individuality:

> An entire distinct individuality, in the social state, is neither possible nor desirable. Our happiness is so connected with the social and family ties as to prevent it; but, if it be possible to render ourselves miserable by aspiring to an independence that nature forbids, it is also possible to be made unhappy by a too obtrusive interference with our individuality. (p. 175)

"Templeton in 1837" was planned as a book about the ways in which American society tries to interfere with individual rights. That is one subject of *Home As Found. Homeward*

---

[14] Quoted by Beard, *L/J*, III, 249, n. 2.

Bound, however, is preoccupied with the force of family ties and the misery of aspiring to an independence that nature forbids, a subject with which Cooper was very familiar. He had struggled to free himself completely from the Judge, but now he considered victory undesirable as well as unattainable, now he wanted literary testimony to his efforts to carry out his father's "will." Yet before he could castigate the villains of the Point affair, men, he said in the *Freeman's Journal*, "who would rudely thrust themselves, between a parent and his children!" (*L/J*, iii, 278), it was imaginatively necessary to reconcile himself with that parent. Fulfilling this psychological prerequisite meant that the Effinghams' homecoming had to be delayed.

As published, *Homeward Bound* can be characterized as half a comedy of manners and half a narrative of adventure. It is set almost entirely at sea, but Cooper uses the nautical environment, as he wrote a friend, "quite in a new way" (*L/J*, iii, 300). On board the packet *Montauk* are the Effinghams, cousins Edward (Ned) and John (Jack) and Ned's daughter Eve; after twelve years in Europe they are homeward bound to the family estate in Templeton. Among the other passengers are three men travelling under false names—a bogus Sir George Templemore, a Mr. Blunt (who does not himself know his true name), and a Mr. Sharp (the real Templemore). The master of the packet is Captain Truck, whose comic foible is introducing people. Identity thus becomes a major theme in the novel. One character whose name is both his own and apposite is Steadfast Dodge, Yankee, editor of the *Active Inquirer*, New York neighbor of the Effinghams, and the caricatured embodiment of every American vice that Cooper could think of. Dodge and the Effinghams are the central figures in the book's humorless comedy of manners. For most of the novel's first half the London packet functions as a sea-going drawing room, in which Cooper stiffly poses the Effinghams as the model of all refinement, and rather desperately sets Steadfast Dodge up as a target for all his complaints against his vulgar neighbors and the nosy newspaper editors. Halfway through the novel the *Montauk* should have reached America, where Cooper would have transferred the drawing room ashore and continued to vivisect his countrymen's manners. In his chapter on *Homeward Bound* in *Studies in Classic American Literature*, D. H. Lawrence does a wonderful job of interpreting the book that Cooper intended to write. But at the novel's midpoint (which may have been as far as Lawrence got in it) the ship is still on the far side of the ocean, and *Homeward Bound* begins to plot its own course. The Effinghams and Dodge have subordinate roles in the second half; the analysis of society is replaced by a narrative of adventure.

The adventures seem straightforward. The novel is subtitled *The Chase*, which begins immediately. As the *Montauk* leaves Portsmouth a British cruiser follows in pursuit. No one knows why, but Captain Truck, worried about charges of tobacco smuggling, is not disposed to submit to a boarding in peacetime. Driven far off its course by the chase and later by a storm, dismasted by a freak of wind, the packet winds up on the coast of Africa. To refit the ship the crew and passengers go ashore, where they are surrounded by hundreds of hostile natives who threaten to plunder the ship and sell the whites into slavery. But the *Montauk*'s party defeats the Arabs and manages to get up a set of jury-masts. After all this, they reach Sandy Hook only to discover that the cruiser, last seen at the height of the gale, is waiting for them. Anchored in American waters, Truck finally allows the British captain to come aboard, and the reader at last learns the reason for the chase.

Homeward Bound does prove that the five years in retirement had not weakened Cooper's narrative skills. The several excitements—the pursuit, the storm, the battle—are competently handled. Yet we may wonder why such a conventional series of adventures forced Cooper from his avowed literary purpose: depicting the infamy of the Point controversy "as an incident of an ordinary tale." This ex-

plicitly happens in *Home As Found*, when Edward Effingham asserts his title to the "Fishing Point." But just as
interesting is the way in which Cooper's complicated feelings about the controversy reveal themselves in *Homeward
Bound*. Far from being irrelevant, the action of this novel
is in fact an emotional scenario, a transcript of Cooper's
state of mind. The most obvious example, although Cooper
himself appears not to have been conscious of its meaning,
is the fight with the Arabs for possession of the *Montauk*,
which is an imaginative transmutation of the struggle over
a piece of land in Cooperstown.

Leaving the packet in a natural harbor, Truck, the crew
and most of the passengers take the ship's boats up the
coast several miles to the beached wreck of a Danish vessel,
where they hope to equip themselves with its rigging. Only
the Effinghams, Mr. Sharp, and Mr. Blunt remain on board.
Though everyone is aware of the imminent danger of an
attack by the natives, no weapons are left with the *Montauk*. When masses of Arabs begin gathering around her,
the Effinghams and their friends are forced to escape at
night in the launch. After several hours of aimless drifting
and a couple of perfunctory "close calls," the launch joins
Truck and the others returning with the spars from the
wreck. By this time, Truck is informed, the Arabs are in
command of his ship. The vastly outnumbered whites have
two alternatives: try to reach the Cape Verde Islands in
the boats or put up a fight for the *Montauk*. Like Cooper,
Truck believes in taking the path of most resistance; having
offered his passengers a chance to leave, he announces that
he intends to fight: "The nature of a seaman is to stick by
his ship, and of a ship to be treated like a vessel, and not
to be ransacked like a town taken by storm" (*HB*, p. 390).
Everyone but Dodge readily agrees to stand with him. Their
rallying cry is "The Montauk and our own!" (*HB*, p. 395).
The men are armed, the boats arranged in a line, and the
attack begins. "An order had been given," Cooper says, "to
fire the first shot over the heads of the barbarians" (*HB*,

p. 396), but the Arabs shoot first—"This assault changed the plan," and a fierce volley is fired directly into their midst.

Just as Cooper's first notice warning the public about mistreating the Point was replaced by a stronger one after he was "menaced" by some of the villagers, so the barbarians' bullets only make the *Montauk's* men more determined to retake their own. Working unconsciously, Cooper allowed the packet to fall into the hands of the Arabs solely to be able to depict its recapture, and in doing so he reveals the psychic rewards which a fantasy, in this case a legitimate (i.e. artistic) fantasy can provide. In real life, as we have noted, Cooper was incapable of confronting his opponents; in the world of his imagination, however, he was less circumscribed. By replacing a group of men in Cooperstown with a horde of nameless Arabs, he could characterize the people who tried to take something that did not belong to them as coarse, foul-smelling, foul-looking barbarians, epithets he could not hurl at his neighbors. The pitched battle —"Men fell at this discharge; but how many was never known" (*HB*, p. 396)—proves that vicariously Cooper could be more violent than his father in defending his honor. Necessarily, Edward Effingham's defense of the Point in *Home As Found* is quiet and dignified; it had to conform to reality. But in the first Effingham Novel Cooper could appropriate the conventions of a genre to his own end, could satisfy his readers' appetite for adventure at the same he fulfilled his buried impulses. His imagination gave him a glorious triumph: by means of the pen, violence was repelled by the strong hand.

In this wishful version of the Point controversy, Edward Effingham, the man Cooper's contemporaries recognized as the author, properly remains with his daughter instead of joining the fray. It is Captain Truck, a fellow sailor and the true "owner" of the *Montauk*, whom Cooper invests with his own emotions. When the Arabs on deck are raked with cannon fire they promptly abandon ship—" 'Hurrah!'

shouted Captain Truck; 'that grist has purified the old bark! And now to see who is to own her! "The thieves are out of the temple," as my good father would have said'" (*HB*, p. 398). Truck's words about repossessing his ship echo Cooper's about buying back his father's house: five years earlier, we may remember, he wrote his nephew about driving the Jews from the Temple. To Cooper, the Three Mile Point was similarly sacred: "The recollections associated with the spot," he said in the *Freeman's Journal*, "the records on its trees, the scenes of my boyhood, produce on me, who stand, as it were, between the present and the past, sensations that no man of sentiment will require language to explain" (*L/J*, III, 278). Suddenly made a man of sentiment himself, Truck seems to feel the same way about the *Montauk*:

> The instant Captain Truck retrod the deck of his ship was one of uncontrollable feeling with the weather-beaten old seaman. . . . he sat down on the coamings of the main hatch, and fairly wept like an infant. So high had his feelings been wrought that this outbreaking was violent, and the men wondered to see their gray-headed, stern, old commander so completely unmanned. (*HB*, p. 404)

In *Home As Found*, Ned is much calmer during the crisis, preserving a refinement that no doubt Cooper also strove to maintain in public. But I suspect that the vehemence of Truck's "outbreaking" corresponds more closely to Cooper's private reaction.

In 1840, attempting to disprove the identification of Edward Effingham as Fenimore Cooper, the novelist wrote that "I can recall no incident so closely resembling what has happened to myself, as one connected with Capt. Truck" (*L/J*, IV, 86). He repeats this in *Brother Jonathan* (1842), adding that "I never thought of describing myself in Captain Truck!" (*L/J*, IV, 267-68). Cooper's exclamation point indicates how absurd he considered the idea that he had described himself in the captain. As I said, Cooper was not consciously aware of the relationship between the African and the Cooperstown conflicts; his unconscious, working through his imagination, was dictating to his pen. And for this reason he could and did describe more of himself in Truck than he would ever have expressed in his own person, or in the recognizable person of Ned Effingham.

In the thick of the battle Truck quotes his "good father," an image that would certainly have been in the back of Cooper's mind while he was writing the scene—as an executor he was, after all, fighting his father's battle. Truck's father, as we learn near the middle of the novel, was a priest, and Truck himself a prodigal son: "I ran away from him at twelve, and never passed a week at a time under his roof afterwards" (*HB*, p. 260). Since then he has been at sea, but once the barbarians have been repulsed he begins, apparently for the first time, to repent his youthful transgressions. He tells the Effinghams, "I have always owed my parents a grudge for bringing me up to a dog's life."

> "I had understood [replies Ned] it was a choice of your own, captain."
> "Ay—so far as running away and shipping without their knowledge was concerned, perhaps it was; but then it was their business to begin at the bottom, and to train me up in such a manner that I would not run away. The Lord forgive me, too, for thinking amiss of the two dear old people; for, to be candid with you, they were much too good to have such a son; and I honestly believe they loved me more than I loved myself." (*HB*, pp. 414-15)

If in this passage Truck's feelings toward his parents are still mixed, a few pages later, in one of the strangest scenes in any Cooper novel, the aficionado of introductions is forced to make his own acquaintance in a new identity. One of the passengers, Mr. Monday, has been fatally wounded in the fight. It takes several days for him to die, and throughout this period Truck becomes increasingly anxious. As he tells Blunt, "We must offer the poor man the consolations of religion" (*HB*, p. 412); as captain, Truck feels that this duty is his. His apprehension is caused by his doubts of his adequacy, "seeing that my father was a priest." Cooper prepares the scene carefully, out of all proportion to its contextual significance (cf. *HB*, pp. 414-17 and 420-21), and the scene itself, beside Monday's death-bed, can only be explicated in terms of Cooper's psychic drama.

Quoting his "worthy old father's" advice on such solemn occasions, Truck, accompanied by his first mate Leach, nervously enters the dying man's room. He knows that he must perform his father's office. A few words are exchanged, a passage from the Bible read aloud by Truck, then Leach reminds the captain that they must also pray with Monday. Earlier Truck had confessed that prayer was another part of his childhood that he had left behind (*HB*, p. 261), but now he has to remember his parents' lessons. Cooper describes him struggling to do so with these words:

> The old man looked awkwardly about him, turned the key of the door, wiped his eyes, gazed wistfully at the patient, gave his mate a nudge with his elbow to follow his example, and knelt down with a heart momentarily as devout as is often the case with those who minister at the altar. He retained the words of the Lord's prayer, and these he repeated aloud, distinctly, and with fervor, though not with a literal conformity to the text. Once Mr. Leach had to help him to the word. When he rose, the perspiration stood on his forehead, as if he had been engaged in severe toil. (*HB*, pp. 456-57)

The passage sounds as if it ought to be comic, but I want to suggest that in one respect it is as serious as Cooper could make it. What Truck struggles to accomplish is a reconciliation with the father he had run away from, the

178

father who, like Cooper's, is in heaven. The captain's fervor
and perspiration attest to the severity of Cooper's toil.
Cooper had started this novel for one reason: to demonstrate how well he had obeyed his father's will, how well
he assumed his father's role. First, however, he had to sweat
through this scene. Between its lines, Truck (and Cooper)
are on their knees asking for forgiveness, they are acknowledging the father's authority, they are declaring themselves
to be the father's son. The novelist's account of Truck's
reaction after the Lord's prayer has been said applies equally well to himself:

> The captain rose . . . with the feelings of a man who
> had done his duty, and, from that moment, he had a
> secret satisfaction at having so manfully acquitted him-
> self. Indeed, it has been remarked by those who have
> listened to his whole narrative of the passage, that he
> invariably lays more stress on the scene in the state-
> room, than on the readiness and skill with which he
> repaired the damages sustained by his own ship, . . .
> or the spirit with which he retook her from the Arabs.
> (*HB*, p. 457)

Reading Cooper's whole narrative of the passage homeward
will convince anyone that he also lays the most stress on
the scene in the stateroom, in which the father's blessing
is begged, wrestled for, and received.

There was, however, still one more scene that Cooper had
to write before he was psychically ready to let Edward Effingham set foot on American soil. Pardoned for his prodigality, Truck is allowed the secret satisfaction of successfully
emulating his father. On board the *Montauk* is another
prodigal who must be punished.

After Mr. Monday's death the Atlantic is crossed without
incident until Navesink is in sight, where the British cruiser
that had chased the *Montauk* through the novel's first half
again appears. This time, his ship within the jurisdiction
of the United States, Truck heaves to and the English

captain comes aboard. The real Sir George Templemore,
Mr. Sharp, guesses the reason for the pursuit: "Some one
has been a defaulter," he asks Captain Ducie; "is it not
so?" (*HB*, p. 495). It is—the man who has been masquerad-
ing as Sir George is really Henry Sandon, a minor employee
of the British government. Hoping to find asylum in America, he has absconded with forty thousand pounds of the
exchequer's money. Cooper consistently calls him a "defaulter," a word which can mean embezzler, but which particularly refers to a person who has failed in a duty. Even
more than taking the money, that is Sandon's crime. He is
the only son of the man who originally held the very position that Sandon abused; he got the post, Cooper tells us,
solely "out of respect" for his father's honest service (*HB*,
p. 501). "To identify the fugitive," Captain Ducie is accompanied by Mr. Green, "a cold, methodical man, every
way resembling the delinquent's father, whose office-com-
panion he had been" (*HB*, p. 502). This surrogate father,
when he confronts Sandon, immediately names his real
sin: "What would your upright and painstaking father
have said, had he lived to see his only son in this situation?"

"He is dead!" returned the young man, hoarsely.
"He is dead, and never can know anything about it."
The unhappy delinquent experienced a sense of
frightful pleasure as he uttered these words. (*HB*, p.
508)

But when Sandon pleads for mercy, Green sternly reminds him that he has committed "a crime that might
almost raise your upright father from his grave" (*HB*,
p. 509). Having reached America, Sandon finds retribution
instead of asylum. The cruiser carries him home to England, where, we are informed, he commits suicide before
he can be tried. The long chase across the Atlantic ends
with the arraignment of a man who has defaulted in his
duty as his father's son.
Sandon made himself miserable by illegally aspiring to

an independence that nature forbids. He has been pursued by more than the British government: as he faces Mr. Green, "Guilt, that powerful vindicator of the justice of Providence, as it proves the existence of an inward monitor, conscience, was painfully impressed on [his] countenance" (*HB*, p. 508). I believe that Cooper decided on the details of Sandon's crime only while he was writing the scene— his sense of his own guilt created and punished the defaulter. It was not a coincidence that Sandon chose to hide his identity behind the name *Temple*-more, or rather, that Cooper chose to convict the person who has hidden behind that name of betraying his father. Fifteen years earlier he had called his father Marmaduke Temple. In *The Pioneers* and most of the books that followed he had tried to assert himself by denying his father's achievements and values, going so far in 1826 as to try, as Sandon did, to deny his father's name. Now he was attempting to come home. There is a moment in *Homeward Bound* that perfectly symbolizes his emotional fix. The Effinghams, Sharp, and Blunt have escaped in the launch from the Arabs surrounding the *Montauk*. The night is incredibly dark, and for hours they float in circles, helplessly lost. At last they decide to examine the compasses by striking a light: "These faithful but mysterious guides, which have so long served man while they have baffled all his ingenuity to discover the sources of their power, were, as usual, true to their governing principle" (*HB*, p. 386). On his own return from Europe Cooper was equally lost, his identity uncertain, his future obscure. At some point during this time he found a governing principle for himself—to be again his father's son, a Cooper of Cooperstown. But there was an obstacle in his path homeward; knowing their course does not really help the men in the launch: "Paul [Blunt] was at the helm, steering more by instinct than any thing else, and occasionally nodding. . . . Strange fancies beset men at such moments; and his busy imagination was running over some of the scenes of his early youth" (*HB*, p. 387). Cooper does not elaborate, yet we can imagine the memories that would have beset *him* as he contemplated his return home: his hostility toward the Judge, his ebullitions and prodigalities—these stood between him and his new definition of himself. If in his imaginative version of the homeward journey one man, Truck, is reconciled with his father, Cooper's conscience demanded that another, Templemore-Sandon, be condemned for failing his father. With his own rebellion thus self-punished (even as "Templemore" takes his own life), Cooper was free to assert publicly the bond between William and James Fenimore Cooper. The Effinghams could now go back to Templeton.

When they get there, a third of the way through *Home As Found*, Ned voices what was doubtless Cooper's initial response to his homecoming: "What a lovely spot!" he sighs, standing on Mount Vision and looking over the lake and the village, with the Mansion House squarely at its center. "This is truly a place where one might fancy repose and content were to be found for the evening of a troubled life" (*HAF*, p. 151). To find this security Cooper had fallen back on his past, but he learned almost as quickly as Edward Effingham that in the outside world the past was not there to fall back on. Ned has only been in his house, called "the Wigwam" in the novel, a few minutes before he must chase away a group of boys noisily playing ball on his lawn, and a little later he is informed that the village barber he had sent for would rather not make a special trip to the Wigwam to shave him. For Ned, these are not trifles: "Here Mr. Effingham rose . . . and went to his own room, doubting, in his own mind, from all that he had seen, whether this was really the Templeton he had known in his youth, and whether he was in his own house or not" (*HAF*, p. 185).

This confusion may seem like an overreaction, but after all, Judge Temple's commands had always been obeyed promptly and respectfully, and after all, Ned was now installed in Judge Temple's house. The conclusion that Ned reluctantly reaches—that this is not the same Templeton— is actually a comforting one. It would be far worse to conclude that he was not the man Judge Temple had been. And it was, I believe, this unconscious logic that helped convince James Cooper that the home he found was not the one he had left. Or, as cousin Jack puts it, broadening the point of reference, "I have told you, Ned, that you were not to expect the America on your return, that you left behind you on your departure for Europe. I insist that no country has so much altered for the worse in so short a time" (*HAF*, p. 256). This indictment of the nation is the theme of *Home As Found*, which Cooper originally thought of calling "At Home" (*L/J*, III, 305). Needless to say, the book angered its American readers as much as his local behavior on the Point issue angered his neighbors. But throughout all the ruckus that followed its publication, Cooper refused to retract a word, writing in 1840, "I will never excuse myself for having manfully exercised the noblest prerogative of literature, that of exposing the follies and vices of *society*" (*L/J*, IV, 79). At home, Cooper was more constantly aware of the stature of the original owner of his house; where he merely exposed the villagers' trespasses, Judge Cooper, he knew, would have punished them; his frequent use of such words as "manfully" and "manliness" to describe his role in the quarrel with his country indicates how seriously he in fact doubted his manhood.

John Effingham's assertion, which is of course Cooper's, that American civilization has declined so steeply over the last decade does not account for the contradiction between the eulogistic *Notions of the Americans* and the excoriating *Home As Found*. Even the qualities that Cooper then praised are now deprecated. As Lounsbury says, "the change was not really in the people; it was in himself."[15] The world of *Home As Found* is essentially Cooper's projection of his own preoccupations onto an American landscape. Lounsbury cites the seven years Cooper had spent in Europe as a chief reason for his disenchantment with the character

[15] Lounsbury, p. 118.

of life in the United States; a number of passages from the novel, particularly in reference to New York "society," support this conclusion. In addition, the novelist was still disgusted with the nation that had earlier forced him to retire; much of the book is an acrid satire on America's enslavement to foreign opinions. But juxtaposing *Notions* and *Home As Found* brings the most drastic change in Cooper's perspective into relief. The leading motif in the first book is the promise of America's future: each of the European bachelor's reservations is met by Cadwallader's glorious portrayal of what America *will be*. In the second, however, Cooper's strongest complaint against his countrymen is that they are insensitive to their national and individual pasts, that they have broken faith with what America *was*.

Beginning with the jeremiads of the Puritans, the notion that America had failed to live up to the standards of its founding has been a pervasive one in its politics, its religion, and its literature. But the terms of Cooper's indictment are particularly personal; they reveal, I think, more about him as an individual than they do about America as a culture. In the Preface he states the charge generally:

> That the American nation is a great nation, in some particulars the greatest the world ever saw, we hold to be true, and are as ready to maintain as any one can be; but we are also equally ready to concede, that it is very far behind most polished nations in various essentials, and chiefly, that it is lamentably in arrears to its own avowed principles. Perhaps this truth will be found to be the predominant thought, throughout the pages of "Home As Found." (*HAF*, pp. vii-viii)

But once the novel reaches Templeton, he looks at what he has found with a much narrower focus. What he had hoped to find is indicated by the quotation from Bryant that he placed at the head of Chapter Ten, the chapter in which Ned Effingham reoccupies the Wigwam.

"AT HOME"

It is the spot, I came to seek
My father's ancient burial place—
It is the spot—I know it well,
Of which our old traditions tell. (*HAF*, p. 159)

William Cooper's grave of course remains, but in place of
the Americans he had expected, people like the Canajoharie
Dutchman with deep attachments to a locality and its traditions, Cooper discovers a new species of man, "birds of passage," a restless nation of migrants who discount tradition
and put dollar signs on every plot of land. "I don't believe,
sir," one old resident of Templeton tells Captain Truck,
"that in all this region you can find a dozen graves of sons,
that lie near their fathers. Everybody seems to have a mortal
aversion to stability." This circumstantial evidence damns
America in Cooper's eyes: "It is hard," Truck replies, "to
love such a country" (*HAF*, p. 481). And though Ned finds
it so hard even to reside in such a country that at the end
of the novel he is planning a speedy removal to Europe,
an idea the novelist often entertained in his letters from
this period, we know that neither he nor Cooper will ever
stray that far again from the family bones.

As the Effinghams proceed up the Hudson toward Templeton, John, who has recently been back, tries to prepare
the others for the shock of returning. He tells Eve, "When
he reaches his own home, your father will not know even
the names of one-half his neighbors. Not only will he meet
with new faces, but he will find new feelings, new opinions
in the place of traditions that he may love, an indifference
to everything but the present moment" (*HAF*, pp. 137-38).
The representative specimen of this distasteful newness is
Aristabulus Bragg. Self-made as a man, self-taught as a
lawyer, Bragg has a selfish respect for majority opinions
and the main chance. In his eyes, America's greatest virtue
is that it is not weighed down by any economically foolish
sentiment about the past: "The man who should resist an
improvement in our part of the country, on account of his

185

forefathers, would fare badly among his contemporaries" (*HAF*, p. 35). Ned Effingham is exactly that man, but he moves back to a Templeton filled with Aristabulus Braggs. When Fenimore Cooper bought space in the *Freeman's Journal* to explain to his neighbors the way he felt about the Point, he made a distinction between himself and them; he stood, he said, "between the present and the past." In *Home As Found* he unequivocally announces in which of those two directions he is facing:

> In Templeton and its adjacent district, . . . the descendants of the fathers of the country [are] beginning to make a manly stand against the looser sentiment, or the want of sentiment, that so singularly distinguishes the migratory bands. The first did begin to consider the temple in which their fathers had worshipped more hallowed than strange altars; the sods that covered their fathers' heads, more sacred than the clods that were upturned by the plough; and the places of their childhood and childish sports dearer than the highway trodden by a nameless multitude. (*HAF*, pp. 191-92)

From the strange and faceless present Cooper turns away, preferring instead to worship his household gods, and accusing America of a failure to show the proper respect for them.

Actually, what Cooper denounces in the actions of his countrymen is nothing more than what he had himself tried to do. If they resist the rule of the propertied class of gentlemen, had not Cooper earlier counseled that they should? If they insist that their responsibility is toward the future, not the past, had not Cooper earlier upheld the same priority? If they refuse to define themselves as the son of a particular man, had not Cooper earlier attempted to achieve the same independence? Now, however, he could no longer identify with the nation that had betrayed him. America had forced him to find a new bond upon which he could center his affections. Never psychically sturdy enough to be *himself*, he became a Cooper of Cooperstown. As his father's son he had a fresh stake in a particular class and a particular past. As his father's son he chastised the men who claimed to be, or behaved as if they were, nobody's sons. According to John Effingham, here is the most alarming symptom of contemporary America's disease:

> "Look into the first paper that offers, and you will see the young men of the country hardily invited to meet by themselves, to consult concerning public affairs, as if they were impatient of the counsels and experience of their fathers. No country can prosper where the ordinary mode of transacting the business connected with the root of the government, commences with this impiety." (*HAF*, pp. 257-58)

John's contention is characteristically overstated, if not a bit hysterical; yet he is responding to a real and pervasive cultural impulse at large in the America of his time. Two generations after the Founders, most Americans tended to have as little patience as Aristabulus Bragg with an appeal to the authority of the Fathers, of the Past in general. The most eloquent philosopher of Jacksonian egalitarianism, Ralph Waldo Emerson, was also the most persuasive spokesman for this radical impulse. *Home As Found* appeared in 1838. Emerson's first book, *Nature*, had appeared in 1836; in it he laments the hold that the Past has on his age: "It builds the sepulchres of the fathers," he wrote, using a phrase that Cooper would have underscored. Nowhere in any of his writings does Cooper refer to Emerson (though it hardly seems possible that he could have remained oblivious to the Orphic breeze that was blowing from Concord, even in his own intellectual seclusion at Cooperstown), but had he looked into any of Emerson's writings he would have been deeply disturbed. In *Nature*, and in such lectures as "The American Scholar" (1837), Emerson invited the young men of the country to reject all authority but the promptings of their intuition, to build their own world. Thoreau, who was graduated from Harvard in 1837, was one of the young men who accepted Emerson's invitation, and he spoke for many of his contemporaries when he said in *Walden* that "I have lived some thirty years on this planet, and I have yet to hear the first syllable of valuable or even earnest advice from my seniors. They have told me nothing, and probably cannot tell me any thing, to the purpose." Emerson and Thoreau were representative men of the generation whose disrespect for tradition so shocked John Effingham and James Fenimore Cooper.

Of course, Cooper's own attempt in the first half of his career to create a distinctly indigenous literature, to shake off the influence of English ideas on American thought, and his avowed faith in the individual's independence and the nation's future, had anticipated a number of the attitudes which New England's Transcendentalists and New York's Young Americans would take in the 1830s and 1840s. By that time, however, instead of welcoming these trends he stood firmly opposed to them. His unconscious awareness of his complicity in such filial "impiety" only made him a more severe critic of the period's assault on inherited conventions. Exposing the vices of society was not simply the noblest prerogative of literature, it was at the same time a means of assuaging his own guilt. That *Home As Found* would be unpopular did not matter. Unconsciously, he was more concerned with expiating his own sins than with correcting his country's. In fact, his tremendous literary outburst in 1838 (the most prolific year of his career) —*Chronicles of Cooperstown, The American Democrat, Homeward Bound, Home As Found*—can be traced entirely to the same psychic need: in his own mind these four books were necessary to establish his new identity.

Home As Found has no real plot. Cooper apparently felt on such bad terms with his readers that he did not bother to supply one. But it does end with two conventional elements: an uncovered identity and a marriage. In both cases, however, even these stock situations partake of Cooper's latent purpose. The discovery involves the young man who had called himself Paul Blunt on the *Montauk*, who had taken the name Powis, who had been called Assheton as a child, and who is really, it turns out, Paul Effingham, the son of John. The denouement is more than conventionally ludicrous. Cooper had been referring to John as a bachelor through two novels; to make him Paul's father he must abruptly and awkwardly invent a short-lived and secret marriage. Yet psychologically it is appropriate for one of the novel's characters to learn to think of himself as some-one's son—that is what had happened to Captain Truck, that is the new identity Cooper is trying to establish. And the discovery has an additional benefit. The wedding with which *Home As Found* concludes joins Paul to Eve Effingham. By that time they have already become first cousins once removed, and their marriage, though not legally in-cestuous, is perfectly endogamous: the Effinghams—fathers Ned and Jack, children Paul and Eve—close ranks within the walls of the Wigwam, where they can keep family tradi-tions alive and the world at a distance.

In fact, once the ball-players have been thrown off the lawn, the only time the citizens of Templeton seriously penetrate the Effinghams' defenses is during the Fishing Point dispute, which occupies three chapters at the middle of the novel. After the protracted struggle of *Homeward Bound*, however, there was little left for Cooper to say about the incident. It is introduced in an apparently arbi-trary manner: Eve, John, "Blunt," and Templemore are boating on the lake one day when John suddenly warns his cousin's daughter that "the public—the all-powerful, omnip-otent, over-ruling, law-making, law-breaking public—has a passing caprice to possess itself of your beloved Point; and Ned Effingham must show unusual energy, or it will get it!" (*HAF*, p. 236). Informed of this threat, Mr. Effing-ham remains calm—indeed, half a dozen times during the three chapters Cooper emphasizes Ned's steadiness—and acts quickly, although for all his energy he never leaves the Wigwam. Aristabulus Bragg is dispatched into the village to tell the people that they do not own the Point. He returns to report that they defy Ned's claim. Ned's response leaves Bragg "filled with wonder at seeing a man so coolly set about contending with that awful public which he himself as habitually deferred to, as any Asiatic slave defers to his monarch" (*HAF*, p. 239); Ned's response is to write a notice against trespassing and to instruct Bragg to have it published in the local paper. Next evening Bragg is back in the library. The notice, he says, is "awfully unpopular," and he is "staggered" by the way Ned dismisses this dread judgment: "I suppose it is always what you term an unpopular act, so far as the individuals opposed are concerned, to resist aggression" (*HAF*, p. 240). Mr. Effingham could not fight the savage Arabs, but he valiantly challenges the populace in this nonviolent struggle for the Point and his own.

Cooper calls the public's behavior toward Ned an "outrage on all his rights, whether as a citizen or a man" (*HAF*, p. 246). John suggests that his cousin's resistance to their tyranny is analogous to William Tell's to the tyrant Gessler (*HAF*, p. 274). Clearly, the villagers were grossly in the wrong, but since, as Edward often says, no one can affect his legal title to the Point, it is not so clear how they have grossly abused his rights. Like Cooper, but unlike William Tell, Ned will not deign to confront his oppressors, not even to prove his title, and the continued misunderstanding becomes as much his fault as theirs. Beyond question, Cooper wanted it that way. The actual dispute over the land provided Cooper with the opportunity to do two things at once. One was literally carrying out his father's will, by means of which he could reconcile himself with the man he had run away from. But this meant that his antagonism toward his father had to be either repressed or transferred onto a substitute. For this reason, Cooper cast the people of Cooperstown, and later the newspaper editors, in the op-

pressor's role. By resisting them he could submit to his
father without sacrificing any portion of his manhood.
Therefore it was in his best psychic interest that the controversy be prolonged. As long as he could picture himself
standing up to the "all-powerful, omnipotent, over-ruling,
law-making, law-breaking public" it was easier for him to
acknowledge the Judge's authority. "Are you reconciled
with your country?" is the question that almost everyone
asks Eve Effingham (*HAF*, pp. 15 and 85). As far as Cooper
is concerned, the answer is no—reconciling himself with
his father necessarily put him at odds with his country.

Cooper seized upon the Three Mile Point controversy
because it served his various psychic needs so well. In *Home
As Found* the same public meeting is held, the same resolutions passed. As before, Bragg visits Ned in his library to
describe the event:

> "It resolved, sir, that it was your duty to carry out the
> intentions of your father."
> "In that, then, we are perfectly of a mind; as the
> public will most probably discover, before we get
> through with this matter. This is one of the most pious
> resolutions I ever knew the public to pass." (*HAF*, p.
> 250)

The alternation in this statement between obedience to
the father and defiance of the public epitomizes the way
Cooper reoriented his mental energies. Between these two
impulses he found a viable identity.

Almost every line in the four books we have been discussing indicates how thoroughly Cooper redefined his identity. He even calls the Effinghams Federalists, although that
party had long ago ceased to exist (cf. *HB*, pp. 64-67).
There is, however, reason to believe that he was less comfortable with his new role as William Cooper's son than I
have so far suggested. As I have said, the Fishing Point
dispute begins on Lake Otsego when John oracularly announces that the villagers plan to wrest the spot from Ned.

Immediately preceding John's warning, however, Cooper introduces Natty Bumppo's name into the novel.

In their boat, the Effingham party pauses to talk with the "old commodore," a resident figure who has fished the lake for decades, a man who is deeply attached to local tradition. The commodore is the person who evokes the Leatherstocking: "He was a great man! They may talk of their Jeffersons and Jacksons, but I set down Washington and Natty Bumppo as the two only really great men of my time" (*HAF*, p. 229). By intruding this famous product of his imagination into his second novel about Templeton, Cooper subtly, I believe unconsciously, resurrects the moral issues of *The Pioneers*. He is fairly explicit about this. John Effingham tells the commodore that they are on their way to admire the celebrated echoing rocks of Lake Otsego. The commodore replies: "Some people maintain that there is no echo at all, and that the sounds we hear come from the spirit of the Leather-stocking, which keeps about its old haunts, and repeats everything we say, in mockery of our invasion of the woods" (*HAF*, p. 230). In the realm of Cooper's fiction, that invasion had of course been led by Marmaduke Temple. With his parting words, the commodore seems to remind Temple's descendants of how Natty had been driven from his old haunts—"the time has been when we could boast of a Natty Bumppo" (*HAF*, p. 231). In this setting, still inhabited by the defiant figure of the Leather-stocking, the meaning of Eve Effingham's reply to John's eruption a few pages later is ambiguous: "That Point," she says, "has been ours ever since civilized man has dwelt among these hills" (*HAF*, p. 236). Theirs, that is, since the great man Natty Bumppo was forced to flee the oppressive and wasty ways of Judge Marmaduke Temple.

In *The Pioneers* Natty represents the imagined realization of James Cooper's hostility toward his father. His presence at this point in *Home As Found* reveals that Cooper had not entirely overcome that antagonism. Almost the last thing John says before mentioning the threat to the

Point is that "we will now hold a little communion with the spirit of the Leather-stocking" (*HAF*, p. 233). Even in this novel written to demonstrate how well he had done his father's bidding, Cooper could not exorcise the rebellious spirit of the Leather-stocking from his imagination. In fact, the very next novel he wrote is *The Pathfinder*, the penultimate Leather-Stocking Tale. And two years later he again gave literary existence to Natty, returning him in *The Deerslayer* to his old haunts around Lake Otsego.

CHAPTER VI

═══════════════════════════════════════

"KING OF THE WOODS"

═══════════════════════════════════════

ONE OF the lies often printed by Cooper's newspaper critics was that he had abused America in the Effingham Novels in order to insure their sale in Great Britain. Apparently the editors believed this. Richard Bentley, Cooper's English publisher, knew better. The novelist's work as a social commentator appealed only to himself; his readers, whether English or American, bought his books with different expectations, and lately they had not been buying his books at all. Bentley also knew what those readers wanted. On April 6th, 1839, he wrote Cooper:

> I wish I could persuade you to undertake a naval story on your own inland Seas.—The late unfortunate war gave rise to many gallant encounters on your lakes, which wrought up into a story could scarcely fail to be interesting to readers on both sides of the water. It would unite pictures of the border country, and possess a fresh interest. Do me the favor again to think of this, which I believe I previously had the pleasure of proposing to you.[1]

A naval story, gallant encounters, pictures of the border country (i.e. the frontier)—these were the ingredients of which Cooper's reputation had been made. The idea for a tale of the Great Lakes was an old one. Cooper had initially proposed it to Bentley's partner early in 1831, but had put it off to write the European trilogy. From time to time Bentley had tried to reinterest Cooper in the subject, but the author insisted instead upon writing unpopular novels

───────────────

[1] Quoted by Beard, *L/J*, III, 370, n. 3.

of purpose. Now, after almost a decade, after the protracted quarrel with his countrymen, Cooper quickly replied to Bentley, writing on June 18th that "your idea has been followed, and I have got to work on a nautico-lake-savage romance" (*L/J*, III, 393). The eagerness of Cooper's response sufficiently suggests the extent of his own misgivings about his recent novels. A nautico-lake-savage romance would unequivocally return him to his role as a storyteller, would certainly remove him from the arena of his controversies, would perhaps restore the popularity of J. Fenimore Cooper the novelist. In a troubled time, Bentley's phrase "a fresh interest" must have stood out from the rest of his letter.

About half a year later, *The Pathfinder; or, The Inland Sea* was published. In writing it, Cooper returned to more than the romance genre: the novel's setting is Lake Ontario, where over thirty years previously he had served as a midshipman, and its leading character is once again Natty Bumppo, who, as an eighty-year-old trapper, had been buried at the end of *The Prairie* (1827). Cooper had misgivings as well about resurrecting the Leather-stocking seventeen years after his literary death. The reading public, it was believed, was less receptive to sequels than to novelties. When he sent Bentley the first half of the manuscript, in November 1839, Cooper was somewhat defensive about the reappearance of "your old acquaintance the Leather-stocking in the person of the Pathfinder"; he hoped that the tale had enough *"interest"*—by which he meant basically enough gallant encounters and narrow escapes—and then added, "But the *idea* is in the Pathfinder" (*L/J*, III, 443-44). The idea, as David Howard has noted, "is one of Cooper's general themes, that of being true to oneself."[2] And this theme is most fully articulated by Natty, who expounds at length upon his doctrine of "gifts." According

[2] "James Fenimore Cooper's *Leatherstocking Tales*: 'without a cross,'" in *Tradition and Tolerance in Nineteenth-Century Fiction*, ed. David Howard et al. (London: Routledge & Kegan Paul, 1966), p. 25.

to Natty, human nature is always, everywhere, essentially the same, but gifts are what people acquire individually by belonging to a particular race, sex, class, and profession. A gift is a moral imperative: to be true to himself, a man must be true to his gifts. Yet although, as Natty puts it, "when a man has his gift from Providence, it is commonly idle to endeavor to bear up ag'in it,"[3] throughout *The Pathfinder* it is the Leather-stocking who threatens to be false to his own unique set of gifts.

Cooper told Bentley that in the second half of the book his old acquaintance would "fully maintain his own, though in an entirely new point of view." Love provides the new perspective. Each of the Leather-Stocking Tales has a romantic subplot, but in this one Natty is for the first time directly involved in the love story, and suddenly it becomes difficult for him to maintain his own. Almost forty, the Pathfinder discovers the attractions of the opposite sex in the buxom person of Mabel Dunham, daughter of a regimental sergeant who, like Natty, is stationed at Oswego. The English and French colonies are at war, the garrison is tensely on the alert. But rather than prowl around the fort for signs of the hostile "Mingos"—the kind of mission he had eagerly undertaken in *The Last of the Mohicans* or *The Prairie*—Natty chooses to spend his time in Mabel's charming company, a choice that nevertheless brings its own hazards. *The Pathfinder* is the only Tale in which Natty ever blushes:

> "Well, Pathfinder, [says the surprised sergeant,] this is the first time I ever knew men on the trail of the Mingos, and you not at their head!"
> "To be honest with you, serjeant," returned the guide, not without a little awkwardness of manner, and a perceptible difference in the hue of a face that

3 *The Pathfinder*, p. 196. Throughout the remainder of this chapter the titles of the individual Leather-Stocking Tales will be abbreviated as follows: *The Pioneers—Pi; The Prairie—Pr; The Pathfinder—Pa; The Deerslayer—D.*

had become so uniformly red by exposure, "I have not felt that it was my gift this morning." (*Pa*, p. 128)

Natty knows that he has sinned against himself. A few days later, when Mabel asks him about Chingachgook, he specifically acknowledges his transgression:

> "And our own Delaware, Pathfinder—the Big Serpent—why is he not with us to-night?"
> "Your question would have been more nat'ral had you said, why are *you* here, Pathfinder?—The Sarpent is in his place, while I am not in mine. He is out . . . scouting." (*Pa*, p. 204)

The love story is of course a conventional element, but Natty is hardly a conventional lover. His declaration to Mabel reveals just how much he is out of place, and out of his place, in that character. "I never know'd it afore, Mabel," he commences, "but girls, as you call them, though gals is the name I've been taught to use, are of more account in this life than I could have believed" (*Pa*, p. 301). The question, though, is whether they belong in Natty's life— he goes on to tell her that lately he has been unable to sleep, that when he does sleep his dreams are disturbed by the image of "a cabin in a grove of sugar maples," and that worst of all, in one dream he had tried to shoot a deer and Killdeer, his celebrated rifle, "Killdeer missed fire" (*Pa*, p. 302).

The interpretation of Natty's dreams is so obvious that even he recognizes their meaning. To him that cabin among the maples would be a prison. Providence made him a scout, a hunter, and a warrior; to be a husband he would have to sacrifice his gifts, nothing short of sacrificing his life. Of course he does not settle down with Mabel Dunham. At the end of the novel he and Chingachgook disappear into the lonely depths of the forest, where his sleep is undisturbed, where Killdeer never misses, where the Pathfinder is again in his place—just as in writing *The*

Pathfinder Cooper was again in his. George Dekker suggests that the novel should be read as "an autobiographical document,"[4] and applies the moral of Natty's projected misalliance to Cooper's decision to re-create the character of the Leather-stocking. Like Natty upon returning to the woods, Cooper, in Dekker's words, "must have been aware that, in returning to Leatherstocking, he was again being true to his own best gifts."

Cooper kept returning to the Leather-stocking. His involvement with this figure of his imagination spanned most of his literary career: Natty first appears in *The Pioneers*, which was published in 1823, last in *The Deerslayer*, published in 1841, and in 1850, a year before he died, Cooper told George Washington Green that he had considered writing a sixth Leather-Stocking Tale. According to Green, who met Cooper on one of the novelist's visits to New York, "He confessed his partiality for Leather-stocking. Said he: 'I meant to have added one more scene and introduced him in the Revolution, but I thought the public had had enough of him.' "[5] Cooper however was wrong about the reading public—it has expressed the same singular partiality for Natty Bumppo. Out of Cooper's nearly fifty books, the five Leather-Stocking Tales remained popular longest. For almost a century they were among the most widely read American novels. Even today, when the novels themselves no longer appeal to an audience, James Fenimore Cooper is remembered primarily as their author, as the creator of Natty Bumppo. The amount of time that Cooper and his readers have spent in Natty's company suggests that we should look more closely at this character.

As I tried to demonstrate in my analysis of *The Pioneers*, the figure of the Leather-stocking was conceived out of a specific, personal conflict. Even in *The Pathfinder* Cooper is thematically dealing with a personal preoccupation. And yet, if we examine what has been said about him, Natty

[4] Dekker, p. 166.   [5] Quoted by Phillips, pp. 332-34.

Bumppo seems completely to transcend the limitations of his meaning for Cooper. For example, the first man to review the collected edition of Cooper's novels, Francis Parkman, had this to say about his most enduring creation: "The tall, gaunt form of Leatherstocking, the weather-beaten face, the bony hand, the cap of fox-skin, and the old hunting frock, polished with long service, seem so palpable and real, that, in some moods of mind, one may easily confound them with the memories of his own experience."[6] Parkman is not the only reader to respond so personally. Discussing the first three Leather-Stocking Tales, an anonymous critic in the *New York Mirror* wrote in 1827:

> It is not sufficient praise to say the character of Leatherstocking is natural and original. We often meet with delineations which we pronounce to be natural, because we observe nothing in them decidedly the reverse —and original, because we do not remember to have seen any thing drawn precisely like them before; but this personage is not only totally different from every thing we have ever before looked upon, but he is sketched with such indefinable skill—possesses so much peculiar individuality, that we at once *know* him to be true to nature, even though we have never seen his counterpart in real life, and can scarce persuade ourselves that he does not possess actual existence.[7]

More recently, critics have used terms like mythic, epic, and archetypical to define the dimensions of the Leatherstocking, terms, I believe, that more succinctly imply the same reaction. It will be necessary for us to define how Natty Bumppo satisfies the requirements of a "mythic figure," one who exists, to quote Richard Chase, "like Don

6 Parkman, p. 148.

7 Quoted by Marcel Clavel, *Fenimore Cooper and His Critics: American, British and French Criticisms of the Novelist's Early Work* (Aix-en-Provence: Imprimerie Universitaire de Provence, 1938), p. 153.

Quixote, apart from any and all books,"[8] but even Parkman's simply drawn outline—the fox-skin cap, the deer-
skin jerkin—describes a presence that is at once familiar
and attractive to us. So far my study of Cooper has exclusively focused on the relationship between the novelist's
life and his work. I have tried to analyze how his imagination served his psychic needs, to interpret the texts of his
novels in terms of his unconscious impulses and attitudes.
But the tremendous popularity of the Leather-Stocking
Tales underscores the fact that a work of art has a cultural
as well as a personal significance. If Natty Bumppo was to
an extent created in the privacy of Cooper's psyche, he has
been appropriated by other individuals who respond to
his imaginative existence out of the depths of their own
psyches. In this chapter I shall also try to analyze that response—the way in which one man's aesthetic fantasies
fulfill the desires of his readers. The Leather-stocking provides the best material for this examination: since Cooper's
culture has received him with such enthusiasm, more than
any of his other characters must he represent a common
desire.

Though Natty remains fundamentally unchanged in each
of the Tales, most critics have agreed that it is in *The Deerslayer*, the last of the five, that he finally and fully attains
the stature of a mythic figure. To understand the source of
Natty's appeal we must understand the meaning of this
novel, which D. H. Lawrence has called the "most fasci-
nating Leatherstocking book."[9] Part of its fascination is its
failure as a novel. It cannot be assessed by the standards
normally applied to a piece of fiction. "I may be mistaken,"
writes Mark Twain (who does not really think he could
be), "but it does seem to me that *Deerslayer* is not a work
of art in any sense; it does seem to me that it is destitute
of every detail that goes into the making of a work of art;
in truth, it seems to me that *Deerslayer* is just simply a

[8] Chase, p. 55.　　　　　　[9] Lawrence, p. 60.

literary *delirium tremens*."[10] In this famous essay on "Fenimore Cooper's Literary Offenses," Twain has a good deal
of fun with *The Deerslayer*, but other critics, using kinder
language, have made the same complaint about the book.
Donald Davie sums up their judgment: "No one, not Winters nor Wilson nor any other, pretends that the plot of
The Deerslayer is anything but very bad indeed. . . . What
is wrong with the plot is that it does not hang together;
has no internal logic; one incident does not arise out of
another."[11] These adverse reactions suggest the difficulty of
attempting to interpret this tale, a problem that George
Dekker very accurately defines:

> the fascination of this novel is in some respects the
> fascination of a puzzle: how can a work of art that is
> so often gauche, improbable, crowded, bigoted, puerile
> —how can such a work form, as I believe *The Deer-
> slayer* does, an aesthetic whole which is intensely mov-
> ing and convincing?[12]

"In my experience at least," Dekker goes on to say, "*The
Deerslayer* is the most moving of all the Leatherstocking
Tales," and many others have acknowledged a similar ex-
perience.

Like *The Pioneers* and *Home As Found*, *The Deerslayer*
is set on and around Lake Otsego. This, too, is a piece of
the puzzle, "for," as Cooper states in the course of his narrative, "we are writing of real scenes" (*D*, p. 157), yet in
this instance the site of his childhood, which was realisti-
cally re-created in the first book, the site of his present life,
which was charged with the anger of his personal quarrel
in the second, is here transformed into the spaceless realm
of a myth that his readers can recognize as their own. Natty

[10] Mark Twain, "Fenimore Cooper's Literary Offenses," *North American Review* 161 (1895), 12.
[11] *The Heyday of Sir Walter Scott* (London: Routledge & Kegan
Paul, 1961), p. 125.
[12] Dekker, p. 170.

Bumppo had originally been imagined on this ground as the aged outcast from the pioneer settlement, but now Cooper restores both Natty and Otsego to an earlier period. Natty is in his twenties. In a sense, the lake is also young. The novel's action takes place about 1740, when, Cooper wrote Bentley, "all this region of country *was in a state of nature*" (*L/J*, IV, 112), or when, Cooper writes in the novel, "the hand of man had never yet defaced or deformed any part of this native scene" (*D*, p. 33). Not having been formally named by the white man, Otsego is known as the "Glimmerglass" to the few hunters and trappers who have visited it. The pristine quality of the region seems almost prehistorical; seeing it for the first time leads the youthful Natty to exclaim:

> "This is grand!—'tis solemn!—'tis an edication of itself, to look upon! . . . not a tree disturbed even by redskin hand, as I can discover, but everything left in the ordering of the Lord, to live and die according to his own designs and laws!" (*D*, pp. 33-34)

Prehistory is the appropriate context for myth, and the Glimmerglass, we sense immediately, the perfect setting.

The story set here, the story of the Leather-stocking as a young man, has two themes: a rite of passage and the right of possession. The book's subtitle—*The First War-Path*—refers to the passage. War between England and France has just been declared. After a long peace, the frontier is once again filled with armed parties of Indians. Deerslayer has come to the Glimmerglass to meet his Delaware friend Chingachgook. Together they intend to track down the Mingos who have kidnapped Wah-Ta!-Wah, a Delaware maiden to whom the Big Serpent is betrothed. But before Natty can be joined by Chingachgook, the lake is surrounded by the same band of Mingos. Neither youth has yet trodden the warpath; Natty's skill at the hunt has earned him the name Deerslayer among the Delawares, but as a warrior, a slayer of men, he is untried. He is soon put to the test. At sunrise on the novel's second day, Natty faces a lone Mingo on the margin of the lake and kills him. More than his courage and his aim is being tried—the encounter is his initiation into manhood, marked by a change of name when the dying Indian bestows the title "Hawkeye" upon his victorious enemy. The ritual episode is described in one of Cooper's best scenes, but Natty's victory seems tangential to the major concern of *The Deerslayer*. Cooper's initial choice for a subtitle was "A Legend of the Glimmerglass." It would have been a better one, for symbolically that clear sheet of water is obviously more important than the blood which Natty spills. Even the chapter in which he takes his first human life is headed by a passage from Byron about the pure and placid beauty of Lake Leman.

It was, in fact, Otsego itself that prompted Cooper to write *The Deerslayer*. Susan Fenimore Cooper gives an account of that decision, and though we have to make some allowances for her prose, the incident seems accurately reported. She and her father were driving along the lake shore one evening. Her father was singing.

> Suddenly he paused, as an opening in the wood revealed a sweet view of the lake. His spirited gray eye rested a moment on the water, with that expression of abstracted, poetical thought, ever familiar to those who lived with him; then, turning to the companion at his side—the daughter now writing these lines—he exclaimed: "I must write one more book, dearie, about our little lake!" Again his eye rested on the water and the banks, with the far-seeing look of one evoking imaginary figures to fill the beautiful scene. . . . A few days later the first pages of the Deerslayer were written.[13]

One of those figures was of course the Leather-stocking, who, in the world of Cooper's imagination, had been driven

13 *Pages and Pictures*, pp. 322-23.

from Otsego after forty years in residence by Marmaduke Temple's settlers and laws. The opening pages of *Deerslayer* recount Natty's primal contact with the lake. When he arrives, however, one family has already settled there—a father, Floating Tom Hutter, and his two daughters, Judith and Hetty. As far as anyone knows, Hutter is the only man, red or white, ever to live in the region. Both the Delawares and the Mingos, Natty believes, claim the lake as common territory. "Hurry Harry" March, the huge woodsman with whom Natty has travelled to the Glimmerglass, and a violent Indian-hater, insists at the outset upon setting his companion straight:

> "Common territory!" exclaimed Hurry. . . . "I should like to know what Floating Tom Hutter would say to that? He claims the lake as his own property, in vartue of fifteen years' possession, and will not be likely to give it up to either Mingo or Delaware without a battle for it." (*D*, p. 20)

Possession of the Glimmerglass is the real theme of the novel. A few hours after Natty and Hurry get there, they and the Hutters are indeed attacked by Mingos, and the battle for the lake begins. Yet the most significant contest is not the physical one between the whites and the Indians, but the ethical one among the whites themselves.

Once before Natty Bumppo had been involved in a moral struggle for the right to the land at Otsego. The Leatherstocking's antagonist was Judge Temple, who could produce the requisite documents to support his title; the Deerslayer's is the squatter Tom Hutter, whose title, backed up by his rifle, is more tangible. Even the Mingos recognize him as "king of the lake" (*D*, p. 262), and his hut, actually built on a shoal halfway across the water, is called appropriately "Muskrat Castle." As a trapper, Floating Tom values the land in muskrat furs and dollars, unlike the Deerslayer, who prizes most its untouched beauty. The incidents on and around the lake become, just as they had in *The Pioneers*, a series of moral tests. Natty fights the Indians to prove himself true to his training and gifts; Hutter and Harry March, for their property and their lives, although England and France have also made it possible for them to profit from the war. The Kings' officers have offered a bounty for Indian scalps which their colonists may collect as well as their Indian allies. Both Hutter and Hurry are eager to add a few Mingo scalps, preferably from women and children, to their income. Natty refuses to accompany them. Scalping, he declares, is an Indian's gift: "for them it's *lawful* work; while for *us*, it would be grievous work" (*D*, p. 48). To Hurry Harry, who asserts that the colony has made it lawful, Natty replies: "Laws don't all come from the same quarter. God has given us his'n, and some come from the Colony, and others come from the king and parliament. When the Colony's laws, or even the King's laws, run ag'in the laws of God, they get to be onlawful, and ought not to be obeyed" (*D*, p. 49).

Which authority to obey and which to resist are questions that confront Natty throughout the novel. At one point, after he has foiled an attempt by Hutter and Hurry to abuse a truce with the Mingos, they accuse him of being untrue to his friends. " 'I should have been ontrue to the right, had I done otherwise,' returned the Deerslayer, steadily; 'and neither you nor any other man has authority to demand that much of me' " (*D*, p. 277). Two men, however, try to claim that authority: the King of England, who by his agents has ordered Natty to violate the rules of combat, and the king of the lake, Tom Hutter. Because the Glimmerglass belongs officially to no one, each "king" could be considered its owner. As Hurry Harry tells Natty, the King "may pretend to some right of that natur', but he is so far away that his claim will never trouble old Tom Hutter, who has got possession" (*D*, p. 35). Since Hutter has got possession, he presents the greatest threat to Deerslayer's moral purity; he is the king referred to in the following selection from Chatterton, which Cooper used for the epigraph to Chapter Fifteen:

> As long as Edwarde rules thys lande,
> Ne quiet you wylle know;
> Your sonnes and husbandes shall be slayne,
> And brookes with bloode shall flowe.
>
> You leave youre goode and lawfulle kynge,
> Whenne ynne adversitye;
> Like me, untoe the true cause stycke,
> And for the true cause dye. (*D*, p. 272)

While Deerslayer and Hutter work together "ynne adversitye" to defeat the Mingos, Deerslayer alone struggles to remain true to the right, and the true cause requires him to rebel against Hutter's dominion.

A violent, greedy, small-minded man, Hutter would like to rule the small community at the lake as autocratically as Judge Temple had earlier ruled the village of Templeton, as autocratically as Judge Cooper had originally ruled Cooperstown. We have already noted the many similarities between Marmaduke Temple and William Cooper. No such overwhelming resemblance exists between William Cooper and Floating Tom, yet I believe that the trapper must be understood as another fictional representative of the novelist's father. Cooper himself was not consciously aware of this identity, but there are a number of clues to it throughout the novel. When Hetty Hutter seeks to identify her father to the Mingos, she asks Wah-Ta!-Wah, who is serving as a translator, to describe him as the man "who owns the castle and the ark, and who has the best right to be thought the owner of these hills, and that lake. . . . They'll know whom you mean by Thomas Hutter, if you tell them *that*" (*D*, p. 202). If the ark—Hutter's boat—is omitted, *that* would also describe Judge Cooper. The Judge acquired the deed to those hills and that lake about forty

years after the imaginary tenure of their first white "owner";
he even had his own "Castle," the name by which the resi-
dents of Cooperstown often referred to the Mansion-House.[14]

That Tom Hutter did stand for the Judge in Cooper's
imagination is, I believe, revealed in one particularly suggestive sentence. About two-thirds of the way through the
story Hutter is ambushed in his Castle by a party of Mingos.
Dying both from a knife wound and from being scalped,
he is discovered by his daughters at the end of the twentieth chapter. At the beginning of Chapter Twenty-One,
Cooper pauses to recount the ambush, prefacing the brief
passage by stating that "the facts were never known until
years later, in all their details, simple as they were; but they
may as well be related here . . ." (*D*, p. 384). Since Cooper
never explains the reason for the delay, this reference is
confusing. Since Hutter could easily have related the details—simple as they were—to his daughters before he died,
it seems superfluous. Since by the end of the novel Hutter
and nearly all the Indians who attacked him are dead, it
is meaningless. In the book's penultimate paragraph, in
fact, Cooper flatly contradicts it: "Time and circumstances,"
he writes, "have drawn an impenetrable mystery" around
the life of Thomas Hutter, and "none connected have felt
sufficient interest . . . to withdraw the veil" (*D*, p. 597).
Had Cooper reworked the manuscript of *The Deerslayer*,
the problematic sentence might have been crossed out. But
he always believed in publishing what was written "at the
first heat," and in the careless heat of composition Cooper
wrote that the details of Hutter's death remained unknown
for several years. This puzzling, unnecessary statement did
not get into the text accidentally (the writer's imagination
can work without care, but never without motivation), and
if it is nonsense in the immediate context of the story, it

[14] James Cooper also referred to it by that name—cf. his letter to
Mrs. Cooper, *L/J*, 1, 26. In *The Pioneers*, the novelist similarly refers
to "the castle, as Judge Temple's dwelling was termed in common
parlance" (*Pi*, p. 44).

makes perfect sense in another context. William Cooper was also murdered. Though not scalped, he did die from a blow to his head. And the facts of his death are doubtful. James Cooper, who was in New York when his father was slain in Albany, may very well have learned exactly how it happened only several years later, perhaps when he moved to Cooperstown after his marriage. Certainly he would have felt sufficient interest to uncover all the details, details that have remained hidden from the historians. By a common psychic process—a parapraxis, a mental slip— Cooper's unconscious intention disclosed itself: at the deepest level of his mind, Tom Hutter was his father.

The most interesting aspect of this relationship, however, is not the way Cooper treats the death of the "father," but the way he repeatedly removes the father from the scene. Where Judge Temple's authority is omnipresent, Hutter is most often absent, at least from the field of Natty's vision. Almost immediately the trapper is captured by the Mingos, and soon after his release two days later, Deerslayer is himself captured, and by the time Deerslayer returns, Hutter is dead. This change of places leaves the young man master of his conduct, unlike the aged Leather-stocking, who was consistently in direct conflict with Temple. Therefore, the Deerslayer, except when he refuses to abet Hutter's mercenary schemes, need not be openly rebellious. His other actions are hard to characterize: for the most part it is Natty's behavior that has confounded the novel's critics. He is constantly in motion about the lake, but seldom to any specific purpose. Within four quick days he fights off an ambush, chases canoes, kills an enemy, meets Chingachgook, rescues Wah-Ta!-Wah, gets captured by the Indians and paroled by them, shoots an eagle, returns to the Mingos and tries to escape, is recaptured and tortured, and is finally saved. With all this, he has time leisurely to explore a chest full of the Hutter family's secrets, innocently to win the heart of a pretty girl, and firmly to decline two marriage proposals. *The Deerslayer* is beyond question the most episodic of the Tales. Dekker calls its plot crowded and puerile. Davie describes it as illogical. To me, the series of incidents on the Glimmerglass suggests nothing so strongly as the make-believe play of a child, which can be undirected but which must always be busy. We know that as a boy Cooper was infatuated with the lake and the woods around it, and that his love for "our little lake" inspired him to write *The Deerslayer*. To the middle-aged novelist, no doubt the lake seemed little, but to the boy, it would have been large enough. There Cooper could be free of his father's oppressive authority, which was doubtless exercised often within the Mansion-House. There Cooper could indulge in his own fantasies of manhood, could come of age in his play. In this last Leather-Stocking Tale, he bestows the same privilege on the Deerslayer. With the father-figure, stern Tom Hutter, safely out of the way, the young Natty is free properly to take possession of the pristine Glimmerglass and heroically to assume the stature of a man.

The childhood world to which Cooper returns imaginatively in *The Deerslayer* is of course unlike the one revisited in *The Pioneers*. The first Leather-Stocking Tale is usually cited as the most realistic, the last as the most mythic; in D. H. Lawrence's well-known phrase, the series represents "a *decrescendo* of reality, and a crescendo of beauty."[15] Yet in Cooper's mind both worlds had their own remembered reality. If the inhabitants, buildings, and events of "Templeton" once existed in the shared space and time of history, so the Glimmerglass—fraught with danger and splendor, offering countless opportunities for courage, for the light-hearted pose of heroism—once had a personal existence for the young Cooper. Whenever he scouted the bushes around Lake Otsego for Indians waiting in ambush, he was on the Glimmerglass. To make those Indians real, it was necessary merely to believe in them, and that every child can do. So can every artist. In *The Deerslayer* life provides the infi-

[15] Lawrence, p. 50.

nite possibilities for action and expression that belong uniquely to the writer's imagination and the infant's make-believe. Mark Twain, pretending not to believe, points out how incredible the action of the novel is. And he is right. But what moves the rest of us, even in our disbelief, is precisely this unambiguous aesthetic projection of child's play as a vision for ordering reality. This is the meaning of *The Deerslayer*'s myth.

Actually, the book with which *The Deerslayer* can best be compared is *Home As Found*. Written four years apart, set on the same scene, the two books offer antithetical ways of perceiving the world. Cooper set both in his own back yard, and wrote both directly from his own experience, but the visions presented in each have their equivalents in everyone's personal experience. That property and social position pass from father to son, that the father's grave is to be respected, that his counsel is to be followed, that his will is to be obeyed—these are the implicit themes of *Home As Found*. Cooper treats them not simply as facts of life, but as the foundations of society. When these tenets are called "tradition," they have an equal weight with the majority of adults; a large part of the process of maturing in any society involves the recognition of the values and accomplishments of one's ancestors. The exigencies of Cooper's psyche caused him to distort the meaning of social heredity—in his eyes, behaving as though they were "nobody's sons" is the most serious of his countrymen's vices, and America's duty to its forefathers becomes synonymous with its duty to itself—but every defense of tradition or appeal to past values exists essentially in the same context as the polemical *Home As Found*.

The world posited in *The Deerslayer*, however, is entirely separate. It is a moral world in which "tradition" would retain its original meaning of surrender and betrayal. On Lake Glimmerglass, as opposed to Lake Otsego, the father's authority is perceived as tyrannous, corrupt, illegitimate; the son does not inherit the world, but takes possession of it firsthand, fresh from the creator, earning his right to it solely by his own actions, not his ancestors'. In the novel this is accomplished by Natty Bumppo, but each new generation of men has believed it could accomplish the same thing. As adolescents we have all asked ourselves the great question put by Emerson in *Nature*: "The foregoing generations beheld God and nature face to face; we, through their eyes. Why should not we also enjoy an original relation to the universe?" In *The Deerslayer*, the moral authority of history does not predate the present moment: all that has gone before, epitomized by the reign of Tom Hutter, is invalid; by the purity of his acts, by his steadfast refusal to betray or surrender his ideals, Natty is entitled to enjoy an original relation with God and nature.

Shortly after Hutter's death, his daughters and the Deerslayer examine the trapper's property. One item—the long rifle named Killdeer—is particularly attractive to Natty:

> ". . . this is a lordly piece, and would make a steady hand and quick eye, the King of the Woods."
> "Then keep it, Deerslayer, and become King of the Woods," said Judith, earnestly. (*D*, p. 422)

Natty's hand is steady and his eye true because his heart is pure and his cause always just. He does accept the rifle, and as the King of the Woods he succeeds the false king of the lake. Yet he need not ever accept the burden of succession. Ned Effingham's father, like Cooper's, left a will as well as an estate, and both the fictional and the real sons felt themselves bound by the terms of that will. But the Deerslayer owes nothing to Tom Hutter. In the child's fantasy, no responsibilities come with the crown—being King simply means being free from anyone else's, and especially parents', authority. Natty will not look through any but his own eyes. He will not recognize even the real King's authority whenever he cannot in good conscience do so, for conscience, as he tells Judith, "is king with me" (*D*, p. 452).

A civilization cannot be founded upon this vision. Natty

Bumppo's initiation into manhood is an individual, not a social rite, "accomplished appropriately," notes R.W.B. Lewis, "in the forest on the edge of a lake, with no parents near at hand, no sponsors at the baptism."[16] Nor is he baptised with the name of the father. The laws of descent with which society joins its past to its future—the laws that became commandments in *Home As Found*—do not apply to the Leather-stocking. Natty earns his various names as he ultimately earns his salvation, alone in the wilderness, without the intercession of other people or their institutions. "Evidently uneasy at the idea of being too near the world" (*D*, p. 25), Natty puts as much wilderness as he can between himself and society. Throughout the Tales he retreats from what he calls "the uproar of clearings" to seek "the honesty of the woods" (*Pr*, p. 264). Natty states this dichotomy in *The Prairie*, the third Leather-Stocking Tale. In it, he has been forced to retreat even beyond the woods "to escape the wasteful temper of my people"—from the hills around Otsego he has fled westward across the Mississippi to the Great Plains. Westward was also the course of American civilization, but Natty remains ahead and outside the pale of that progress. When one of the other white characters in *The Prairie* simply mentions "the practices of men, as connected with their daily intercourse, their institutions, and their laws," Natty hastily interrupts him: "And such I call barefaced and downright wantonness and waste" (*Pr*, p. 295). Over eighty years old, alone among the Indians, Leather-stocking dies at the conclusion of the novel facing west, the hated practices of mankind at least for the moment far behind him. With this final gesture of repudiation Natty's career ends. It is, however, a gesture he has made before: in the last chapter of *The Pioneers* he refuses the offer of Oliver and Elizabeth to live with them and renounces the domestic comforts of Templeton; turning his back on the clearings, he steps briskly into the woods.

[16] *The American Adam: Innocence, Tragedy, and Tradition in the Nineteenth Century* (Chicago: Univ. of Chicago Press, 1955), p. 105.

The same gesture is repeated at the end of *The Deer-slayer*, although there the particular circumstances define most clearly what Natty renounces. It is the fifth day of his stay on the Glimmerglass. The Mingos have been beaten, Wah-Ta!-Wah has been reunited with Chingachgook, Tom and Hetty Hutter have been killed. No one remains on the lake but Deerslayer and Judith. Natty has proved himself worthy of the glories of the Glimmerglass and has been deeply touched by its beauty. Quite unexpectedly, at least to him, he is given the opportunity to take permanent possession. Five days earlier, after Hurry Harry had told him that Tom Hutter considered himself its owner, Natty had said:

> "I invy that man!—I know it's wrong, and I strive ag'in the feelin', but I invy that man! . . ."
> "You've only to marry Hetty to inherit half the estate," cried Hurry, laughing. (*D*, p. 35)

Hurry laughs because he knows that Hetty is an imbecile and because he is firmly convinced that Judith's proud beauty would have nothing in common with Deerslayer's humble plainness. Judith has in fact been too proud of her attractions. Sometime earlier she has been seduced by one of the gallant English officers stationed at the nearby garrison: if the Glimmerglass is unsullied, she, as Cooper tactfully but repeatedly hints, is not. Faced with the Deerslayer's upright honesty, she realizes that she is a lost woman; yet that truthfulness appears to her as her last chance for salvation. Judith is brave enough to propose marriage to Natty, and shrewd enough to put her proposal in its most irresistible form:

> "You love the woods and the life that we pass, here, in the wilderness, away from the dwellings and towns of the whites."
> "As I loved my parents, Judith, when they was living! This very spot would be all creation to me, could

this war be fairly over, once; and the settlers kept at a distance."

"Why quit it, then? It has no owner—at least none who can claim a better right than mine, and *that* I freely give to you. Were it a kingdom, Deerslayer, I think I should delight to say the same. Let us then return to it, after we have seen the priest at the fort, and never quit it again." (*D*, p. 590)

The man whom Natty had envied is dead, he has only to marry Judith to inherit the entire estate, Judith's beauty can even compete with that of the Glimmerglass—the King of the Woods is offered a kingdom and a queen. But Natty, once he has figured out Judith's intentions, is not at all tempted by the offer. He intuitively knows about her indiscretion, yet had she not been corrupted by civilization he would still have said no. Again, it is a question of his gifts. As he had said earlier in the story, when he told his Indian captors that he would not marry the squaw of the warrior he had slain, and that therefore they might as well begin torturing him, "Most likely Providence, in putting me up here in the woods, has intended I should live single" (*D*, p. 514).

Like *The Pioneers*, *The Deerslayer* ends with Natty's departure from Otsego, for in rejecting Judith's hand he also rejects the kingdom she would "freely give" him. In the first novel, however, Oliver Effingham remains behind in possession of the inheritance that in 1823 Cooper himself had lost. By 1841, when he wrote the second, Cooper had managed to buy back much of that inheritance, and a large percentage of his earnings went to pay for further purchases. But in *The Deerslayer* Natty abandons the lake and the hills to nature; he refuses to accept Tom Hutter's estate. It is not difficult to understand why Cooper wrote such an ending. For him, the land at Otsego had been anything but freely given. First there had been the anxieties and failures connected with his initial management of his fa-

ther's estate, which had broken down his health and left
him in debt for a decade. Even in 1841, when once again
he could sit in his father's house, now as its owner, there
were still anxieties. The quarrel with the villagers that began with the Three Mile Point controversy continued to be
bitter. James Franklin Beard cites, for example, a lengthy
libel suit brought by a grocer and a lawyer in Cooperstown
solely to embarrass and annoy him,[17] and Cooper's own
libel suits against the newspapers' coverage of that controversy took up more and more of his time and energy. Fi-
nancially, the land he had worked so hard to reacquire
continued to be a source of trouble. As he confessed in a
letter to an old family friend late in 1839,

> had it not been for an unexpected Godsend, in receiv-
> ing a little back rent, the other day I should now be
> literally without money enough to keep the devil out
> of my pocket. Thank God, I see better times before
> me. I have paid several thousands on account of my
> father's estate, for which I am yet only $80 in pocket.
> (*L/J*, III, 441)

Yet better times remained just out of reach. Early in 1841
he wrote Bentley to renew his previous request (cf. *L/J*,
IV, 102) for an advance on *The Deerslayer*: "I have been
repurchasing a good deal of old family property, and have
a last payment of £1000 to make shortly, which consumes
my ready cash" (*L/J*, IV, 112). His psychic investment in
that old family property had forced him to antagonize his
neighbors, his financial investment forced him to write *The
Deerslayer* as rapidly as possible, and still he could not
claim to have the authority, the power, that had been William Cooper's—he had been unable to restore his father's
name to its original station in Cooperstown. In this context,
Natty's freedom to turn his back on Judith's proposal had
an obvious appeal to the novelist.

More interesting, however, is the way in which Natty's

[17] Beard, *L/J*, IV, 5.

iterated renunciations have appealed to the novelist's readers. For the commencement of Natty's apotheosis into a
mythic figure was his rejection of civilized life with the
newlywed Effinghams in favor of the solitary hardships of
the wilderness. Carl Van Doren writes about the Leather-
stocking's first appearance: "In *The Pioneers* he is not of
the proportions which he later assumed, and only at the
end, when he withdraws from the field of his defeat by
civilization, does he make his full appeal."[18] In a letter to
Cooper shortly after the publication of *The Pioneers*, Richard H. Dana called this scene "the most touching in the
book," and added, "A friend of mine said at Natty's departure, 'I longed to go with him.' "[19] Each of the subsequent Leather-Stocking Tales ends with a similar withdrawal from the society of men and women. What Natty
gives up to live in the woods makes an impressive list—
marriage and a family, social success and position, personal
property, even something so simple as a place, however
meager, which he can call his own. These are what we
would ordinarily call the pursuits of happiness, these are
our inalienable rights. Yet in repudiating them all, Natty
somehow makes us long to go with him. Yet as R.W.B.
Lewis says, the story of Natty's life represents "some image
of experience we know to be fundamentally our own, or at
least could wish that it were."[20] For all Natty's renunciations, what does he get back?

Natty Bumppo's presence, to summarize the reactions and
judgments of the commentators, it at once real and mythic,
at once something we seem to remember and something we
seem to desire. Vague memories and unstated desires suggest the realm of the unconscious, which tenaciously preserves the life of the child in all of us. And of course until
recently the audience to which the Tales did appeal was

18 *The American Novel* (New York: The Macmillan Company, 1921),
p. 68.
19 Quoted by Clavel, p. 149.   20 Lewis, p. 102.

basically an adolescent one. Whether we read them as children or as adults, the Leather-Stocking Tales are "boys' books." I have already said that in *The Deerslayer* the world is ordered by the vision of a child at play. But what do children play at? Almost invariably, they play at being adults. And that, I want to suggest, is what Natty Bumppo does, or more precisely, he embodies a preadolescent conception of adulthood. Cooper himself says at one point that the Leather-stocking possesses "a mind that was almost infantine in its simplicity and nature" (*Pa*, p. 304), a characteristic that has bothered some of the critics. Robert H. Zoellner, for example, is right to insist that throughout the Tales "the infantile conflicts with the epic-heroic."[21] Zoellner doubtless has in mind an epic like *The Iliad* and heroes like Hector and Achilles, for in Homer the hero is forced to make mature choices—Hector, between his family and his city; Achilles, between his pride and his duty. In both cases the choice is between personal desires and social obligations, and the Trojan and the Greek each knows what he must sacrifice to be a true hero: they make their decisions as responsible adults. Natty never needs to decide between such delicate alternatives; as Cooper says, "while, in moments of danger, he acted with the wisdom of the serpent, it was also with the simplicity of a child" (*Pa*, p. 438). This simplicity certainly denies Natty the particular stature that Hector attains in the great scene within Troy's walls, when he takes off his helmet to play with his frightened son while Andromache cries at his side, both he and his wife knowing that he must don it again to resume the ill-fated battle. Yet I believe that Zoellner is exactly wrong when he concludes that Natty's immaturity "constantly undercuts his attempt to develop into a dominant mythic archetype."[22] On the contrary, the deepest source

[21] Robert H. Zoellner, "Conceptual Ambivalance in Cooper's Leather-stocking," *American Literature* 31 (1960), 419.
[22] Ibid., p. 401.

of Natty's mythic appeal is precisely that his actions are guided by, to quote Zoellner again, "a system of moral imperatives essentially infantile."

What we remember and respond to in the figure of the Leather-stocking is our own childhood projection of the adults we imagined we would become. Though in our make-believe we often modeled ourselves upon the adults we knew, especially our parents, we had a blissfully distorted conception of adulthood. To the child, there are no limits on the power of the grownups: adults are accountable to no one but themselves. Children's fantasies are always about adults because they seek to appropriate that power —so often directed against them—for themselves. If there is seemingly no end to the authority that a parent has over a child, why should there be any to the parent's authority over the world?

I said earlier that Natty Bumppo was originally imagined by Cooper out of his opposition to his father. In *The Pioneers*, Judge Temple is the real adult; he must make the difficult decisions that actual adulthood forces upon a man; he must, for example, decide as a Judge to prosecute the the hunter to whom, as a father, he owes his daughter's life. In making this decision, less grand certainly than Hector's, he nonetheless has to make the same compromise between his desires as a person and his responsibilities as a member of a community. Themselves exempt from this kind of choice, children are incapable of understanding it. But adults have learned too well that such compromises with reality—to meet the demands of family, social position, civilization in general, even growing older—are the cost of adulthood, of membership in an adult community. But in the character of Natty Bumppo Cooper created a man who makes no compromises, who recognizes no authority but his own conscience, who never sacrifices his gifts. By refusing to acknowledge the authority of the community, Natty gains his freedom from its demands. Natty is defiant, but his stance is not that of a rebel with a social cause. When he

breaks out of Judge Temple's jail, when he exiles himself
from the clearings, he is simply asserting his own independence. To the same end has every child at least once tried
to run away from home. Natty, however, succeeds in running away, and so forever preserves his inviolate selfhood.
In that sense, he never grows up. Natty's virtues—purity
of motive, courage of heart, virtuosity in action, fidelity to
his gifts—define a fundamentally juvenile sensibility. And
by remaining true to them, Natty keeps a clear conscience.
And as Sergeant Dunham tells the Pathfinder, "A good conscience will keep one like you a mere boy all his life" (*Pa*,
p. 141).

Yet only in the pathless wilderness, only alone, can Natty
remain faithful to his virtues. As *The Pathfinder* reveals,
marriage would put an end to his freedom. He must stay
emotionally unattached to anyone else. At one point in *The
Pathfinder* Cooper offers this list of Natty's characteristic
qualities: "his truth, integrity of purpose, courage, self-de-
votion, disinterestedness . . ." (*Pa*, p. 308). These traits do
not conflict with each other, at least not as long as Natty
confines himself to the roles of warrior and hunter. Yet his
virtues would hardly make him a good husband, a good
father—his truth would have to include the recognition of
someone else's truth, his integrity would have to be strong
enough to admit the possible necessity of change, his self-
devotion and disinterestedness both would have to acknowledge the inconvenient right of others to demand his devotion and his interest. The morality of our emotional life is
more complex, more suspect, than that which will serve
Natty in the woods. Even he recognizes this fact. "Fri'nd-
ship's an awful thing!" he admits to Judith Hutter; "Sometimes it chides us for not having done enough; then ag'in
it speaks in strong words for havin' done too much" (*D*,
p. 491). His one lasting relationship is with Chingachgook,
but that is a special case. Natty explains it to Judith: "he
is my fri'nd; and all the better fri'nd, perhaps, because
there can never be any hard feelin's atween us, touchin'

our gifts; his'n bein' red, and mine bein' altogether white" (*D*, p. 479). Because it can never require a sacrifice, because it involves no compromise of either man's selfhood, Natty and the Big Serpent can safely be fri'nds. They can both be self-devoted and true to themselves, because they meet, in D. H. Lawrence's words, "across an unpassable distance."[23]

In his "Preface to the Leather-Stocking Tales," Cooper describes Natty Bumppo as "a being removed from the every-day inducements to err, which abound in civilized life" (*D*, pp. viii-ix). Natty cannot go astray, because life in the wilderness does not force him to make choices; and by investing his emotions exclusively in himself, he is safe from the danger of suffering from another's errors. For the rest of us, hopelessly, happily, or miserably caught in the web of our loves, our fears, our needs, and our desires, life is not that simple. But there was a time when we could imagine that it would be. That time was our childhood and preadolescence, when only the adults stood between us and the world. That is why we played at being adults, un-grownup adults, who enjoyed a pure and original relation with the glories of the universe. Reading the Leather-Stocking Tales and vicariously experiencing the Leather-stocking's "courage, truth, nobleness of soul and conduct" (*Pa*, p. 499), we reacquaint ourselves with our once-shining vision of the adults we would have become . . . had not the demands of adult life again come between us and the world. By marrying, having children, accepting a social role, we have of course taken those demands upon ourselves, but that does not make them any less restrictive. That does not make Natty's autonomy any less attractive. Few of us would actually follow him into the forest, but fewer still have never wanted to. Adult society can push Natty westward across the continent, but not once can it force him to betray his integrity. People feel that Natty Bumppo must exist because he did exist, for each of us, in our childhood dream of the future. Our dream did not

23 Lawrence, p. 61.

recognize the independent existence of other people whose claims upon us we could not ignore. No one else was included. Alone, uncompromised, we would reign as the King of the Woods.

CHAPTER VII

"FILIAL PIETY"

TODAY almost no one reads Fenimore Cooper, not even the boys. The image of Natty Bumppo has passed into our culture, but his actual presence in the Tales is seldom encountered. There are several reasons for this neglect, for the dust that the five Leather-stocking books are gathering on library shelves and in attics. Cooper's style is archaic. The literary conventions he subscribed to have largely passed out of favor. His narrative pacing cannot compete with television's. Yet I suspect that the chief cause of Cooper's unpopularity is the fact that the present generation of children does not need to experience Natty's inviolate freedom vicariously. American society, instead of denying the child's selfhood, now directs its efforts to fostering it. In most families, the American father no longer represents an overbearing but unimpeachable source of authority. The Leather-Stocking Tales survived many shifts in the craft of writing, but I doubt they can survive this pervasive cultural change: the child who can influence the adults in his real world has no motive to join Natty in his imaginary one.

The erosion of the father's status might make it hard in our time to understand the full dimensions of Cooper's psychic fix. "Paternal authority" had meaning in Cooper's culture, and the particular character of his father only reinforced that meaning. Stern as a judge, despotic as a patriarch, violent as a man, William Cooper made a deep impression on the politics of New York, the county of Otsego, on everyone who met him. His son's unconscious attitude toward that father was the predominant force behind his behavior and beneath his imagination. At no time was the extent of this influence more clear than at the end of the son's life.

I have already tried to explain the way in which Cooper, in the four books published in 1838, sought to redefine his identity, to declare publicly that he had become a Cooper of Cooperstown. His various efforts to free himself from the figure of his father—which had included the open rebellion of his youth, the financial and political efforts to surpass his father's achievements in his young adulthood, and the sweeping rejection of his father's principles, even of his name, in his early years as an author—were replaced by an equally powerful need to identify himself with William Cooper. Analyzing the last decade of the novelist's career, Robert E. Spiller concludes: "He saw himself as his father's son, as his wife's husband, as a property owner, as the head and founder of a family of his own, as himself a man of culture and reasonable wealth."[1] The first term in Spiller's list is the most important. Cooper described himself similarly in a letter of 1848 from Cooperstown to a former Yale classmate. Like Spiller, he begins by citing his place on the family tree: "My descent in this country runs thus, William (emigrant), James; William; James; William James Fenimore Cooper" (L/J, v, 304). That is how he punctuated the sentence; there is no syntactical break between the father and the son; this slip of his pen graphically illustrates the dominant relationship between the two in the son's unconscious.

The unconscious, however, is a conservative force: every impulse that is fixed there continues to demand some kind of gratification. In the Oedipal conflicts of the infant son, two attitudes toward the father are permanently internalized. One is active, one passive. The first seeks the overthrow of the father's authority and his privileged position with the mother; this is the best-known phase of the Oedipus complex. Yet the second can often be just as active in the mental life of the child. It seeks to supplant the mother in

[1] Spiller, pp. 299-300.

the father's affections; it can only be satisfied with complete submission to the father. During the last dozen years of his life, Cooper's psychic stance toward his father was, as I shall try to prove, determined by this second need. Finally he ceased to resist the domineering presence of the Judge. But acknowledging his father's supreme authority left the active psychic impulse unfulfilled. We have already dealt with a similar problem in Cooper's life. In the 1820s he was in revolt against everything that William Cooper represented to him. Then he satisfied the passive impulse by replacing the real father with General LaFayette, a father-substitute; in his own words, like a dutiful child he set about doing the General's bidding and serving the General's causes. After the mid-1830s he perceived that his duty was defined by the will of his actual father, and he made himself subservient to that will. Now to satisfy his need to resist he again found a substitute for his father. This time, though, it was not an individual, but a group of men. Cooper chose to defy the newspaper editors.

As early as 1832, in the midst of the Finance Controversy, Cooper told a friend that he would not submit quietly to the assaults on his actions published in the American press. "I care nothing for the criticism, but I am not indifferent to the slander. If these attacks on my character should be kept up five years after my return to America," he promised, "I shall resort to the New York courts for protection."[2] More than he would ever admit Cooper was sensitive to simple criticism, but he never hesitated about avowing his determination to protect his character or his honor. Ten years earlier, in a passage I have already quoted, he wrote his father-in-law that he would "defend my character against every assault," and his unnecessarily hostile insistence upon this point prevented the De Lanceys and their in-law from patching up their quarrel. Still earlier, in the December 19th, 1808, letter to his brother Richard, midshipman Coop-

2 Quoted by Beard, *L/J*, II, 231.

er said that he was willing to forget any "family dissensions"—"could it be done consistent with my own honor." Richard was the eldest brother, a sibling often associated by the younger ones with the father, and John Peter De Lancey was of course a father-in-law. The original source of Cooper's touchiness about his character was, I believe, his father himself: it was a defensive reaction to Judge Cooper's almost overwhelming desire to dictate to all his dependents, be they his children or his settlers. By standing firm on his honor James Cooper helped himself stand up to His Honor the Judge.

It is in this light that the novelist's struggle against the editors should be considered. From the beginning of his literary career Cooper had been suspicious of the press, which, for its part, had cautiously followed the lead of the English critics in praising the first real American novelist. Toward the end of his stay in Europe, however, that press became increasingly unfriendly to him. The reasons for this antagonism are not entirely clear, but certainly they included partisan politics: Cooper's most relentless critics were uniformly Whigs. Since then both he and the newspapermen had grown more and more vituperative, and it was exactly five years after his return in 1833 when the novelist filed libel suits against three upstate New York editors. These first suits were brought on the basis of local coverage of the Point dispute, but soon Cooper was suing other editors for their reviews of the Effingham Novels, their reviews of his *History of the Navy of the United States of America* (1839), even their published comments on the libel suits themselves. In all, Cooper took half a dozen editors to court, many of them more than once. Among the defendants were such famous men as Park Benjamin, Horace Greeley, and Thurlow Weed. They appeared to enjoy battling the novelist in person as much as they enjoyed panning his latest novel—either way they got lively copy, and though Cooper consistently won in the courtroom, the amount of the verdicts was always small.

Cooper's attitude toward the trials was more serious. In 1841 he claimed that he was ready to devote his life to this cause (cf. *L/J*, iv, 202)—a claim well supported by his actions. Before attempting to interpret those actions, we must acknowledge that Cooper had objective grounds for his complaints; or, as James Grossman says in his article on Cooper's libel suits, "When we read Cooper's strictures on American life we are likely to believe them exaggerated because of a certain intrusive vehemence of his rhetoric, but when we read the venomous newspaper rhetoric directed against Cooper, we realize some of the force of Cooper's arguments."[3] Beyond question, the press slandered Cooper. Some of the editors seemed to feel that anything could be said about a man with a public personality. And no doubt their abuse eventually hurt the sale of Cooper's novels. Yet Cooper's compulsion to take the editors to court did just as much damage to his popularity, and his disgressive rantings against the press in the later novels probably put off more readers than all the bad reviews. A fight against the American press was one he could not win, but he continued to wage it long after it was apparent even to him that it served no objective purpose—no courtroom victory would help to defend his character. He continued to wage it because the struggle served a compelling unconscious purpose.

That purpose is indicated by the rhetoric with which Cooper sought to explain his motives to the public, although he meant the rhetoric quite literally. "I have brought these suits," he wrote in a letter published in the *Tompkins Volunteer*, March 21st, 1843, "because I am sick of being a freeman in name only. The man is a slave, who lives in dread of calumny, and I choose to struggle for my liberty" (*L/J*, iv, 370). "At all events," he wrote in *Brother Jonathan*, January 1st, 1842, "I am determined, in my own person, to make an effort to be the freeman we all profess to be, but which no man can be, while he lives in terror of

[3] James Grossman, "Cooper and the Responsibility of the Press," *New York History* 35 (1954), 514.

tyranny like that exercised in this country by so large a portion of the press" (*L/J*, IV, 222). "The world would be surprised," he wrote in *The American Democrat*, "to learn the
tyranny that the press has exercised, in our own times, over
some of the greatest of modern names, few men possessing the
manliness and moral courage that are necessary to resist its
oppression."[4] By now we are perhaps too familiar with the
particular vocabulary used in these passages. To struggle for
liberty,[5] to make an effort to be free, to resist oppression—
this was the psychological battle in which Cooper had been
engaged since childhood. That portion of his psyche which
had rebelled against William Cooper's rule in Cooperstown,
or against the fathers of Yale College, or against England's
attempt to dominate the States, or against the public's claim
to the Three Mile Point, now fought for Cooper's independence from the newspapermen. It almost did not seem
to matter who was perceived as the oppressor—as Cooper
said in the *Arcturus* on December 6th, 1841, "to me, it is a
matter of indifference whether he who wishes to tyrannize
over me, be a prince by birth claiming to make me his slave
by inheritance, or a blackguard who edits a newspaper"
(*L/J*, IV, 202). Or, we can add, an overbearing father.

But in this psychic drama that Cooper still needed to
enact, to perform on the stage of the real world, "the editors" were not cast as the villains arbitrarily. The unconscious operates by its own rules of logic, and to serve the
novelist's unconscious purpose the editors had to be accept-
able as substitutes for the father who could no longer be
resisted. In a way that can only excite our admiration at the
workings of the mind, the editors were made to serve that
purpose.

When *Homeward Bound* and *Home As Found* were published, the newspaper critics immediately, and justifiably,
identified Edward Effingham as James Fenimore Cooper.

---

[4] *The American Democrat*, p. 125.

[5] Appropriately, it is specifically slavery that Captain Truck and the
Effinghams must defend themselves against in *Homeward Bound*.

This identification became such an important issue in the suits and quarrels that followed that the entire episode is often referred to by Cooper's biographers as "the Effingham libels." It upset Cooper tremendously, and he took great pains to demolish it. In a letter published in the *Evening Post* late in 1841 he wrote:

> You well know that a widespread attempt has been made to persuade the public that I wished to represent, or rather to misrepresent myself in the character of Mr. Effingham. Perhaps there is not a case in the annals of literature, in which one of these imaginary resemblances has been supposed to exist, that is susceptible of being so triumphantly disproved ⟨of⟩ as this between myself and Edward Effingham. (*L/J*, IV, 198)

Cooper's naiveté might appear pathological. Ned Effingham, after all, exactly like Cooper, had returned from Europe to a town on Lake Otsego where he quarreled with his neighbors about a point of land—resemblances that were anything but imaginary. Even Cooper's strenuous efforts to disprove the identity, which resulted in the two long letters to *Brother Jonathan* that I have already discussed, only reinforce the many similarities—Cooper admits, for example, that he and his character live in the same house, but insists that they have different noses! Yet his heated response to the attempt to call Edward Effingham by Cooper's name suggests that a much deeper issue was involved. I believe that it was: in effect the editors were claiming the right to bestow a name upon the novelist, a right that belonged only to his father. Cooper had to defeat such an attempt. Unfortunately the outrageous logic of the *Brother Jonathan* letters convinced no one. Cooper only got angrier when the editors began calling *him* Edward Effingham.

The most obvious way in which "the editors" could represent William Cooper in the novelist's unconscious can be mentioned quickly. "The upright judges of American literature" (*L/J*, IV, 273) is one variation on a scornful phrase that Cooper used several times to describe his opponents. His father, of course, had been First Judge of Otsego County; according to L. H. Butterfield, who was writing in Cooperstown in 1954, Cooper's father is "still known in these parts as 'The Judge.' "[6] The son, in his struggle with the newspapermen, could simply and economically replace The Judge with "those who have set themselves up as judges of all things in heaven and earth" (*L/J*, IV, 82).

For Cooper, therefore, "the editors" wished to tyrannize over him by both naming and judging him. To these two quasi-paternal claims Cooper added a third, unquestionably the most important: the newspapermen, Cooper states in *Brother Jonathan*, claimed to possess the most awesome of the father's powers. Here is what he said:

> Messrs. Weed, Benjamin, and others of the press, including, I believe, the "Three Colonels," (Messrs. Stone, Webb and King,)[7] have pronounced my works "trashy," "worthless," "overrated," "balderdash," "disgrace to American Literature," &c. &c. And some of them, if not *all* of them, with others of their league, have affirmed that any little reputation I may have gained, *has been owing to the American press.*—They have accused me—some, I do not say *all*—of ingratitude, by turning on the *power that made me*, because I have sued some of the fraternity for libels. In private, I am told, they boast they will let me feel the power of the press; and as *they made* me, so will *they destroy* me. In answer to all this, I have said, both in public and private, that I will make *them* feel the power of the law. In the end, we shall see which will prevail. (*L/J*, IV, 272)

This passage carries the issue beyond the mere problem of resisting oppression; here it is transmuted into the desperate psychological struggle of the infant son for survival

---

[6] Butterfield, "Cooper's Inheritance," p. 387.

[7] Of these five, Charles King was the only editor whom Cooper did not sue.

in the face of the father who, he knows, made him and who, he fears, can actually destroy him. Cooper goes on promptly to disprove this audacious assertion by the members of the press, but the passage reveals unmistakably the extent to which in his unconscious the editors did stand for William Cooper.

At the end of the paragraph Cooper cites "the power of the law." Libel suits, as he himself had pointed out in *Notions of the Americans*, were "astonishingly rare in America,"[8] and no one was more surprised than the editors when Cooper began serving processes. Early in 1842, again in the pages of *Brother Jonathan*, the novelist troubled to reply to the people who "say I might defend myself with the pen" (*L/J*, IV, 222). That would be easy enough, he says, but would require too great a "sacrifice of time." Yet having decided to prosecute the editors in court, Cooper not only continued to publish scores of explanations and accounts in various papers, he also took complete charge of the cases. With his nephew Richard as counsel, Cooper spent an incredible number of hours preparing and personally conducting the trials. Saving time was not the real issue in his decision to employ the power of the law. "Besides," he continued in *Brother Jonathan*, "I have learned to know that the refutation of a lie, in this country, is of little importance. It must be *punished*, to do any good." Cooper certainly did try to have the editors punished. Unlike the Three Mile Point affair, when he refused to meet his opponents face to face, the Effingham libels revealed Cooper as a man of action. By most accounts, even many presented by his adversaries, he was eloquent and very forceful in the courtroom. These trials were the only instance among the many controversies of Cooper's life in which he acted directly, not through the written word, in his own behalf. But as he had said in 1832, he looked to the New York courts for protection, and it was only in a courtroom that he could act under the eyes of a judge. Once he had firmly decided

8 *Notions*, II, 105.

to behave like Judge Cooper's dutiful son, once he had atoned for his ebullitions and executed the Judge's will, the presence of a New York judge apparently provided him with the kind of security he needed to open up in public.

We shall return to this topic when we examine Cooper's last novel, *The Ways of the Hour*; there Cooper appears to advance a plan to abolish juries entirely in order to let the judge be the sole arbiter of a defendant's fate. About the relationship between Cooper and the press only one thing remains to be noted—the disturbing evidence that it provides of Cooper's tendency to paranoia. In one sense there obviously was a kind of conspiracy among the Whig editors to annoy and abuse Cooper: on the basis of his political statements they ranked him with the Democrats and considered him fair game. Journalism was a rough profession at that time, and invective a common way to fill column inches; editors insulted each other as frequently as they insulted political opponents.[9] Cooper, however, felt that the papers' hostility was malign and personal, that he had been singled out for persecution: "Perhaps there is no instance of a similar, atrocious invasion of private right, as connected with the press, to that of the attacks on me" (*L/J*, IV, 222). For example, he could angrily refer to "a combined attack in the newspapers—one, so little concealed, as to induce its agents to write and promise a moneyed contribution to maintain it" (*L/J*, IV, 222). By moneyed contribution he meant the "Effingham Libel Fund." This was proposed in jest by an editor after Cooper had announced yet a new libel suit: he suggested that all the editors in the country could contribute one dollar. Needless to say, Cooper was not amused. As he got older, Cooper became more convinced that there was a secret conspiracy against him.

[9] The journalists, according to Van Wyck Brooks' account of this period, occasionally went beyond invective in their attacks: "The most respectable editors, Bryant, for instance, assaulted one another on the streets" (*The World of Washington Irving* [N.Y.: E. P. Dutton & Co., Inc., 1944], p. 326).

The year before he died he wrote one friend that "for years" there had been "a *concerted plan* among the news paper men and the leaders of the Whigs, with here and there an exception, to put me down by apparent neglect. I have been distinctly notified of the existence of such a plan, and have had proof of its being carried out in several instances" (*L/J*, VI, 198). The facts suggest, however, that the papers neglected Cooper's novels because at last they got tired of answering his subpoenas.

Despite the court cases, Cooper managed to publish about three novels every two years. More prolific during the 1840s, he was also poorer and apparently less popular. The silence of many of the papers after the last libel suits ended in 1843 and the cheapness of the new English novels still being pirated by American printers, the turn in literary taste from the romances of Scott to the urban melodramas of Dickens and the confused image in the popular mind of the irascible author, all contributed to a substantial reduction of Cooper's literary income. And of course he remained sore at his countrymen. When one of them wrote him an admiring letter in 1841, Cooper replied that he was touched, and surprised. "This is the only country," he told the man, "in which I have found it a positive personal disadvantage to be a writer" (*L/J*, IV, 195). He was not complaining, he said; he merely wanted his admirer to understand "how little inducement I can have to write except according to own convenience and benefit." Writing was an activity that he could not abandon, but now he felt free to write every book exclusively to please himself.

After *The Deerslayer* he wrote thirteen such novels. To me, the most interesting of them is *Wyandotté* (1843). Depicting a series of episodes in the early life of a small upstate New York settlement, the book represents a darker, more ambiguous version of *The Pioneers*. Cooper himself, in the introductory pages of *Wyandotté*, suggests a parallel between the two novels:

They who have done us the honor to read our previous works, will at once understand that the district to which we allude is that of which we have taken more than one occasion to write; and we return to it now less with a desire to celebrate its charms than to exhibit them in a somewhat novel, and yet perfectly historical aspect.[10]

Charms the book has not. The historical period is the Revolutionary War, but though there are sufficient battle scenes and reconnoiterings, *Wyandotté* is not another martial adventure story. The first sentence of Cooper's Preface states that "the history of the borders is filled with legends of the sufferings of isolated families, during the troubled scenes of colonial warfare" (p. v). The book's real interest centers on the family—even the colony's war is called "a family quarrel" (p. 138), and it functions in the novel less as an actual historical event than as a metaphor for the tensions and struggles of the leading characters. "What a thing is a civil war!" laments one of them. "Here is husband divided against wife—son against father—brother against sister" (pp. 140-41).

The husband and father is Captain Willoughby. In 1765 he retires from the English army to found a settlement in the wilds of New York. Cooper quickly recounts the Captain's work as a pioneer, then advances the action ten years, to the commencement of the Revolution. By that time Willoughby is the patriarch of a fairly large community, composed mainly of emigrants from New England. Living with the Captain are his wife, his daughter Beulah, and his adopted daughter Maud, who has, however, always been strictly considered by the family as his own child. On the day in May 1775 when the story reopens, two more of the Captain's dependents return home. The first is an aging Indian warrior named Wyandotté, though everyone calls

[10] *Wyandotté; or, The Hutted Knoll*, p. 10.

him "Saucy Nick." Nick's relationship with Willoughby
dates back thirty years: he had originally pointed out the
site of Willoughby's patent, and has lived with him off and
on ever since. After a long absence, Nick returns to the
Hutted Knoll (the name of the Willoughbys' house) with
the news that their only son, Robert, is following just behind him. Robert, who has been away serving as a Major
in the British army, comes with the news that England and
the colonies have at last come to blows. The Major com-
municates this alarming information privately in the Captain's library, where the following exchange occurs:

> " . . . I beg you to remember the awkwardness of my
> position, as a king's officer, in the midst of enemies."
> "The devil! . . . Do you call lodging in your father's
> house, Major Willoughby, being in the midst of en-
> emies? This is rebellion against nature, and is worse
> than rebellion against the king."
> "My dear father, no one feels more secure with you
> than I do. . . ." (p. 88)

Robert's bland rejoinder is sincere, yet this misunderstanding is one of many ambiguities that create an underlying
tension, a tension that builds throughout the story and is
resolved only by violence, a tension that is only superficially
connected with rebellion against the king, but one which in
fact implies rebellions against nature.

Cooper did not plan what eventually happens to the narrative. *Wyandotté* is another novel that seemed to write
itself. Its original title was "The Hutted Knoll," but two
months after the printers began setting its first volume
Cooper told Bentley that he would probably rename it: "A
few chapters remain to be written, and the incidents have
led me away in such a manner, that I am not certain a more
pithy title can not be found" (*L/J*, IV, 388). Had not the
incidents dictated a new plot, "The Hutted Knoll" would
have been a story of the greed and treachery of New Eng-

land demagogues, and its most dramatic episode would have
been the assault by Willoughby's settlers against their landlord, using the pretext of the Revolution to seize his property unlawfully. That subject of course had a personal
meaning for the novelist. But *Wyandotté's* most dramatic
moments are still more personal, and its most significant
psychological conflicts occur within the palisades that ostensibly protect the Willoughby family.

The first of these is the relationship between Robert Willoughby and his foster sister Maud. Their romantic love for
each other is more than a conventional plot element. Although Bob has always known, and Maud for several years,
that there is no familial tie, they feel separately ashamed of
their emotions, and this has produced a false estrangement
which no one else in the family comprehends. As Cooper
says, "Two minutes of frank communication might have
dissipated all these scruples for ever" (p. 279). At the one
point when a conversation between them turns in this direction, however, Bob abruptly breaks off a sentence and
Maud starts "as if some frightful object glared before her
eyes" (p. 278). Guilt keeps the young lovers apart—for Bob
"had ever shrunk from the direct avowal of his own sentiments, lest he might shock her; as a sister's ear would nat-
urally be wounded by a declaration of attachment from a
brother"; and Maud "struggled with her feelings, as against
a weakness" (pp. 278-79).

Much later their struggle is finally rewarded with understanding. Frank communication, however, is not the means
Bob chooses to declare his attachment. Rather he presents
Maud with a riddle to solve. Held prisoner by the rebellious tenants besieging his father's house, the Major manages to get a message, and a gift, sent in to Maud. The gift
is a silver snuff-box; the message: "When you get at the contents of this box, dear girl, you will learn the great secret of
my life" (p. 407). No ordinary snuff-box, this one can only
be opened by finding its "secret spring" (p. 406). After a lot
of trepidation and a long search for the secret spring, Maud

does "get at" the contents of the box—and of Robert's
heart, for inside is a lock of her hair: "It was a memorial of
herself, then, that Robert Willoughby so prized, had so long
guarded with care, and which he called the secret of his
life!" (p. 410). Given the way Cooper has handled their
attachment, it is impossible not to regard Bob and Maud's
suppressed emotions—so long guarded with care—as one of
the class of "life secrets" which all people keep hidden beneath the "secret springs" of the unconscious. I have already said that among the strongest forces in Cooper's
psyche was his repressed incestuous love for his sister Hannah. I believe that love, so close beneath the surface of *The
Pioneers*, here pushes its way, through the unguarded working of his imagination, into the text of *Wyandotté*. Of
course the love shared by Bob and Maud is not incestuous,
but Cooper treats it as such, the lovers consider it as such.
Even after the riddle of the box has been solved, the guilt
remains. For if "from that moment, [Maud] ceased to feel
shame" for her passion, "She might still have shrunk a little
from avowing it to her father and mother, and Beulah"
(p. 411), and in fact she carefully conceals from them both
the box and its secret.

As it turns out, neither she nor Bob must reveal their
passion to the others. By the end of the novel, Captain and
Mrs. Willoughby and their daughter are dead. The women
are brutally killed by some Indians who have joined the
traitorous settlers in the effort to dispossess their landlord,
an effort which, thanks to the timely arrival of a detachment of upright Colonials, is at the last second defeated.
But this rescue is an anticlimax: Captain Willoughby's
death, as James Grossman points out, "is the heart of the
book,"[11] and the Captain is murdered somewhat earlier,
murdered not by a grasping outsider, but by his old acquaintance Wyandotté.

Wyandotté kills for revenge: revenge for the times over the
last thirty years that Willoughby, a bit of a martinet, had

11 Grossman, *Cooper*, p. 180.

flogged him. The Captain has the bad habit of reminding Saucy Nick of these floggings. He does so once too often. "Wyandotté's back don't ache now" (p. 446) is the Indian's response once he has done the deed. Edgar Allan Poe, reviewing the book in *Graham's Magazine*, calls the murder "a species of poetical justice. We may observe here, nevertheless," Poe continues, "that [Willoughby's] repeated references to his flogging the Indian seem unnatural, because we have otherwise no reason to think him a fool, or a madman, and these references, under the circumstances, are absolutely insensate."[12] Poe's objection is well-taken. But the particular circumstances surrounding the Captain's death can explain what otherwise would be absolutely insensate.

Deserted by almost all his dependents, encircled by enemies, Willoughby determines at least to rescue his son. To accomplish this he sets out from the Hutted Knoll with a small party of faithful servants to the buttery shed where the Major is being kept. Their passage through hostile territory is quiet and careful and safe. Fifty feet from the buttery Willoughby leaves his party and proceeds with Wyandotté to reconnoiter the remaining distance. There he suddenly chooses, despite the need for absolute silence, to threaten Nick with another beating. There he dies. "He had breathed his last, within six feet of his own gallant son, who, ignorant of all that passed, was little dreaming of the proximity of one so dear to him, as well as of his dire condition" (p. 440). This lamely written protestation of the son's innocence cannot disguise the fact that Cooper has brought the father across a number of miles to die within six feet of his son. A little later, in fact, again first establishing Robert's "utter ignorance," Cooper describes the slaying as "the dire event that had so lately occurred, almost within reach of his arm" (p. 463). Since Cooper renamed his book after the Indian, this was beyond question that most significant of the incidents that led him away from his first inten-

[12] Edgar Allan Poe, "Review of *Wyandotté*," *Graham's Magazine* 23 (1843), 262.

tions. The incident's biographical significance is very well noted by Grossman: "The novelist, whose own father, also the founder of a settlement, was murdered, treats with deep respect the savage's ritual need to kill the patriarch."[13] What is really depicted in this scene is parricide. That the Major, although only an arm's length away, did not actually wield the knife that killed his father is psychologically irrelevant. Neither did the novelist actually kill his father. But the wish to get rid of the Judge was fixed in his unconscious, and when another man carried out that wish Cooper would still have felt guilty. In the son's unconscious the murder of his father must always be a parricide.

Wyandotté reveals that this was true for Cooper. Wyandotté himself, having killed the Captain, says of the Captain's wife, "She my moder, too!" (p. 474). And the real son is made to lose his "utter ignorance," and with it his innocence, in regard to his father's death. For years, Cooper informs us (reminding one again of William Cooper's death), no one knows the details of Willoughby's death. In the book's last chapter, however, Robert discovers Wyandotté and his father's former chaplain beside his father's grave. The chaplain has converted Saucy Nick to Christianity, and heard his confession for the Captain's slaying. With Wyandotté's approval, he informs the Major that he has "a secret to communicate" to him. We are not allowed to overhear their conversation; instead Cooper tells us that "Willoughby had yielded to [the chaplain's] expostulations and arguments a forgiveness, which came reluctantly, and perhaps as much for the want of a suitable object for retaliation, as from a sense of Christian duty." But when the Indian then hands the son his tomahawk, bares his breast, and commands, "Strike—Nick kill cap'in—Major kill Nick," he unmistakably presents the son with an apparently suitable object of retaliation (pp. 520-21). Yet Robert cannot strike, and his failure to strike ratifies his complicity in

<hr />

[13] Grossman, *Cooper*, p. 180.

his father's murder. He cannot find a psychically suitable object for retaliation because he is, as Cooper knew below the conscious level of his mind, equally guilty. As Freud pointed out about Hamlet's similar inability to avenge his father, he cannot kill the man who in his unconscious represents himself.

I am tempted to take more time with *Wyandotté*, especially with the way Cooper runs the father's murder and the son's marriage together—Robert proposes to Maud only seconds before Maud informs Robert of the slaying (cf. pp. 469 and 471-74). We have already discussed how closely Cooper linked the Judge's death with his own marriage a year later. I think, though, that enough has been said about a novel that is hardly ever read. It is a very difficult book to read: gloomy, confusing, unrelieved. I am not entirely certain why Cooper decided, even against his conscious will, to write it at this time—unless merely returning to the region of *The Pioneers*, to the early life of a frontier settlement, stirred up the powerful impulses of his own early life that were repressed in his unconscious, so that they demanded imaginative release. At the beginning of the book, after Robert's homecoming, he teases his sisters about their love affairs and demands to be made "*au fait* of all the family mysteries" (p. 85). By the end, the reader feels uncomfortably aware of those mysteries, all of them indeed. How Cooper felt after finishing *Wyandotté* is not recorded in any of the extant letters, but one may hope that he experienced the catharsis which the reader is denied.

Two years and two more novels after *Wyandotté* Cooper again decided to write about the settlement of land in upstate New York. This time he kept clear of family mysteries, concentrating instead on the theme he had started to develop in *Wyandotté*: the rights of property versus the greed of tenants. To treat this issue properly, Cooper felt, required the most deliberately extended literary project he had undertaken. "The Family of Littlepage," he wrote Bentley in 1845, describing his plans,

239

will form three complete Tales, each perfectly distinct
from the others as regards leading characters, love story
&c, but, in this wise connected. I divide the subjects
into the "Colony," "Revolution" and "Republic," carrying the same family, the same localities, and the same
things generally through the three different books, but
exhibiting the changes produced by time &c. In the
Colony, for instance, the Littlepage of that day, first
visits an estate of wild land, during the operations of
the year 1758, the year that succeeded the scenes of the
Mohicans, and it is there that the most stirring events
of the book oc[c]ur. In the "Revolution" this land is
first settled, and the principles are developed, on which
this settlement takes place, showing a book, in some
respects resembling the Pioneers, though varied by localities and incidents—In the "Republic" we shall have
the present aspect of things, with an exhibition of the
Anti-Rent commotion that now exists among us, and
which certainly threatens the destruction of our system
— (*L*/*J*, v, 7)

As published, "The Family of Littlepage" became "The
Littlepage Manuscripts," the "Colony" *Satanstoe* (1845),
the "Revolution" *The Chainbearer* (1845), and the "Republic" *Red Skins* (1846). Otherwise Cooper's letter gives
an accurate description of the series. Each of the novels is a
first-person account by a Littlepage (Cooper had first used
the first-person narrative form in the two preceding tales,
Afloat and Ashore and *Miles Wallingford*); the three novels
cover four generations of that family's adventures and
achievements on the Mooseridge and Ravensnest patents.

Cooper planned the series in response to contemporary
events. The Anti-Rent War of the 1840s had its beginning,
like the Littlepage Manuscripts, in the early days of New
York colony, in the policy of the Dutch West Indies Company to grant patroonships to wealthy colonists. These men
received feudal rights over vast patents. They leased their

land in small portions to tenants from whom they annually claimed rent in produce, money, or labor. This system of landholding was confined to New York, where for many years the position of the patroons was undisturbed. But in 1839 the falling price of wheat and the rising spirit of democracy combined to incite the patroons' tenants to rebellion. They could not afford the rents, and besides, they argued with good reason, feudal rights were opposed to the principles upon which the country was founded. With less reason they insisted that they were entitled to outright ownership of their farms. Ragtag armies of tenants banded together to prevent the landlords and sheriffs from evicting the nonpaying renters, and at one point the Governor had to mobilize the militia to restore order. For Cooper, as he indicates in the letter to Bentley, the real issue was nothing less than the survival of the United States. Writing to his friend William Shubrick while he was working on the trilogy, Cooper added a postscript: "You see what anti-rentism is about? It is the great American question of the day" (L/J, v, 52). It was to deal with that question, and if he could, to settle it, that Cooper wrote the Littlepage Manuscripts.

Also in the letter to Bentley Cooper suggests analogies between these novels and two of the Leather-Stocking Tales. In a later letter he makes a broader comparison, telling Bentley that he intends to connect "one or two characters with the three books as Leatherstocking appears in different tales" (L/J, v, 56). But a comparison between the two series —Cooper's two most sustained fictional productions—reveals primarily a striking difference. As a whole, the Tales are ambivalent about the American goal of populating the wilderness, and the life of Natty Bumppo, as he appears in the different Tales, represents a morally clear as well as an aesthetically convincing denial of that goal. The Manuscripts, on the other hand, affirm that clearing the forest for society is unequivocally good, and that the men who lead this enterprise, the landlords, are the very capital on the column of American civilization.[14] As a hero, a landlord is much less palatable to us than a backwoodsman, but it is not difficult to account for the novelist's desire to present him in that pose.

Though Cooper did own several acres in Cooperstown, he was by no means himself a landlord. Granville Hicks makes a common error when he describes "the roots of Cooper's indignation against the antirenters" in these words: "he was specifically defending the class to which he belonged, the class of large landlords." Yet Hicks's characterization of the three novels is exact and perceptive: "The antirent trilogy is starkly and one might almost say uniquely class-conscious, for it is both a theoretical defense of a class and an emotional expression of class-feeling at a high pitch."[15] The class he was defending, however, and impersonating, was not his; it was his father's. David M. Ellis' explanation of Cooper's emotional indignation is the more persuasive one: "The [anti-rent] *jacquerie* seemed to be undermining not only the institution of property but also repudiating his family background."[16] That his family background was foremost in Cooper's mind is even revealed in the way he chose to approach the issue of anti-rentism. The Littlepage Manuscripts are the only instance in his fiction where he deliberately planned to write sequels, or where he depicts the generational succession of a family. In this respect one analogy with the Leather-Stocking Tales seems very appropriate. The two series cover much the same period of American history. But in the first Cooper himself attempts to repudiate his family background; in the second, then, he rewrites that story from the antithetical perspective. Just as the meaning of the Tales and the presence of Natty Bumppo can be traced to the novelist's latent hos-

[14] Cf. Preface to *The Chainbearer*, pp. viii-ix.
[15] "Landlord Cooper and the Anti-Renters," *The Antioch Review* 5 (1945), 98.
[16] "The Coopers and New York State Landholding Systems," *New York History* 35 (1954), 412.

tility toward his father, the man who by 1807 had settled
more acres than any other American, so the meaning of the
Manuscripts and the presence of three landlord-heroes can
be traced to the novelist's psychological submission to his
father. That submission was so complete, so prostrate was
Cooper, that he seriously believed the framework of the republic was threatened by the behavior of a few thousand
destitute tenants. After all, they were defying the figure of
the landlord, a sin that was now beyond Cooper's contem-
plation. What Hicks describes as the high pitch of Cooper's
feelings is, in *The Redskins*, closer to hysteria. Surely, he
felt, if a New York landlord could successfully be overthrown, the end of civilization must be near.

The Littlepage Manuscripts offer strong circumstantial
evidence of Cooper's submission to his father. From his
letters, from his behavior, can be cited direct evidence. For
example, on June 1st, 1848, Cooper wrote his niece, Mrs.
Charles Woolson (née Hannah Cooper Pomeroy), to invite
her to visit the Mansion-House. He does not exactly say that
he would be pleased to see *her*, but that

> I have great pleasure in seeing any descendant of my
> father in this house, for I think it would have given
> him pleasure to know that his posterity meet in this
> spot, where I should think they must be induced to
> think of its founder. I have embellished a little, but
> he founded the place, and it is the first man who be-
> comes identified with any thing of this sort. (*L/J*, v, 369)

This extraordinary passage exhibits to a remarkable degree
the way Cooper had invested his emotional energy in the
Judge. In Cooper's mind the father has become "the founder," "the first man." "This spot" has become almost a
shrine to the founder's memory. The world-renowned novelist appears to advance his father's fame ahead of his own.
The claims he makes for himself—"I have embellished a
little"—are self-effacing; those he grants his father—"he
founded the place"—seem all-inclusive. The son's pleasure

has become synonymous with the father's. It was for this reason, because "it would have given him pleasure," that his son wrote the anti-rent trilogy. Now a middle-aged man, James Cooper was that determined to be a dutiful child, to be the kind of son he had originally not been.

"In this house" he remained until his death. "I have had a good deal of difficulty in keeping possession," he goes on in the letter to Mrs. Woolson, "there being a very strong disposition in this country to make common property out of any thing that takes the fancy of the public. I suppose one half of this village would gladly pull down this house, because they can not walk through the hall whenever it suits them; but I am firm. . . ." His firmness on this point is attested to by all his biographers. As Spiller puts it: "when the small boys and girls of the village stole into the Hall garden for roses or berries, they were likely to find its owner descending upon them with stick in hand; and if he caught them, he would not let them go until he had lectured them on the crime of theft."[17] This figure would be merely funny did we not recognize the impulse to which Cooper was responding. The man whom the village children no doubt considered the neighborhood grouch was actually serving a sacred cause: to protect the shrine he had erected in his unconscious from desecration. The descendants of his father—fellow-worshippers—could always be admitted, but the profane had to be kept out.

I have already said that Cooper made the Hall a sanctuary. He himself said in 1850 that "I am so much of a recluse when at home, seeing and hearing so little of the outer world" (L/J, VI, 172). The outer world began at the walls of the Mansion-House, and included the people of Cooperstown. Describing the novelist's aloof behavior in the village, S. T. Livermore also tries, charitably, to explain it:

The amount of labor which he performed left him but little time for sociability. When he walked the streets

17 Spiller, p. 293.

his mind, abstracted from present scenes and passers-by, was doubtless threading the forest, wandering over the prairie, or engaged in a sea fight. This, with the fact of his spending so much time in his study, accounts for the seeming distance there was between him and many of his fellow citizens.[18]

That distance, however, was real, and it separated the novelist from his fellow Americans as well. Cooper's unsociability, his withdrawal from present scenes, excepting members of the family and old friends, excepting contemporary events that had a personal significance, should be traced to his psychological, not his literary, preoccupations. "As he advanced in years he narrowed instead of broadening," writes Lounsbury of Cooper, characterizing a man who was unable "to project himself out of the circle of his own feelings."[19] At the center of that tight circle was William Cooper, whose centripetal presence in Fenimore Cooper's unconscious ruled his relationships with the rest of mankind. Cooper himself, using the persona of Miles Wallingford, gives a better and more suggestive account than Livermore of the motive behind his aloofness: "Certain I am, that all the real, manly, independent democrats I have ever known in America, have been accused of aristocracy, and this simply because they were disposed to carry out their principles, and not to let that imperious sovereign, 'the neighborhood,' play the tyrant over them."[20] If William Tell would not lift his cap to the tyrant Gessler, neither would Cooper lift his to the tyrant neighbors. The real manly independent stance that he took with the villagers, like the struggle to resist the editors, satisfied the active impulse of his psyche. In a way, he was putting Tocqueville's "tyranny of the majority" to its ultimate emotional uses. His manhood constantly reaffirmed on his walks through

[18] Livermore, *History of Cooperstown*, p. 202.
[19] Lounsbury, pp. 256 and 259.
[20] *Miles Wallingford*, p. 213.

the village, he could return once more to his father's study and his role as his father's obedient son.

The last years of his life indicate that the passive impulse of his unconscious made greater and greater demands for submission. "Filial piety" is a phrase that Cooper used in a number of contexts during these last years,[21] but I want to use it to stand for the most striking reorientation of Cooper's psychic posture in the late 1840s. His daughter Susan describes this change as follows:

> Through life the religious convictions of the author of "The Pathfinder" had been clear and sincere. . . . He ever yielded a full and honest assent to the great doctrines of Christianity. . . . But . . . he had not until a comparatively late day fully submitted to those sacred influences.[22]

Susan's choice of the words "fully submitted" is a very perceptive one, but she was much too conventional to suggest how radically different her father's new-found susceptibility to "sacred influences" in fact was from his previous attitude toward religion. In 1848 he began reading the Bible for the first time, at least for the first time with interest, as the journal he kept reveals. For example, the March 16th, 1848, entry includes this comment: "Genesis. What an extraordinary history!" (*L/J*, v, 312). What had before been simply an unthinking assent to the doctrines of Christianity, a kind of cultural piety, became an active, thoughtful, and persevering exploration toward their meaning. And the meaning Cooper found was determined by the terms of his psychological history. In discovering and vesting his faith in God the Father, he was more fully submitting to the real

21 Cf. for one example *L/J*, v, 168. Cooper writes on September 18th, 1846, to accept an honorary membership in the Historical Society of New Jersey, where he had been born: "I shall not consider labour expended in behalf of New Jersey as time thrown away, but as a simple exhibition of natural filial piety."

22 *Pages and Pictures*, p. 391.

father. Or, in other words, in the son's unconscious, the stature of William Cooper grew so large, his presence so commanding, that he underwent an apotheosis: the father became the Father.

This type of transformation is a common psychological process, one that in Cooper's case can be closely followed; the interpretive step from Father to father is easy to take. As early as 1838, in a section of *The American Democrat*, Cooper associated the earthly and the divine fathers within the same thought, within the space of one sentence: "The first direct mandates of God, as delivered on Mount Sinai, were to impress the Jews with a sense of their duties to their Heavenly Father; the next to impress them with the first of their social duties, that of honor and obedience to their parents."[23] To obey William Cooper had he protected the Three Mile Point, to honor William Cooper had he written the *Chronicles of Cooperstown*, and these "social duties" had acquired, as his letter to Mrs. Woolson reveals, an increasing value in his eyes. On January 17th, 1847, writing to Shubrick about a mutual acquaintance, Cooper said, "By the way, he spoke of Conner reverentially, as one ought to speak of a papa" (*L/J*, v, 190). Not respect, but reverence— a state of mind usually reserved for a deity—reverence was the emotion with which he regarded his papa. Cooper had come full circle: from defying William Cooper's authority to deifying it.

It was more than a decade previously, after he had been forced to conclude that the American public had betrayed and traduced him, that Cooper had begun to reassess his father's authority. Popularity was the psychic armor which he had worn in his struggle for mental and psychological independence. When public approval appeared to be withdrawn, he renounced the struggle and put on the hand-me-down clothes of a Cooper of Cooperstown. This, I believe, is the latent meaning of the following homily from *The*

23 *The American Democrat*, p. 80.

Crater (1847), one of his late novels, and consequently one which reflects his nascent faith in his Heavenly Father:

> Success is all in all with the common mind; and we daily see the vulgar shouting at the heels of those whom they are ready to crucify at the first turn of fortune. In this good land of ours, popularity adds to its more worthless properties the substantial result of power; and it is not surprising that so many forget their God in the endeavor to court the people. In time, however, all of these persons of mistaken ambition come to ex-claim, with Shakespeare's Wolsey—
>
>> "Had I but served my God with half the zeal
>> I served my king, he would not in mine age
>> Have left me naked to mine enemies."[24]

One of these persons was of course J. Fenimore Cooper, who stated in a letter a year before writing *The Crater* that "I can say with Woolsey, 'if I had served my god with half the zeal I've served my *country*,' it would have been better for me" (*L/J*, v, 132). Two changes are therefore necessary in the passage from *The Crater*. Just as Cooper, writing in his own person, substituted country for king, so we must conclude that in his mind he had substituted God for father. Because his countrymen had let him down, he turned to his father for support; because he felt he had let his father down, he became the more thoroughly dedicated to carry-ing out his father's will, to trying to please his father; and because only a divinity can properly claim that degree of subservience, he at last turned his father into God.

Oak Openings (1848) followed *The Crater*. For the first time in his career Cooper chose a religious theme: the case history of a conversion to Christianity. Though the convert is a Michigan Indian named Scalping Peter, the penulti-mate paragraph of his story offers an insight into the causes of Cooper's own recent conversion. No longer a "heathen,"

[24] *The Crater*, pp. 361-62.

old Scalping Peter now looks back "upon his [aboriginal] traditions and superstitions with a sort of melancholy interest, as we all portray in our memories the scenes, legends, and feelings of an erring childhood."[25] Cooper had reason to equate the memories of a rebellious childhood with the guilt of a converted pagan toward the period before he had found God: in his case, the Prodigal Son had come home to the Father.

Cooper kept a journal at the time he was reading the Bible, and the musings that he entered there reveal the way in which unconsciously he applied the truths of sacred history to his own behavior. On March 16th, 1848, reading Genesis, he wrote: "It is impossible for us to appreciate conduct, when a power like that of God is directly brought to bear on it—Obedience to him is our first law" (L/J, v, 312-13). Resistance to oppression, rebellion against authority, insistence upon self-determination—these once characteristic acts, these once commendable virtues, are overruled in the face of the incomprehensible but omnipotent commands of Jehovah. Two days later, still in Genesis, he wrote: "The more I read of this book the more I feel convinced that sin is 'transgression against the Law,' and nothing else" (L/J, v, 313). At the end of his life, the Judge's son made "Obedience to the Law" the supreme human virtue. The Law was God's, of course, but the God was recognizably Cooper's. In *The Sea Lions* (1849), his thirty-first novel, his second religious novel, Cooper described that God as "the Dread Being who had created all, who governed all, and who was judge of all"[26]—a Being, in fact, very much like the founder of Cooperstown.

What Cooper did in his thirty-second and last tale was, in effect, to turn God back into the Judge. When he wrote Bentley about *The Sea Lions* he mentioned that it would be the last, "though there may be an exception in favour of a long cherished project, which will require time to execute"

---

[25] *Oak Openings*, p. 496.   [26] *The Sea Lions*, p. 456.

(*L/J*, v, 374). Whether *The Ways of the Hour*, published in 1850, was actually the fulfillment of that project, Cooper did not say, though it obviously deals with a subject he had long pondered. All he told Bentley at the time was that "my story is one of to-day, and does not so much relate to the *manners* of Manhattan, or pictures of its ordinary society, as to certain peculiarities connected with its justice, and its mode of administering the law" (*L/J*, vi, 43-44). The story is, in Grossman's words, "an improbable murder mystery"[27] whose plot evolves around the courtroom trial of Mary Monson. Grossman convincingly argues that this plot was based on the real trial several years earlier of a woman named Mary Bodine, but Cooper thoroughly transforms the issues of the real case to underscore what he called "certain peculiarities."

And in any case, Cooper had always been preoccupied with the themes of justice and judgment. In 1833 he termed the newspapers' adverse response to his participation in the Finance Controversy "putting an American on his trial, at the bar of public opinion." He then took the newspapers to trial at the bar of New York State, relying on the judgment of the courts for his justice. In the middle of *The Ways of the Hour*, Cooper even describes life as "this condition of trial."[28] That is a metaphor often used by religious men, but Cooper, I believe, had a secular meaning in mind: almost every one of his novels contains an unmistakable "judgment scene," a scene in which, to quote from one such book, "the whole arrangement [has] a most uncomfortable air of investigation and justice."[29] We have already examined the judgment scene in *The Pioneers*. These episodes, however, do not uniformly take place in an official courtroom before a duly constituted judge and jury. Certainly the most fa-

[27] Grossman, *Cooper*, p. 238. Grossman also reads *The Ways of the Hour* from a biographical perspective. His focus and conclusions are different from mine; his interpretation is extremely interesting.

[28] *The Ways of the Hour*, p. 313.

[29] *Wing-and-Wing* (1842), p. 262.

mous and the most impressive of Cooper's judgment scenes
occurs in Chapter Thirty-One of *The Prairie*, before what
Henry Nash Smith calls "Ishmael Bush's primitive court of
justice."[30] Himself a lawless squatter, Bush nonetheless, to
quote Smith again, "deals out justice as a self-constituted
patriarchal law-giver and judge";[31] convened hundreds of
miles into the desolate space of the Great Plains, the court
nonetheless conforms to society's mode of administering the
law.

Before discussing *The Ways of the Hour*, the novel in
which the judgment scene expands to fill the story, I want
to look briefly at *The Prairie*'s thirty-first chapter. The action of the tale has left most of its important characters in
Ishmael's power. He believes that all of them have committed some wrong against himself or his family. At the
chapter's beginning, the novelist carefully heightens the
squatter's moral stature: he is pictured moving "through his
little encampment, with the seriousness of one who had
been unexpectedly charged with matters of a gravity exceed-
ing any of the ordinary occurrences of his irregular existence." In the next sentence the narrator's perspective suddenly shifts to enable us to see the squatter through his
sons' eyes:

> His sons, however, who had so often found occasions to
> prove the inexorable severity of their father's character,
> saw, in his sullen mien and cold eye, rather a determi-
> nation to adhere to his resolutions, which usually were
> as obstinately enforced as they were harshly conceived,
> than any evidences of wavering or doubt.[32]

Next these sons, "in obedience to an order from their father,
conducted the several subjects of his contemplated decisions
from their places of confinement into the open air," and the
prisoners are "placed in situations that were deemed suit-

[30] Smith, Introduction to *The Prairie* (New York: Holt, Rinehart
and Winston, Inc., 1950), p. x.
[31] Ibid., pp. xviii-xix.   [32] *The Prairie*, pp. 423-24.

able to receive the sentence of their arbitrary judge" (pp. 424-25). So far, as the novelist states, Bush's authority is solely a "species of patriarchal power," but it excites "a degree of awe" even in his prisoners (p. 425). Ishmael proceeds, in fact, to appropriate a higher power by declaring: "I am called upon this day to fill the office which in the settlements you give unto judges, who are set apart to decide on matters that arise between man and man" (p. 426).

With this announcement the trial opens: Cooper has set up the inexorable father as the arbitrary judge. One by one the prisoners are brought before the "Judge," their cases weighed by him, and eventually their liberty restored by him, until only one prisoner remains. That prisoner is "the old trapper," the eighty-odd-year-old Natty Bumppo, who had similarly been arraigned in Judge Temple-Cooper's pioneer courtroom. Here on the prairie the charge against him is more serious: Ishmael accuses him of having murdered his oldest son, and declares his intention to take Natty's life in return. There is a pause, and then the trapper realizes that "he was expected to vindicate himself from the heavy imputation." Natty's speech for the defense reminds us of both his role in *The Pioneers*, and the attitude of all Cooper's early heroes, the rebels against authority: "For myself, I hope, there is no boasting in saying, that though my hand has been needed in putting down wickedness and oppression, it has never struck a blow of which its owner will be ashamed to hear, at a reckoning that shall be far mightier than this" (p. 436). Natty, innocent of the charge, had actually witnessed the crime, and he proceeds to confront the real murderer, Ishmael's brother-in-law, with his deed. The criminal's face immediately betrays his guilt; the squatter asserts his terrible authority:

> The voice of Ishmael was deep, and even awful, as he answered—
> "It is enough. Let the old man go. Boys, put the brother of your mother in his place." (p. 438)

As before, the magistrate is at once the head of the family, the head of the family, the magistrate.

This synthesis of the roles of father and judge—characters that William Cooper also had in common—is without question among the most significant aspects of this dramatic judicial *and* familial scene. Equally significant is the fact that Cooper deliberately arraigns his hero before such a father-judge. As I have said, these episodes, with their uncomfortable air of investigation and justice, appear in the majority of Cooper's novels. Repeatedly his heroes must account for themselves before some kind of tribunal presided over by some kind of judge. In Cooper's fiction, as in his life, resisting wickedness and oppression—the "gift" claimed by Natty in Bush's court—required one to stand up to the judge. Although there is no record of such a scene, we can be confident that the young Cooper was often forced to vindicate his actions before the commanding figure of his father, a man who did not hesitate—either within or without the Mansion-House—to pass judgment, to deliver a sentence. We have the testimony of the Judge's character, the son's behavior, and not least the novelist's fictions.

The last of his novels explicitly reveals how deeply Cooper had been impressed by his own appearances before the Judge. "The ways of the hour" are evil ways, and *The Ways of the Hour* reads like a recapitulation of all Cooper's complaints about the actions and principles of his countrymen. But the various details of these accusations need not occupy our attention; nor do we need to attempt a summary of the book's complex, digressive, confused, and absurd plot. For according to Cooper, there is one specific problem which demands our attention as "the crying evil of the times";[33] there are also only two forces to which we can look for salvation—"the Deity" (cf. p. 19) and "the judiciary" (cf. p. 29). And about the Deity he has in this novel little to say.

The crying evil of the times is the threat that Cooper perceived to the authority of the judges. Part of the threat

[33] *The Ways of the Hour*, p. 282.

was contained in a recent law that provided for the popular election of judges to fixed terms, but Cooper's uneasiness cannot be traced to any one particular change. Everything that has happened in the last fifty years is equally responsible. In one passage near the middle of the book he comes closest to defining his fears and objections. "The judges of this great republic," he asserts, "may lay claim to be classed among the most upright of which history furnishes any account." At least, this was true "down as late as the commencement of the present century." It was in 1801 that William Cooper had retired from the bench, and it was, I suggest, his father that the novelist pictured as he described the former glory of the legal system and lamented its passing: "The sheriff appeared with his sword, the judge was escorted to and from the courthouse to his private dwelling with some show of attention and respect, leaving a salutary impression of authority on the observer. All this has disappeared" (p. 280). How all this was once done for Judge Cooper in Cooperstown is indicated in James Cooper's account of such a procession in *The Pioneers,* although there the description is only part respectful, and part comic. Now Cooper is wholly serious. The entire system, and with it the rights of every American, are at stake. The absence of the salutary impression presumably produced by this dumb show has had dangerous consequences, the worst of which is "in the lessening of the influence of the judge on the juries; the power that alone renders the latter institution even tolerable" (pp. 280-81).

Juries are the special target of Cooper's invective. What to many people forms the special genius of the jury trial—that a man is judged by his peers—to Cooper comprises its most blatant offense. Jurors, he rightly insists, are ordinary people, and ordinary people, he righteously insists, "are not all fit to be trusted," are especially not fit "to utter the fearful words of 'guilty,' or 'not guilty' " (p. 83). Throughout Cooper's legal fight against the press, the various juries had consistently declined to levy the large fines Cooper had asked for, but more than a grudge lay behind his animosity toward his "peers." The full force of Cooper's contemptuous distrust of his fellow citizens erupts in the entry he made in his journal on January 25th, 1848:

> Drove wife as far as Myrtle Grove [the Three Mile Point], by the new road, which is a very pretty drive, and a great addition to our outlets. But the Grove is spoiled. This place is a monument of the "people's" honesty, and appreciation of liberty! I know them and would as soon as confide in convicts. (*L/J*, v, 262)

Had known them, in fact, since the controversy over Myrtle Grove. The source of Cooper's distrust is suggested by one of Miles Wallingford's bitter reflections: "As for myself, I can safely say, that in scarce a circumstance of my life that has brought me the least under the cognizance of the public, have I ever been judged justly."[34] The Finance Controversy, the Point affair, the reception of the Effingham Novels, the libel suits—the list of unfair verdicts Cooper felt he had suffered is a long one. "I have been so long treated with injustice," he wrote in a letter dated October 30th, 1845, "have got to be so familiar with ill treatment from my own countrymen, that they can no longer hurt my feelings" (*L/J*, v, 93). This confession is perhaps too unreserved, but it is not entirely candid: Cooper's wounds never healed.

That, however, he refused to concede. But he did, in *The Ways of the Hour*, publicly and vehemently declare that the people—the people who had injured him so badly—must not be allowed to injure the judge's infallible and apparently divine authority. Before the novel's trial begins we are warned that juries "have a pleasure in asserting a seeming independence, and of appearing to think and act for themselves" (p. 148). Not surprisingly, the denouement proves his point: by disregarding the judge's instructions and advice, the jury in the case of *The People* v. *Mary Monson* convicts an innocent woman. "There was a morbid

---

[34] *Miles Wallingford*, p. 88.

satisfaction," the narrator intones sanctimoniously, "in the minds of several of the jurors, in running counter to the charge of the judge. This was a species of independence that is grateful to some men, and they are guided by their vanity, when they fancy they are only led by conscience" (pp. 457-58). Cooper worked hard through this crabbed and cloudy novel to allow himself to make this conclusion. Yet I cannot read it without sadness. Throughout his exuberant nonage and the bright early years of his literary career Cooper had struggled even harder for freedom from the orders of the Judge, for the right to think and to act for himself, for a species of independence—psychic freedom from the parents—that would, if ever we could truly know it, be grateful to all men. It is, certainly, a vain fancy—we can never fully outgrow the child within us. But it is a fancy to be honestly and courageously fought for, not one to be dismissed.

*   *   *

Cooper died in 1851, the year after finishing *The Ways of the Hour*. At the time of his death he was working on a nonfiction book, a history of Manhattan. Only his Introduction has survived; in it Cooper himself sounds very sad. He digresses from his historical subject to make a gloomy prediction about his country's future, once so shining in his eyes, and to indicate bleakly the only source of hope that remained to him:

> Nevertheless, the community will live on, suffer, and be deluded: it may even fancy itself almost within reach of perfection, but it will live on to be disappointed. There is no such thing on earth,—and the only real question for the American statesman is, to measure the results of different defective systems for the government of the human race. We are far from saying that our own, with all its flagrant and obvious defects, will be the worst, more especially when considered solely in connection with whole numbers; though we cannot

deny, nor do we wish to conceal, the bitterness of the wrongs that are so frequently inflicted by the many on the few. This is, perhaps, the worst species of tyranny. He who suffers under the arbitrary power of a single despot, or by the selfish exactions of a privileged few, is certain to be sustained by the sympathies of the masses. But he who is crushed by the masses themselves, must look beyond the limits of his earthly being for consolation and support.[35]

This is Cooper's last word on the relationship between him and his countrymen, and probably his wisest. His gloom can be attributed to two decades of anguished misunderstanding between both parties, which he was compelled to characterize as oppression. During those two decades he was driven first inside his father's Mansion-House, and finally to look upward to the Father whose house has many mansions. The very last public gesture of his life was to be confirmed in the Episcopal Church. With this step—taken in July 1851, three months before his death—he formally completed the process, so long deferred, of fully submitting himself.

Cooper's discovery of his heavenly Father was made in the pages of his Bible. After 1848 he read a portion of it daily. Referring to this practice, his daughter Susan says, "The allusions to Melchisedec always interested him particularly."[36] Cooper himself said, in an entry in his journal on March 1st, 1848: "Hebrews—This book is so much superior to the rest of Paul's epistles that I must think some one wrote it for him. The allusion to Melchisidec is most extraordinary and I scarce know what to make of it" (L/J, v, 290). That allusion is found in the fifth chapter of Hebrews. Theologically there is nothing extraordinary about the

---

[35] *New York: Being an Introduction to an Unpublished Manuscript . . . Entitled The Towns of Manhattan* (New York: William Farquhar Payson, 1930), pp. 58-59.

[36] Quoted by Anson Phelps Stokes, "James Fenimore Cooper: A Memorial Sermon," *New York History* 22 (1941), 44.

passage, but psychologically, from the perspective of Cooper's life, it is easy to understand his interest and amazement. Here is the passage which leapt to his eye, which stuck in his mind:

> 5 So also Christ glorified not himself to be made a high priest; but he that said unto him, Thou art my Son, to-day have I begotten thee.
>
> 6 As he saith also in another place, Thou art a priest for ever after the order of Melchisedec.
>
> 7 Who in the days of his flesh, when he had offered up prayers and supplications with strong crying and tears unto him that was able to save him from death, and was heard in that he feared;
>
> 8 Though he were a son, yet learned he obedience by the things which he suffered;
>
> 9 And being made perfect, he became the author of eternal salvation unto all them that obey him;
>
> 10 Called of God a high priest after the order of Melchisedec.

James Fenimore Cooper—though he were a son, yet learned he obedience by the things which he suffered.

CONCLUSION

"THE ECLIPSE"

> The things learned in childhood remain longest
> on the memory. They make the deepest marks.
>
> Cooper, *The Lake Gun* (1850)

As a polemicist and controversialist Cooper often wrote about the details of his public life. As a novelist he often exploited portions of his personal experience. But only once did he set down a piece of pure autobiography. "The Eclipse" is an eight page article which recounts Cooper's recollections of the total eclipse of the sun on June 16th, 1806. Dating its composition requires some conjecture. Susan Fenimore Cooper, who discovered "The Eclipse" among her father's papers after his death, is certain that it was written "at the request of an English friend," and believes that it "must have been written about the year 1831."[1] On May 21st, 1831, Cooper wrote a letter to one English friend, Samuel Carter Hall, in response to such a request: "I shall have great pleasure of presenting Mrs. Hall with some little cadeau for her Annual, if an idea suggests itself, though I cannot promise that it will be either very long or very good" (*L/J*, ii, 85). James Franklin Beard speculates that "The Eclipse" was probably written for Mrs. Hall,[2] and there is no reason to doubt his suggestion. With reasonable certainty, it can be dated near the middle of 1831.

---

[1] "Note by the Editor" to "The Eclipse; From an Unpublished Ms. of James Fenimore Cooper," *Putnam's Magazine*, N.S. 4 (1869), 352. Additional references to this article and to Susan's note will be cited in my text.

[2] Cf. Beard, *L/J*, ii, 86, n. 2.

259

Susan had the article published, in *Putnam's Magazine* in 1869. Chronologically, therefore, the piece lends itself very well to my purposes in this conclusion. "The Eclipse" —Cooper's only autobiographical effort, written in 1831 when Cooper was forty-two years old, describing an event from 1806 when he was sixteen, published posthumously in 1869—can properly be said to span the limits of the life we have been studying. As autobiography, it is almost equally inclusive: I believe that most of the significant psychological preoccupations with which he was forced to deal throughout that life are exposed in this brief article.

Cooper may even have felt the same way. In her introductory note, Susan says: "From some accidental cause, this article was never sent to England." But what Susan Cooper (reminding one of her father) calls accidental was actually, I suspect, very intentional. Just before his death Cooper asked his heirs to forbid an authorized biography, to withhold personal documents from the public. Susan, his literary executor, faithfully followed these instructions, so faithfully in fact that according to family tradition she had many of her father's journals buried in the grave with her. Yet although she apparently felt that "The Eclipse" was exempt from these instructions, it might have been one document that the novelist deliberately suppressed himself. Certainly he undertook to write it for publication. Having finished it, however, he may have had second thoughts. In the article's last paragraph, he does say:

> Men who witness any extraordinary spectacle together, are apt, in aftertimes, to find a pleasure in conversing on its impressions. But I do not remember to have ever heard a single being freely communicative on the subject of his individual feelings at the most solemn moment of the eclipse. It would seem as if sensations were aroused too closely connected with the constitution of the spirit to be irreverently and familiarly discussed. (p. 359)

CONCLUSION: "THE ECLIPSE"

So far as we know, this manuscript was the only one that Cooper, with his habit of considering his prose as both artistic production and financial property, withheld from the printers. As we shall see, Cooper's sensations at the most solemn moment of the eclipse—"the intensity of feeling and the flood of overpowering thought which filled [his] mind" —are very deeply connected with the constitution of his spirit. Reading the completed article, he might well have decided that he had been too freely communicative on this subject, decided not to send Mrs. Hall her "cadeau"—decided never to publish it at all.

When he wrote the piece, Cooper was living in Paris. In one sense, 1831 was the midpoint of his literary career. He had already achieved his greatest contemporary successes, had already enjoyed his greatest popularity. He was just beginning to feel the mortification and the anger that led him, during the next year, to inform his publishers and friends of his retirement, was just beginning to sense the void that distanced him from his countrymen. Five years earlier he had left America in triumph. Two years later he returned in defeat.

This context makes more interesting the idea that suggested itself to him for Mrs. Hall's Annual. In the midst of his busy and absorbing involvement with the European trilogy, the Revolution of 1830, and the Finance Controversy, Cooper paused for the brief space of eight pages to reevaluate a private episode from his earlier life. For it was in Cooperstown that Cooper saw the great eclipse. He was sixteen years old on June 16th, 1806; almost exactly one year before, he had been expelled from college. We can confirm the date of the eclipse from other sources,[3] and so we know that Cooper's daughter has miscalculated both his age and his experience when in her Note she says that at that time "the writer was a young sailor of seventeen, just returned from a cruise." In the article Cooper does call himself a

[3] It is so dated in Theodor Ritter von Oppolzer's *Canon der Finsternisse* as well as the June 19th, 1806, issue of the *Otsego Herald*.

"young sailor," but not until four months later—October 1806—did he actually become a seaman, though it is easily possible that by mid-June his father had already decided and arranged to make him one. I suspect that Cooper's nautical reference, and Susan's subsequent confusion on the point, can be traced to his remembered impatience at sixteen to go to sea: later on he describes himself as a "sailor at heart," and doubtless it was from his heartfelt longing at the time to become a sailor in deed that the ambiguity arose.

Everything that his biographers have learned about the novelist indicates that between 1805 and 1806 he lived at home, where, according to his tutor, the Cooperstown man who took over the role of the Yale faculty, he was at sixteen a "rather wayward" adolescent.[4] Yet if it is certain that he had not been on a cruise prior to the eclipse, there is a second biographical ambiguity in his account of that day that I cannot factually clear up. According to Cooper, on June 16th he was on "a holiday at home" (p. 354), a phrase which clearly implies that he had been living elsewhere. He does not say where. No record of such a residence has survived. And the most likely explanation is that Cooper has confused (as I believe he did in several other places) the events of 1806 with his feelings in 1831. He may temporarily have been on a holiday *away from* home during the spring of 1806, but psychologically, it was in 1831, when he had been away from Cooperstown for fourteen years, that he took this imaginative "holiday at home," that he returned not merely to the site of his childhood, but to the bosom of his family. As he says in "The Eclipse," "I had then a father and four brothers living" (p. 352). This would have been among the last periods during which he could have seen them all together, and one of the last times he could have seen his father, who died three years later, at all. At sixteen, the wayward youth's desire may have been to get away from

Cooperstown, but at forty-two that desire was beginning to reverse itself. Writing the article in 1831 was a kind of emotional prelude, which was restated in a more major key the next year when he determined to buy his father's house; the movement was completed in 1834 when he went back to Cooperstown for good. Now, in Paris, in 1831, recalling the eclipse of the sun after twenty-five years, Cooper went home in his memory to a particularly memorable event in his adolescence.

"My recollections of the great event, and the incidents of the day," writes Cooper at the beginning of the article, "are as vivid as if they had occurred but yesterday" (p. 352). So vividly does he convey these recollections, indeed, that in places "The Eclipse" reads like the record of a dream. Like a dream, it contains startling juxtapositions, abrupt transitions, transformations of objects, changes of scene. But Cooper was not associating randomly. Also like a dream, "The Eclipse" makes perfect sense when we understand its latent meanings.

Regardless of whether Cooper had actually been absent from the Mansion-House prior to June 16th, his recollected feelings on that morning are those of a person who has just returned. After examining the sky for any clouds that might spoil the impending spectacle, he looks around him: "For a moment, my eye rested on the familiar view—the limpid lake, with its setting of luxuriant woods and farms, its graceful bay and varied points, the hills where every cliff and cave and glen had been trodden a thousand times by my boyish feet—all this was dear to me as the face of a friend" (p. 353). This view to which he was so deeply attached was the scene of his childhood play. "His boyish feet" had often carried him into the woods and hills, away from his father's mansion to a realm of freedom from his father's authority. Freedom was what the woods meant to Cooper, both to the boy and the novelist, as he himself indicates in "The Eclipse." He turns next to consider "one object in the landscape which a stranger would probably have overlooked"—

the tall gray trunk of a dead and branchless pine, which
had been standing on the crest of the eastern hill, at
the time of the foundation of the village, and which
was still erect, though rocked since then by a thousand
storms. To my childish fancy, it had seemed an imaginary flagstaff, or, in rustic parlance, the "liberty pole"
of some former generation. . . .

The landscape being depicted here is emotional as well as
physical. The foundation of the village had been the work
of William Cooper, who ruled there as a patriarch. James
Cooper, however, steadfastly refused to submit to his father's
dominion, and in his fancy had raised this emblematic flagstaff to stand over his fight for liberty. It was a fight he had
in one sense managed to win. As he gazes at the tree, the
liberty pole is transformed:

> . . . but now, as I traced the familiar line of the tall
> trunk, in its peculiar shade of silvery gray, it became to
> the eye of the young sailor the mast of some phantom
> ship. I remember greeting it with a smile, as this was
> the first glance of recognition given to the old ruin of
> the forest since my return.

The sixteen-year-old "sailor" had reason to smile. Though
his youth had been rocked by its own kind of storms, through
it he had managed to preserve his selfhood, to keep his identity erect in the presence of his father. The make-believe
independence of the forest would soon become the actual
independence of the sea, the phantom ship would become
the *Sterling*, and before its mast he would be still farther
from his father's commands.

Having read all thirty-two of Cooper's novels, Francis
Parkman came to the conclusion that "it is on the sea and
in the forest that Cooper is most at home. Their spirit inspired him, their images were graven in his heart."[5] Almost
no one disputes this conclusion. Cooper's best and most

[5] Parkman, p. 147.

popular books are set either on the sea or in the forest. But Parkman's phrase should be turned around: Cooper was inspired by their spirit because there he was least at home. Natty Bumppo, Tom Coffin (in *The Pilot*), and Cooper's other heroes of forest and ocean have captured the imagination of his readers because they represent, for Cooper and for us, the fulfillment of the preserved preadolescent wish to run away from home, from the commands of the adults and the demands of adult life. William Cooper was a man who would have made home life seem emotionally very claustrophobic. Because the Judge was such an overwhelming figure, his son knew better than most, and was able to communicate better than most, the psychic rewards of this species of freedom.

How widely the world shared this desire with the Judge's son is indicated by the enormous international popularity of his escapist romances. In Cooper's own lifetime, Natty Bumppo's character was known throughout Europe and as far away as Russia and the Middle East. When Honoré de Balzac, the French novelist, favorably reviewed the appearance of *The Pathfinder* in translation, he echoed the orthodox critical litany of the American novelist's virtues: Fenimore Cooper, he said, "owes the high place he holds in modern literature to two faculties: that of painting the sea and seamen; that of idealizing the magnificent landscapes of America."[6] But impressed as Balzac was with Cooper's descriptions of the forest, he was clearly most impressed with his evocation of the man of the forest, Natty Bumppo, "who will live as long as literatures last." And, after mentioning the imaginative debt that Cooper's tales owe to those of Sir Walter Scott, Balzac goes on to make one particularly suggestive statement about the cultural circumstances of Natty's creation: "We feel that if the great Scotchman had seen America he might have created Leather-Stocking." The

6 Balzac, "[James Fenimore Cooper]," in *The Personal Opinions of Honoré de Balzac*, trans. Katharine Prescott Wormeley (Boston: Little, Brown, and Company, 1908), p. 115.

Frenchman may have meant nothing more than that one needed to have stood beneath the towering trees of the forest primeval in order to have conceived the similarly tall, similarly uncivilized form of the Leather-stocking. His remark, however, can be applied in a larger, more significant context.

Only an American, I think, could have created Leather-stocking, not so much because of the presence here of the primeval wilderness, but because of the absence here of all vestiges of the medieval social order, which unmistakably defined a man by his place in the feudal hierarchy just as it inescapably bound a serf to his master's land. The traditions of feudalism have been a long time disappearing in Europe. After even the serfs were freed, and free to move about, a European was still measured by his membership in a social class. That he could not escape—unless he escaped Europe. The standard reaction of a nineteenth century immigrant arriving on the western shores of the Atlantic was immediately to celebrate his sense that here men were no longer bound and limited by hierarchal social relationships. Here, he was told, a man could make his own place in society. Natty claims a still larger freedom: the right to make a place for himself wholly outside society. And while European readers could respond to Cooper's articulation of that kind of autonomy, no nineteenth century European writer could have imagined it, could have bestowed it upon one of his characters. To create Leather-stocking, Scott would have had to do more than simply see America; he would have had to live here, or at least stay here as long as Tocqueville did. Tocqueville has no superior as a social analyst, and it took him only fourteen months to realize that America's institutionalized equality of conditions provided each American with a degree of individual opportunity entirely unprecedented and almost inexplicable in terms of the Old World's experience. This was an opportunity that Natty, and imaginatively Cooper, and vicariously Cooper's readers, made the most of.

At the pole of the novelist's psyche represented by the

Leather-Stocking Tales, the father could be left behind every time that Natty, like the young Cooper, plunged into the woods. With the father could also be left all the claims of civilization, for in Cooper's particular case the father literally embodied those claims. Founder and patriarch of a settlement as well as a family, party leader and Federal legislator, First Judge of the county—William Cooper was at the center of the society in which his son grew up. The vast amount of wilderness—more than any other American—that William Cooper had sold to pioneers, who cleared its underbrush, cut down its trees, and raised homesteads, crops, and their own families on it, put him also at the center of the American society which was growing out across the continent. From all these impingements on his freedom—from politics, laws, the restrictions of a family, especially from settlers—did Natty Bumppo manage to escape. When he dies at the end of *The Prairie*, in the middle of the prairie, he is hundreds of miles from civilization, and fully 1,500 miles from the site of his birth. "My father lies buried near the sea," he says in the last moments of his life, "and the bones of his son will whiten on the prairies." He has made his solitary westward movement to preserve his autonomy, and he preserves it to the end: when another character offers to carry his remains to the side of his father's grave, Natty quickly and firmly refuses. "Let me sleep where I have lived —beyond the din of the settlements!"[7] The Coopers, father and youngest son, are buried together in Cooperstown. And throughout *his* life, James Cooper's various escapes from his father were only provisional, as "The Eclipse" also reveals. If before the young man on that morning in June lay the "pathless wilderness," behind him stood the Mansion-House.

Occupied by his father, the Mansion-House stood for civilization; given the Judge's political prejudices, in fact, it stood for a civilization in many respects similar to that an immigrant would have left behind in Europe. The opposite

7 *The Prairie*, p. 476.

pole of Cooper's psyche is represented by what Spiller calls the novels of purpose, novels like *Home As Found, The Redskins, The Ways of the Hour.* Their purpose is a simple one: to instill in the reader a proper respect for the values of society which are inherited from society's forefathers. By and large these books have failed to capture the imaginations of their readers. Their failure, however, cannot be attributed to Cooper's inability to involve himself emotionally in his purpose. Rather, I think that both Cooper and his culture must be blamed. To depict imaginatively the claims of society Cooper was forced to use his personal past as his imaginative resource, partly because so much of his emotional energy was fixated on that past, and partly because there were few traditional standards he could use.

Americans have always been more responsive to the idea of personal freedom than to that of social responsibilty. The Declaration of Independence, to cite our culturally most cherished and most resonant political statement, eloquently defines our individual and inalienable rights, but is silent on the subject of our collective and inescapable duties. Cooper's exaggerated point about the American's impulse to behave as though he were nobody's son was not without truth. Few nineteenth century American novels are set in the middle of family life, though this was a favorite setting for nineteenth century British novelists. If the most familiar plot of the European novel during Cooper's lifetime recounts the movement of an inexperienced youth toward an understanding of and a role in his society, fictional Americans more often follow Natty's lead and light out for the Territory. This need not be Natty's or Huck Finn's Territory, or that of Brockden Brown's *Edgar Huntly*—the pathless wilderness of the American West; it may be the Territory of Ahab's ocean, equally pathless, or of any Poe hero's consciousness, equally wild, or even of Christopher Newman's self-fulfillment; but what American literature denies so often throughout the century is a recognizable, valid and tenantable place in the community of men and women.

Cooper was not only the first American novelist to make a success of the genre, but the first as well to assert, as he did in the Preface to *Home As Found*, that "it would be indeed a desperate undertaking, to think of making any thing interesting in the way of a *Roman de Société* in this country,"[8] a complaint that later Hawthorne, and still later James would reiterate. The social relationships between nineteenth century Americans were neither fixed enough to deprive a man of individual opportunities, nor forceful enough to provide a novelist with the opportunity to make those relationships the setting of his story, or the subject of his novel. Realizing this, both Hawthorne and James wound up in Europe. For his part, Cooper was conscious of the aesthetic risk involved in writing a social novel on the barren territory offered by American society, unconscious of the way in which he attempted to resolve the problem. In the Effingham Novels or the Littlepage Manuscripts, Cooper had to spin out of himself the societal and familial values that he wished to affirm, to hold up his father as the forefather. These novels are not set on a shared cultural ground —of which there has always been but little in this country— but on the private battleground of his psyche. There is no room in them for the reader. Yet Cooper's inability to make us respond to the figure of his father as fully as we can to the figure of the Leather-stocking is no gauge of the role that William Cooper played in the drama of his unconscious life. Neither the Leather-Stocking Tales nor any other of the thirty-two novels, neither Fenimore Cooper's problematic behavior nor his self-contradictions can properly be understood unless one appreciates the extent to which his father dominated his life.

We have spent a good deal of time attempting to understand just that. "The Eclipse," I believe, will help to underpin the conclusions that have been reached. In addition to the astronomical one, there is a second spectacle recounted in "The Eclipse"—a spectacle of judgment and guilt. It

[8] *Home As Found*, p. vi.

preceeds the disappearance of the sun. With his father and brothers Cooper is standing on the lawn of the Mansion-House watching the sky when suddenly, abruptly, an unnamed acquaintance insists that Cooper follow him.

> He led me to the Court House, and from thence into an adjoining building, and into a room then occupied by two persons. At a window, looking upward at the heavens, stood a figure which instantly riveted my attention. It was a man with haggard face, and fettered arms, a prisoner under sentence of death. By his side was the jailor. (p. 355)

The prisoner had been the village teacher until, about a year earlier, he beat a student to death because she could not enunciate well enough to suit him. "The wretched man was arrested, tried for murder, condemned, and sentenced to the gallows. This was the first capital offence in Otsego County. It produced a very deep impression." Among the most deeply impressed was James Cooper. Here was a man who, having broken one of society's laws, had been sentenced to death by an Otsego County judge. The sentencing judge in this case was not Judge Cooper; he had retired by that time. But throughout his youth James Cooper had to confront a father who was also a judge, and this added, awesome authority only increased William Cooper's stature as the family disciplinarian. The black robes of the Judge made the father a more dangerous man to rebel against. As Mark Twain (in *Life on the Mississippi*) says about his father, a justice of the peace, "I supposed he possessed the power of life and death over all men and could hang any body that offended him"; Twain is of course stretching the literal truth here, but not the emotional one. Though Cooper never explicitly acknowledged the same fact of life in Cooperstown, he does digress from his account of June 16th, 1806, to recall his feelings on the day—July 19th, 1805, "the day named by the judge"—for which the convicted murderer's hanging was scheduled.

That day would have been at most a few weeks after the

fathers of Yale College had returned the recalcitrant student to his father; Cooper could conceivably have been wondering what, if any, punishment was in store for him. "Looking down, from an elevated position," he watched the convict's journey to the gallows. "Never have I beheld such agony, such a clinging to life, such mental horror at the nearness of death, as was betrayed by this miserable man." At the last moment, however, a pardon from the Governor arrives and the sentence is commuted: "Such was the wretched man who had been brought from his dungeon that morning, to behold the grand phenomenon of the eclipse. During the twelve-month previous, he had seen the sun but once. The prisons of those days were literally dungeons, cut off from the light of day" (p. 356). That particular prison had been built by William Cooper. It was there that, according to contemporaneous records, he repeatedly threatened to send his opponents, which meant anyone who disagreed with the way he governed Cooperstown. As a young man, James Cooper probably felt the dark threat of this dungeon as well. He later said how much he had empathized with La-Fayette's incarceration. He later broke Natty Bumppo out of that very jail. Here is how he responded to the tableau of the fettered murderer gazing out the window:

> That striking figure, the very picture of utter misery, his emotion, his wretchedness, I can never forget. . . . Perhaps human invention could not have conceived of a more powerful moral accessory, to heighten the effect of the sublime movement of the heavenly bodies, than this spectacle of penitent human guilt afforded.

Cooper is not merely looking with the eye of a novelist at a well-arranged scene:

> It was [he continues] an incident to stamp on the memory for life. It was a lesson not lost on me. (p. 356)

Not lost, that is, on the Judge's son. Elsewhere in "The Eclipse" he speaks of his "boyish impatience" with his "elders" and his "boyish love of fun" (p. 354). Translated, these phrases refer to his need to defy the Judge's authority. But the lesson he learned inside the Court House forcefully pointed the consequences of rebellion, although, as we shall see, the danger was not being cut off from the sun, but being cut off from the father.

After leaving the Court House Cooper returns to the Mansion-House. "I once more took my position beside my father and my brothers, before the gates of our own grounds" (p. 356). By now the eclipse is well under way. Stars have started to appear in the noon sky. Several cows, assuming that evening has come, are heading for their barns. Even the birds seem uncertain. The families of the villagers huddle closer together in the gathering gloom, the young children looking to their mothers, the women to their husbands.

To every person, including the unsuperstitious, a total eclipse of the sun is an awe-full experience. Cooper confesses awe and even fear. "We are all," he writes, "but larger children." Yet as the others instinctively draw closer together, seeking strength within their families, Cooper momentarily seeks in his imagination to withdraw from the scene of the darkening village:

> My thoughts turned to the sea. A sailor at heart, already familiar with the face of the ocean, I seemed, in mental vision, to behold the grandeur of that vast pall of supernatural shadow falling suddenly upon the sea, during the brightest hour of the day. . . . And my fancy was busy with pictures of white-sailed schooners, and brigs, and ships, gliding like winged spirits over the darkened waves. (p. 357)

Just as before, when he gazed at the trunk of the lone pine, Cooper transports himself away from the grounds of the Mansion-House. His thoughts anticipate his actions four months later, when, by putting to sea, he would put thousands of miles between himself and his home. The eagerness with which he sought that distance is suggested by how often his "fancy" prematurely embarked on his voyage to England. But he is quickly recalled to the present scene. There can be no escape from home and father, from the moment of darkness.

"At twelve minutes past eleven, the moon stood revealed in its greatest distinctness—a vast black orb, so nearly obscuring the sun that the face of the great luminary was entirely and absolutely darkened" (pp. 357-58). To primitive peoples, who did not recognize the agency of the moon, this was a profoundly traumatic moment. What if the sun's face never reappeared? James Cooper had the benefit of the astronomers' explanations, but his account of his apprehensions retains some of the primitive's fright, and all of the trauma:

> In looking back to that impressive hour, such now seem to me the feelings of the youth making one of that family group, all apparently impressed with a sensation of the deepest awe—I speak with certainty—a clearer view than I had ever yet had of the majesty of the Almighty, accompanied with a humiliating, and, I trust, a profitable sense of my own utter insignificance. That movement of the moon, that sublime voyage of the worlds, often recurs to my imagination, and even at this distant day, as distinctly, as majestically, and nearly as fearfully, as it was then beheld.

The syntax of the passage is confused—the impetus of Cooper's emotions gets the better of his prose—but nonetheless it is very revealing. Part of Cooper's feeling is plainly conventional. His inane reference to profiting by his sense of his own utter insignificance shows just how much latter-day Christianity had enervated the spiritual awe and terror of the earliest men. But Cooper's feelings also belong to the youth making one of a family group. In this context, the humility, the awe and the terror are real. It was this context that made the experience so memorable, as indicated by the latent transition between the passage above and the paragraph that follows—which contains the article's only separate reference to William Cooper:

> A group of silent, dusky forms stood near me; one emotion appeared to govern all. My father stood immovable, some fifteen feet from me, but I could not discern his features. Three minutes of darkness, all but absolute, elapsed. They appeared strangely lengthened by the intensity of feeling and the flood of overpowering thought which filled the mind.

Whatever other overpowering thoughts flooded his mind during those minutes, the only one that he records, and consequently the one that must have reached the deepest mark in his memory, is this inability to determine his father's expression.

The face of the great luminary was entirely and absolutely darkened: the face of his father was obscured. Cooper himself, in his next two sentences, interprets this juxtaposition for us:

> Thus far the sensation created by this majestic spectacle had been one of humiliation and awe. It seemed as if the great Father of the Universe had visibly, and almost palpably, veiled his face in wrath.

There was obvious cause for the father's wrath, both in 1806, when Cooper saw the eclipse, and in 1831, when he remembered it. The sixteen-year-old had spent his adolescence attempting to overthrow the Judge's rule. Tired of his repeated transgressions, William Cooper finally sent his son to sea to be tamed, but before abdicating his authority in this way he unquestionably would have tried to tame the boy himself. The sixteen-year-old must have grown very accustomed to *seeing* the father's face in wrath. We are all but larger children, and even in 1831, the child in Fenimore Cooper, the set of infantile emotions preserved in his unconscious, was still afraid of the Judge's discipline. After all, his father had wielded the power of life and death, as he learned graphically on his visit to the jail.

But what the middle-aged author feared most was the wrathful *absence* of the father's face. One can sense the anxious intensity of feeling behind his abrupt reference to his immovable father. This anxiety, and Cooper's recollected humiliation and awe, his remembered sense of his own utter insignificance, must largely be attributed to the guilt he felt in 1831 for his further prodigalities. Throughout the 1820s he had consistently tried to repudiate William Cooper—by ardently espousing anti-Federalist principles, by dutifully adopting General LaFayette, by defiantly trying to change his name. In this rebellious struggle for independence he had been sustained by his faith in his countrymen's approval. But at the time he wrote "The Eclipse," that approval could no longer be depended upon to make good his new identity. Always insecure, Cooper now began to consider a return home to his old identity as William Cooper's son. What if the father's face remained permanently hidden in anger?

But an eclipse always passes. Hope returns with the renewal of the sun's light. Wanting unconsciously to go home, Cooper expresses his hopes very vividly:

> But, appalling as the withdrawal of light had been, most glorious, most sublime, was its restoration! . . . It seemed to speak directly to our spirits, with full assurance of protection, of gracious mercy, and of that Divine love which has produced all the glorious combinations of matter for our enjoyment. (p. 358)

The face of the great Father is unveiled, demoting the appalling into the enjoyable. Protection—from the abuse and assaults of his countrymen—was precisely what Cooper desired, and remembering the promise—of mercy and love, the qualities that beget forgiveness—which came with the restoration of the light would, in 1831, indeed have spoken directly to his spirits. How badly Cooper needed psychically to retreat to Cooperstown, how much he wanted solace from the wounds he had suffered in the world, is indicated by his apologetic description of the light's return: "I know that philosophically I am wrong; but, to me, it seemed that the rays might actually be seen flowing through the darkness in torrents, till they had again illuminated the forest, the mountains, the valley, and the lake with their glowing, genial touch." Just this warmth and security he sought beside Lake Otsego, a place, as Ned Effingham said, to find "repose and content . . . for the evening of a troubled life."

Yet the terror of the eclipse is much more forcefully described than the sublimity of its passing. This emphasis—a natural way to create narrative suspense—is also appropriate psychologically, for in 1831 Cooper had yet to reconcile himself with his father or to execute his father's will. In going home there was as much to be feared as to be hoped for. And in going home in his memory to recall this episode, Cooper stresses the horrible power of the father's wrath. As he says in his concluding paragraphs, "At such a moment the spirit of man bows in humility before his Maker" (p. 359). "Maker" of course means God, but in the course of this article Cooper refers to God by almost every name but that one. God is the Creator, the Almighty, the great Father of the Universe, the Maker—all words that really describe the figure of his father in Cooper's unconscious.

After 1831 Cooper stood up prouder, straighter, and more defiantly to his countrymen, men, he said, who falsely claimed to have "made him." At the same time, however, he stooped more and more humbly before the figure of his real maker, until at last he had promoted his father fully to the Maker, the great Father of the Universe. To both the father and the Father was he reverent and dutiful. Obedience lessened the guilt for his transgressions, and increased his sense of absolution. By the end of his life, Cooper's hopes for the Father's mercy had almost entirely replaced his fear of the father's wrath. As he said, the feelings associated with the spectacle he had viewed in his father's presence often recurred to his imagination: an eclipse, in fact, is one of the novelist's favorite figures of speech, and in some form or another the disappearance of the sun is referred to in more than half his tales. But eventually it became possible to emphasize the restoration, not the withdrawal, of the light. When in 1848 Cooper wrote *Oak Openings*, he could metaphorically retell the experience, using the persona of the converted Indian, Scalping Peter, in this way:

> "[once Peter was] Afraid of Great Spirit, but didn't love him. . . . Now, all dem cloud blow away, and I see my Fadder dat is in Heaven. His face shine on me, day and night, and I never get tired of looking at it. I see Him smile, I see Him lookin' at poor ole Injin, as if he want him to come nearer; sometime I see Him frown and dat scare me. Den I pray, and his frown go away."[9]

The Indian's broken English cannot disguise the source of Peter's emotions. His lingering fears, his lasting hopes, were Cooper's, and the Father that is in Heaven, he was Cooper's too.

[9] *Oak Openings*, p. 497.

INDEX

INDEX

LIBRARY OF CONGRESS CATALOGING IN PUBLICATION DATA

Railton, Stephen, 1948-
    Fenimore Cooper: a study of his life and
imagination.

    Includes index.
    1. Cooper, James Fenimore, 1789-1851.
2. Novelists, American—19th century—Biography.
PS1431.R3   813′.2   77-85560
ISBN 0-691-06358-3